flat4ever
Specialty cars based on Volkswagen and Porsche

flat4ever
Thomas Braun

The great encyclopaedia of small series and specialty cars based on Volkswagen and Porsche

Summer, sun, a cool lake and a beetle are often enough for the perfect feeling of freedom. Over time, the Beetle has become one of the most versatile vehicles in the world. This Beetle can be hired for a trip around the lake (Ossiachersee, Austria)

Impressum

Copyright 2024 by Thomas Braun

All rights reserved! No part of this publication may be reproduced, transmitted, or copied in any form or by any means, electronic or mechanical, including photocopying, recording, or otherwise, without the express permission of the author.

Cover design and production by Thomas Braun.

Printing and processing by Print on Demand or partner.

Source Reference

The following should be said about image and source references: In general, the book does not use a scientific citation method (short quotations within the text) in order not to disturb the flow of reading. The humanities style of citation in the form of footnotes would also have disturbed the layout. We have therefore decided to place the references at the end of each manufacturer or brand section. The references cover both the content and the images used.

Many of the photos were taken over the last few years during the author's visits to classic car events. Most of the images, however, were found on websites, which are listed as sources in the form of corresponding links. The websites were accessed as secondary sources in the course of the research between 2014 and 2023, but may now be out of date, which does not limit their significance as a valid source ‚at the time'.

Most of the images date from before the internet. In the case of historical images, it is hoped that the original image has survived in a private or institutional archive, but we do not know for sure in each case. Sometimes clues and pictures of vehicles thought to be lost can be found in discussion forums, where descendants of manufacturers sometimes report on the work of their ancestors, keeping alive the memory of great personalities of the scene. Often these are information platforms that aim to cover all types of small-series vehicles, car manufacturers as comprehensively as possible or bodybuilders as completely as possible.

All these efforts share a common goal: to use digital means to create an information offering that can grow organically every day and every hour. This is the advantage of digital media. A book is printed, and perhaps a second, revised version is published a little later. Digital media can be kept up to date much more easily.
If the source is a journal, the title of the journal, the issue and - if available - the title of the article are referenced. If the source of content or images is a book, the author or publisher, book title and page number are referenced. Where „with kind support of…" is given, the source of the content or visual material is indicated.

We would like to thank the many supporters of the project. Many personal connections have been made over the years. What they all have in common is an interest in historic cars, be they made of steel, light metal or plastic. The focus is on the reappraisal of the history and stories surrounding the vehicles covered.

The book is divided into decades. Within each decade, the vehicles and makes are listed in alphabetical order, although there is no guarantee of absolute completeness. New material is constantly being added. Long lost vehicles are constantly being brought to light. We have deliberately refrained from attempting a complete presentation of buggy vehicles, as this would have gone beyond the scope of the book.

We have tried to list all names and sources. However, if a name is missing, please contact the author. The research was carried out to the best of our knowledge and belief and took more than ten years in order to provide another interim status of the research in this second edition.

Acknowledgements

Special thanks are due to all the friends and owners of special models, some of whom provided valuable information in personal conversations at various classic car events.
Bob Blackmans (USA), Alex Boogarts (B), Simon Braker (D), Roman Buchta (A), Paul Bull (GB), Eimo Cremer (D), Pe-

ter Ebeling (D), Phillip J. Fenton (USA), Hannes Fitz (A), Antonio Fleury (BR), Alexander Fritz (A), Christian Grundmann (D), Traugott Grundmann (D), Geoffrey Hacker (USA), R. Herron (USA), Clem Herselman (ZA), Claus Hoppen (BR), William Hough (USA), Matthias Jäger (D), Federico Kirbus (RA), Roman Krcil, (CZ), Günther Ledl (A), Georg Memminger (D), Geir Natvig (N), Felipe Nicoliello (BR), Thomas Otten (D), Daniel Richer (USA), Dirk Rosen (D), Bruno von Rotz (D), João F. Scharinger (BR), Björn Schewe (D), Hartwin Schmidt (D), Wolfgang Seidel (D), Marc Spicer (GB), Dirk Steindorf (D), Ludwig Stolz (D), Alfred Umgeher (A), Raoul Verbeemen (B), Donnie Vivier (GB), Hans Weber (A), Steve Wright (UK), Oliver Zinkann (D)

Table of Content

INTRODUCTION	10
History of Kitcars	12
Working with Plastic	13
Original or Fake – Replica or Self-built?	14
A Typical Conversion	17
CARS of the 1980s	24
AC Sportcar (PT)	26
Akamine (BR)	26
Almenara Buggy (BR)	27
Alto (UK)	28
American Fibre Craft - AFC (US)	28
Angelmar (AT)	30
Aspen 550 RSK (US)	30
Aumann (DE)	30
Avante (UK)	31
BCW Model 52 (US)	32
Beck Replicas (US)	33
Beep Netuno (BR)	34
Belfusca (BR)	35
Bernardi (CA)	36
Blasi Cross (BR)	36
Büffel Koupe (US)	37
CapCar (US)	37
CBP (BR)	38
Chalon (US)	40
Chamonix (BR)	40
Cheda (BR)	42
Chimo (CA)	44
Cintra 959 (BR)	45
Classic Roadsters (US)	46
Corbett Countach 5000S (US)	47
Corsair (US)	47
Countess (UK)	48
Covin (UK)	48
Crosby (US)	50
Crusader (UK)	50
CTC Panzer (US)	51
CWA Targa (BR)	51
Dacon (BR)	52
D´Norbert (BR)	54
DRB Sabre (AU)	55
Dukat Coupé (CH)	55
Eagle (US)	56
Eagle SS (UK)	57
Eagle SS (UK)	59
EMIS (BR)	60
Enseada (BR)	61
Fibrario (BR)	62
Fiera (BR)	64
Fyber (BR)	64
Garra (BR)	67
Griffon LB (BR)	68
Gringo (BR)	69
Jornada (BR)	69
Karma (UK)	70
Kaylor (US)	71
Kestrel / Briton (UK)	71
Kitcar Centre / KCC (ZA)	72
Lalande (UK)	73
L´Autocraft (BR)	74
Lejin (ZA)	76
LeMazone (UK)	76
Letherbarrow (ZA)	77
LN-33 (US)	77
London Roadster (US)	78
Mac Laren (BR)	79
Marauder (US)	80
Marauder (AU)	81
Mikada (AU)	81
Mulholland (US)	82
Orion (BR)	83
Ostermann GR-C (DE)	84
Panache (UK)	85
Pantera (BR)	85

Paragon (AU) 86	Hummbug (CA). 121
Petterson Roadster (SW) 87	Kango Cars (SA) 121
Porrera (AU) 87	Mania Spyder (SW) 123
Procar Van (BR) 88	Mastretta Sports Cars (MX) 123
Proton (BR). 88	Mc Lela / Blaze (US) 126
PS 904 (DE). 89	Nereia (US) 127
Pulmonia (MX) 90	Rudolph (DE) 128
Pulsar (UK) 91	Savana (BR) 129
Quiron SP (BR) 91	Short (BR) 129
Ragge (BR) 92	Total Recall (US) 132
Rawlson (UK) 93	Tukano (BR) 133
Replicar (UK). 94	Vochoneta (MX) 134
Rhino (UK) 96	Vochos Taxi (MX). 135
Ryder Royale (UK) 96	ZF98 (PT) 135
Saier (DE) 97	Delivery Vans (MISC). 136
Samburá Pickup (BR) 98	Woodies (MISC). 137
SAM VW (PL) 99	CARS of the 2000s. 138
Sandbach (UK) 100	Batráquio Anfibio (BR). 140
Sandwood (UK) 100	Bogatti (US). 141
Saphier (LI) 101	Bubbletop Volksrod (US) 141
Scheib (DE) 102	Bugfire (DE) 142
Scorpio GT (US) 102	Chelo Casas GT (PR) 144
Scorpion (CA) 103	Der Wiger Coupé (NO) 144
Seidel GT (DE) 103	Floating T3 Bus (DE) 145
S. H. Design (SW) 103	Gator (US). 145
SN1 (UK) 104	Kübel Lite (US) 146
SPJ Garra (BR) 105	Landrover VW (US) 147
Sportscoupé (FR) 105	Memminger (DE). 147
Tanger (BR). 106	Ora Punk Cat (CH) 148
Tigress (UK). 108	Pirassununga (BR) 149
Town Car (US). 108	Porsche 904 Replica (NO). 150
Tupy Mini 175 (BR). 109	RCH (GR) 151
Vachey (FR) 110	Rolls Royce VW (UK) 153
Van Valen Car (NL) 110	Rosenstiel Roadster (US) 153
Villa GT (BR) 111	Taifun Dream Car (TH) 154
Vision (US) 111	Wittera (DE). 155
Commercial Vehicles (MISC) 112	Stretch Limousines (MISC) 157
CARS of the 1990s. 114	Hunting Cars (MISC) 158
ACE (US) 116	Curiosities (MISC) 159
Alpha Shark (DE) 116	Lively Vintage VW Scene (MISC) 160
Beverly Hills 356 (US). 117	Germany 160
By Cristo (BR) 117	AUSTRIA. 163
Chesil (UK) 118	Puma Col Europe Meeting. 165
Dauphin (US) 118	National Puma Gatherings in Brazil. 166
Delorean Desert (US) 119	Puma Gatherings in South Africa. 167
Fibreglass Designs (SA) 120	Index 168

flat4ever
Thomas Braun

Foreword

What an ingenious design Ferdinand Porsche came up with in the 1930s: a chassis that, with the front axle bolted on and the engine and gearbox fitted, was fully roadworthy even without bodywork!

It was not only the German Wehrmacht that took advantage of these features for the legendary Kübelwagen, but also many thousands of private mechanics and small-series manufacturers. There were no limits to the creativity of hobbyists. Bodies made of sheet metal, aluminium, plastic and even wood were bolted onto new or used Beetle chassis, while at the same time the technology was tweaked to get more power out of the four-cylinder boxer. The result: it was easy to set yourself apart from the rest of the Beetle drivers through looks and dynamics.

Worldwide Activities

Especially for people with a small budget, it was possible to build their own dream car with a little technical understanding. The market quickly recognised this as a new area of business, and many companies around the world offered their services, whether in the body, kit or tuning sector - up to and including complete vehicles of all kinds.

Unfortunately, there are still only a limited number of books and information available on this type of custom car building, which has been popular worldwide since the 1950s, and these are limited to well-known brands such as Hebmüller, Rometsch, Enzmann or Apal, to name but a few.

First comprehensive presentation

It is therefore all the more gratifying that author Thomas Braun, in this book, also highlights the many small coachbuilders and private designers, thus closing the informal gap between the big and the small artists.

Traugott Grundmann
Organiser of the International VW Veterans Meeting in Hessisch Oldendorf
July 2018

Together with his son Christian, Traugott Grundmann runs a private museum in Hessisch Oldendorf displaying early Volkswagens and special models, as well as the legacy of the Rometsch company from Berlin. When Traugott Grundmann started collecting early Porsche and Volkswagen models in 1980 after joining his father-in-law Karl Junker's roofing business, he soon turned his attention to VW-based special bodies and acquired his first Rometsch. When the Rometsch company gave up its accident repair business in 2000, Traugott Grundmann and his son Christian took over the remaining stock from the former special body production.

Traugott Grundmann
Organiser of the International VW Veterans Meeting in Hessisch Oldendorf
July 2017

Thomas Braun studied prehistory and early history in Vienna. His first publication deals with a late Roman burial ground, followed by a book on systemic management theory. In recent years, he has been working on the history of the sports car brand Puma do Brasil.

Foreword of the Author

There have been modified cars almost as long as there have been cars. They range from extravagant to bizarre. No matter how many options a manufacturer has offered or will offer, there will always be enthusiasts who want something faster, more luxurious or more unique. This need has given rise to a wide range of vehicles. Many specialty cars have been created in a hobbyist's back garden or workshop. The sources for this are relatively thin and largely dependent on chance. Manufacturers of small-series vehicles are easier to find. A more comprehensive picture can usually be obtained from advertisements in magazines or from test reports. Manufacturers who produced in the higher price segment often had glossy brochures printed. These luxury goods are well documented through their famous owners.

It Started 1945

This book is the first to cover special models on an international scale, from Europe to Asia, from America to Australia and Africa, based on Volkswagen and Porsche platforms and powered by VW or Porsche engines. These include, for example, former Wehrmacht vehicles converted for civilian use, or spectacular home-made models. Countless vehicles that guarantee more sportiness than the Beetle are shown and described.

Buggies as Trendsetters

The large group of dune buggies represents a separate chapter in the history of automobiles. Buggies are only covered in this book when a manufacturer also offered other special models. The reason for this is that there is already a whole lot of literature on this type of vehicles. Trikes and the Formula Vee are only mentioned in passing; both types are so diverse that they could only be comprehensively documented in special treatises.

A Wealth of Creations

Between 1939 and the early 2000s more than 500 manufacturers and well over 1400 special models are identified until now. There is already literature on the most famous special models and small series, for example from Puma or Rometsch. Beyond that, little was known until now. The wealth of existing creations can only be discovered after years of research on the Internet, in magazines and in a few books. Until now, there has been no comprehensive publication on the subject of „special models based on Volkswagen and Porsche". The situation was, and still is, too confusing for many manufacturers, who often quote large production figures in order to gain more credibility on the market, but who in reality only quote small numbers elsewhere, so that the tax authorities do not collect too much tax.

Structure of the book

It is almost impossible to create a structure that meets all the requirements with the material available. In principle, a chronological structure makes sense. If a manufacturer was present on the market for a longer period of time, the production date of the first special model based on a VW or Porsche is decisive for the assignment to a decade. Within a decade, the data is arranged alphabetically. The designation of the special models usually follows the name of the creator. If there is no specific designation, the name of the vehicle includes its geographical origin, if known.

The first volume covers the earliest models up to the 1950s. The second volume covers special models from the 1960s and 1970s and the third volume covers the 1980s until today.

Research continues

Even after 12 years of research, no claim to completeness and accuracy can be made, given the wealth of material available. Some of the sources are so sparse that it is necessary to evaluate the testimony of the descendants of the creators and their family histories in order to arrive at reasonably plausible information, which is often far from certain. We want to invite everybody to a dialogue. Notes, comments and additions will be posted in the „Durchgeboxt" Facebook group and published as soon as possible.

The story of Volkswagen-based specials is far from over. Almost every day, new and interesting images appear, bringing new things to light. A closer look reveals the complexity of the subject. Only a tiny fraction of the variety of vehicles ever produced is known to the general public.

Note on Sources

For a historian, every source is a valuable piece of the puzzle in reconstructing a possible historical reality. Due to their age and the photographic technology available at the time, some of the pictures in this book are of relatively poor quality. However, these pictures are of great importance in the context of the history. In many cases, the pictures are the only ones known or available to date. The author would be grateful to receive any further information on manufacturers and vehicles covered.

Dr. Thomas Braun
Sankt Poelten (Austria)
29. April 2024

INTRODUCTION

Colorful mix of beetles

Without the invention and development of plastics, the wide variety of special models based on VW would not have been possible. As early as the mid-1930s, Porsche engineers were experimenting with plastic bodies. A car with a body made of soya bean extract was also produced in America. After the war, small and medium-sized manufacturers bolted handmade aluminium or sheet steel bodies onto the undercarriages of discarded Kübelwagen and KdF cars, but it was not until the appearance of the Chevrolet Corvette in 1953 that GRP bodies made their big breakthrough. The development of the Porsche Type 60 is outlined, which was already available from 1938 in variants that would later be called special models. Two plastic bodies were also produced in 1938. Due to the high production costs, the idea of a plastic body was abandoned. In 1939, the first Porsche sports car was built for the journey from Berlin to Rome. After the war, reconstruction was anything but easy. The occupying powers were slow to relax their restrictions. But progress could not be stopped.

Every year, large gatherings of Beetle and Bulli enthusiasts take place all over the world, especially in Europe. This photo was taken in the Styrian Alps in 2012.

History of the Automobile

History of Kitcars

Kit cars have been around since the earliest days of the automobile. In 1896, for example, the Englishman Thomas Hyler-White developed the design for a car that could be assembled at home. Technical designs were published in the magazine „The English Mechanic". In 1900, the same magazine launched a 56-part series of articles with instructions on how to build an automobile. In the USA, the Lad's Car of 1912 could be bought for $160 turnkey or for $140 in kit form.

It was not until the 1950s that the idea of the self-built car really caught on. Slowly, an industry of its own grew up that provided new bodies and, in some cases, chassis so that new vehicles could be built from existing components of mass-produced vehicles. Due to economic considerations, primarily fibre-reinforced plastic (fibreglass) was used for the vehicle parts produced in small series. In the 1970s, smaller manufacturers exported their vehicles in the form of semi-finished products in order to avoid having to comply with the sometimes very complex regulations for series-produced vehicles. The best-known example worldwide is the Puma do Brasil, which was delivered in this way as a kit to America, among others. The dealer in the USA only had to invest a few hours to be able to provide turnkey vehicles for customers.

In the 1970s, kits were mainly designed that could be screwed directly onto the chassis of a VW-Beetle. Since the body of the Beetle can be separated from the chassis relatively easily, it was possible for many ambitious hobby car builders to fulfil their dream of an individually designed vehicle in this way. On the VW-Beetle, practically all mechanical components are attached to the chassis. Once the original body is detached from the floor assembly, almost any type of custom body can be put on. This made the Beetle one of the most popular „donors" for kit cars of all time. Until the 1980s, the kits were produced by the thousands. The Dune Buggy, which became popular in the late 1960s, was also produced in relatively large numbers. Most buggies were bolted onto a shortened floor assembly.

In the 1980s, safety regulations were massively increased, so that only high-quality kits could survive on the market. Many of these kits are replicas of well-known sports cars or expensive classics. As a result, there are more replicas of some classics than original vehicles. The goal of the manufacturers was always a product that was constructed in such a way that anyone with a certain degree of technical skill could build a car at home and with standard tools. To facilitate registration, there were often sample certificates that had to be presented to the TÜV during the inspection. The bodies of these replicas usually look approximately like the prototype, but are almost exclusively made of GRP.

Many manufacturers refrained from buying the right to produce and sell such replicas. This brought the industry into disrepute, because several manufacturers filed injunctions against the producers of the replicas. Nevertheless, a kit car was often the only way to get a sporty-looking car on a limited budget. Particularly noteworthy is the kit developed in England in the mid-1970s for an ultra-flat vehicle that was named the Nova. Shortly after the first version of the Nova appeared, the rights to produce the kit were sold to America. Within a few years, further licensed productions were made in Europe and Africa. Under various names and in different versions, the kit became an absolute blockbuster. The revolutionary exit and entry, made possible by lifting the car roof, fascinated the scene. Even sceptics were convinced that a kit car could be an alternative to the hardly affordable luxury cars, especially since the quality of the kits was steadily increasing. A study carried out in the 1990s showed that, depending on the completeness of the kit, between 100 and 1,500 hours were invested in building the vehicles. The stricter the requirements for operation on public roads became, the more professional the finished vehicles appeared.

In the 1990s, the complexity of the kits increased so that it was hardly possible for amateurs to build such a vehicle. This work was increasingly taken over by professionals who procured donor vehicles on behalf of customers and delivered the finished dream car after a few months. So it comes as no surprise that kits currently on the market require around 5000 hours of work to turn them into an individual car with road registration.

Sources
A small car and how to build it, in: The English Mechanic and World of Science (magazine), 56 articles from year 1900 onwards.
Alan Sutton, „Mr White and his Motor Cars", The Automobile, June 1986.
https://en.wikipedia.org/

Introduction

Working with Plastic

More than 10 years after the first sports cars made of GRP were presented at the Peterson Motorama in November 1951, Robert Cumberford published a first retrospective on the subject of GRP in the automotive industry. In 1962 he came to the conclusion that there was only one reason to build a body from GRP yourself. It is about uniqueness and thus, ultimately, about pride as the driving force for such an undertaking. There are people who will not be happy even by owning a Ferrari, simply because someone else built the car. These people will sit down and make their own sketches, develop ideas and file around until they are really happy with the curves and lines. Sketches should also be provided from all angles, but at least from the front, rear and side. Even better would be a cross-section through the body at significant points.

After drawing, a small model is made to see how the project will look in about 1:14 scale. Robert Cumberford recommends making the model with a minimum length of 30 cm and from a material that does not harden completely so that changes can be made later. This model forms the basis for the development of the moulds for the body parts, which are extrapolated from the appropriate scale to 1:1. It is already recommended in the early 1960s that the body should consist of not much more than five parts. This creates GRP parts that can provide stability and torsional rigidity, and the shapes can be designed with manageable complexity. In his report, Cumberford advises having as large a workshop as possible so that the vehicle in the making can always be viewed from a distance and its effect checked. In this way, errors can be corrected even before the vehicle sees the light of day.

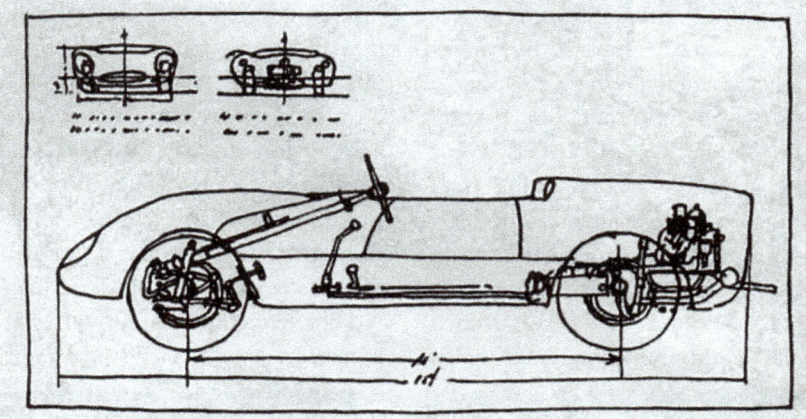

Sketch of the composition of body and chassis created by Robert Cumberford in 1962.

A frame made of wood or wire or a combination of both materials is used to build the production moulds. Cross-sections from the small model, extrapolated to natural dimensions, are arranged slice by slice about every 40 to 60 cm and joined together. Cardboard or similar material is stretched on this grid. The last millimetres are built up with clay, thus creating

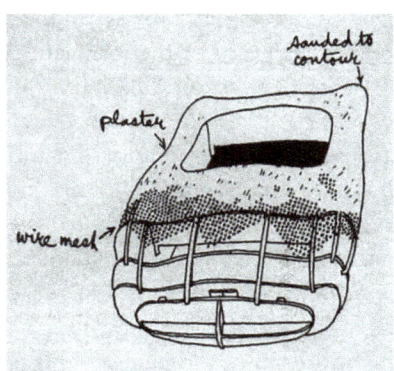

1:1 model skeleton and surface design.

the negative form, so to speak. In the 1960s, the surface of the 1:1 model was still covered with plaster and the surface was smoothed with sandpaper until the moulds could be removed from it.

As soon as the moulds are ready, the release agent and the base coat can be applied. After that, glass fibre mats are laid on, painted with epoxy resin or polyester and hardener and the procedure is repeated until the desired wall thickness of the body part is achieved. Care must be taken to allow sufficient time for curing between the individual layers. After about 24 hours, the part can be removed from the mould and left to air dry.

Some of the individual parts have to be very heavily reworked so that they fit together somehow. The connection between two parts made of GRP is always a critical one. If the components are under tension at the connection points, cracks will appear which will have a negative effect on the whole vehicle later on. The body is built on the chassis of choice and prepared for painting. A primer is applied, which is especially suitable for GRP parts. Afterwards, the last unevennesses are removed by

History of the Automobile

means of filler. Applying the paint is almost a negligible effort compared to the preparation work.

Robert Cumberford sums up his own experience of developing a body by recommending getting one of the 30 custom GRP bodies already available rather than trying to do it yourself. The learning curve to be taken is not in proportion to the quality of the realistically expected result, which will be anything but perfect in the first throw. Despite this rather pessimistic assessment regarding building a body yourself, the market boomed at the end of the 60s. Especially in the 70s and 80s, hundreds of kit cars were created and put on the road by enthusiastic individualists. The fact that time and again - even today - abandoned kit projects turn up in barns testifies to the often underestimated challenge associated with such a project.

Sources
Robert Cumberford, Don't Build That Fiberglass Body! Car and Driver (Magazin), September 1962
With kind support of Geoffrey Hacker (www.forgottenfiberglass.com/)
Robert Cumberford, Don't Build That Fiberglass Body! Car and Driver (magazine), issue September 1962
With kind support of Geoffrey Hacker (www.forgottenfiberglass.com/)

Original or Fake – Replica or Self-built?

In art, an original can only ever be a unique piece, the original of a painting as opposed to a reproduction or print. In the field of automobiles, the term „original" or „originality" must be specifically defined. With regard to historic vehicles, a distinction should be made between originality and gradations in the sense of a degree of originality. To illustrate this, a short anecdote once reported by Martin Schröder is given in advance:

Ray Jones, an American resident in the south of France, is the proud driver and owner of an SSK Mercedes. He speaks quite openly about the fact that he once built a much more desirable Mercedes SSK from a 4-seater Type-S by shortening the chassis and modifying the body. Whether he gave the car a new chassis number and thus its own identity would be an interesting detail. For the purposes of our question, it is necessary to clarify in which respect one should speak of originality or even of forgery.

It is relatively easy to answer the question of originality if there is a definition of „originality" on the part of the manufacturer for the now historic vehicles. If a car has undergone significant modifications, the matter becomes somewhat more complicated.

The highest degree of originality is found in all those vehicles that have made it into the present day over the decades without any special modifications. This includes, among other things, vehicles in an equipment variant that corresponds to a potential state of delivery. In order to be able to assess this, it is necessary to know the basic configuration of a vehicle and the scope of extras for each model and year that could be assembled ex works. Customer requests that were regularly fulfilled before delivery must also be taken into account in this context. These may include, for example, the fitting of a towbar or the installation of a car radio. From the definition of the basic model, the respective available additional equipment and the additional equipment options available before delivery to the end consumer, it can be derived which characteristics a vehicle may have in order to be awarded the highest level of originality. This is also the context of the term „matching numbers", which makes it clear that neither the chassis nor the engine have been replaced. If available, the engine number and chassis number must be entered in the vehicle documents. In addition - if available - the gearbox number, which matches the corresponding year of manufacture.

Special conversions are deemed to have been made if they were or are subject to registration or if they led or lead to the expiry of the road registration. Particularly in the case of historic vehicles, it should be noted that the registration regulations have always changed over time. Modifications may have been legally registered one year and have meant an illegal change to the vehicle one year later. When assessing a historic vehicle, the timing of a modification is therefore essential.

Next to the special modification measures are all those minor modifications that changed neither the technical characteristics of the vehicle nor the basic character of the vehicle and could be carried out without being presented to the authorities. The installation of a steering wheel from the accessories trade or, for example, the installation of an additional shelf under the dashboard of a Beetle can be mentioned here. These accessories are always subject to a trend. The historian knows the typical elements of an era and can judge

whether an accessory fits the life story of a vehicle. In this context, it is interesting to note the tendency to equip originally built classic cars with as many accessories as possible from the period in order to turn a vehicle of the highest originality class into a classic that is as individual as possible. Cars with installations and conversions with components that primarily come from the accessories trade, were not subject to registration and were quite common in the course of a vehicle's life history can thus characterise an „original with authentic modifications".

Significant modifications that were registered in the vehicle documents lead to the fact that one can speak of an original vehicle with contemporary modifications that require approval. These conversions can lead to the creation of a separate type of vehicle. A good example are the conversion kits that turn a standard Beetle into a Baja Beetle, for example. VW Beetles were modified for races through the Californian desert at the end of the 1960s. Subsequently, components were created that could be combined to form a type of vehicle requiring approval, for which there was also a road permit after appropriate presentation to the authorities.

After essential modifications, which led to the expiry of the permit to participate in public traffic, the vehicles always had to be presented to the authorities. This new complete assessment led to „individual approvals". If a VW Beetle was converted into a Dune Buggy, a new vehicle was created that received its own vehicle registration certificate. In the case of these vehicles, the date of the individual approval certificate is decisive for their status as a historic vehicle. For the discussion surrounding the Mercedes converted from Type-S to Type-SSK, what is decisive is what is written in the vehicle documents. If the conversion is registered and the registration is older than 30 years, it is a historic vehicle with special conversions. As soon as an individual approval is available, one can speak of a further „original condition". These vehicles can also be considered to have „matching numbers". Conversions that require approval and those that do not require registration are considered separately, because from the date of the individual approval, one assumes a new vehicle from a legal point of view.

Replica

If the conversion or the construction of a vehicle on an existing basis pursues the goal of imitating another vehicle as closely as possible, one can speak of a replica. There are also several gradations for these types of vehicles.

If a vehicle is restored to its original condition with special conversions, this can be referred to as a replica in the sense of a deconstruction. Here, an attempt is made to identify the „original substance" and around this original core a vehicle is built that is as close as possible to the original delivery condition. This is what happened, for example, when the prototype of the 1938 Beetle underwent a comprehensive restoration. Based on the identified unchanged components from 1938, the reconstruction of the original vehicle was carried out with historical and new components, which were rebuilt according to construction plans from that time. Depending on the extent to which the original substance has been preserved, it must be examined in which case one can speak of a replica or a new construction. If, for example, the chassis and body of a Volkswagen are separated, the question arises as to how far it seems legitimate to build two cars. One of these replicas has an original body and a replica chassis. The second replica has an original chassis and a replica body. This results in a proliferation of vehicles that is not actually desired.

The term „replica" is also used when an alien technical basis is used to build a vehicle with the appearance of another vehicle. In this context, a technical basis that does not correspond to the basis of the intended model is considered foreign. Individually developed components can be used for the replica. Many replicas also make use of the spare parts shelf of the manufacturer of the original vehicle. In the past, both replicas that were tolerated by the manufacturer of the original and those that were created without the approval of the manufacturers of the original vehicles were created. The approval or toleration of a replica meant that the affixing of trademarks and logos was not prohibited, but neither was it forbidden. Thus, our Mercedes is a replica, which was probably created in ignorance of the original manufacturer. Since the vehicle is transparently declared to be a replica, it can be assumed that it is a replica if it has a valid road registration, and that Mercedes at least did not prohibit it. Particularly in the 1980s, there were regular court cases which ended with the destruction of the vehicle in question in accordance with the respective judge's ruling.

History of the Automobile

Degree of Originality

There is a general consensus that the frame of a vehicle establishes its identity. The engine plays a subordinate role in this context, as it may have been replaced in the past or is sometimes missing altogether. In the case of a classic, the question is how original the car still is. Such cars often have more than seven decades under their belt since they were new. A period in which perhaps the engine or an engine part was replaced, the original axle could no longer be saved, or the like. A Porsche from the fifties with the exact leather seats with which it was once delivered is considered original. The same applies if missing parts have been replaced by parts of the same or similar age. However, as soon as you start restoring and reconstructing, things get a bit more complicated.

Originality is present when the vehicle is in a patinated state. This is one explanation why unrestored cars sometimes fetch better prices than fully restored examples. Old cars, meanwhile, are allowed to have patina. They are allowed to look old. This is also reflected in the Turin Charter, where the World Federation of Classic Car Clubs published its guiding principles in 2013 to support and promote the preservation and responsible use of historic vehicles. According to these, as much original substance as possible should be preserved. To check the originality of a vehicle, several steps must be taken. Even the existing documentation on a car can be an indication of originality. Manufacturers can often provide information about the condition on the day of delivery. This roughly sets the starting point for the search. Pictures of the vehicle from previous owners and the current owner also help to draw a picture of a car's history. Specialist literature can also provide clues as to which equipment features were fashionable at which time and can therefore be part of an authentic vehicle. Restoring a vehicle to its as-delivered condition can possibly go too far if important aspects of a car's history

are thereby erased forever. In view of the value trends, it is tempting to aim for a perfectly crafted car when restoring it. However, every new part reduces the degree of originality. In the case of wear parts, it is often advisable to reach into the spare parts store. Depending on the age and rarity of a vehicle, replica components are often the only way to complete a car.

An automobile can only be preserved in its as-delivered condition if it goes from production to the museum, as happens now and then with the last produced example of a series. With appropriate use, the automobile leads to wear and tear. Apart from tyres, there are thousands of other parts or components that are subject to wear. When it comes to spare parts, two terms have become established: N-O-S (new old stock) for original parts that have survived from the time of current production to the present day, and reproduction parts from remanufactures, as offered both by specialised dealers and by the classic departments of the industry.

An example from Brazil: Volkswagens were equipped with Solex Brosol carburettors in the 1960s and 1970s.

Central tube frame of VW30 number 26 plus 1:1 model out of wood.

Replica – Recreation – New Built

Many an automobile museum has vehicles of which only artefacts have survived the test of time. In order to keep the history of these automobiles alive, many vehicles have been rebuilt around the few original components that have survived. Of the Auto Union Type C, for example, only one original chassis has survived. The example in the Deutsches Museum was completely rebuilt on this chassis and marked accordingly. The VW 30 from 1937 was completely rebuilt around the only surviving central tubular frame. Contemporary pictures and documents,

INTRODUCTION

primarily from East German archives, were consulted in order to design the vehicle as closely as possible to the look and feel of the historic prototype of the pre-series KdF car.

The story of Max-Gerrit von Pein is interesting. In the early 1990s, the then director of the Mercedes Museum commissioned a double-digit number of SSK chassis - the numbers vary between 12 and 18 - from Thyssen in the alloy of the 1920s. There was talk in the press at the time that they did not want to have the original SSKs wrecked at the Mille Miglia. Another argument was, „We have the plans and the copyright." Here it is difficult to decide whether the resulting cars are replicas or new builds.

VW30 number 26 recreated after more than four years of work.

Sources
With the kind support of Martin Schröder and family Grundmann.

A Typical Conversion

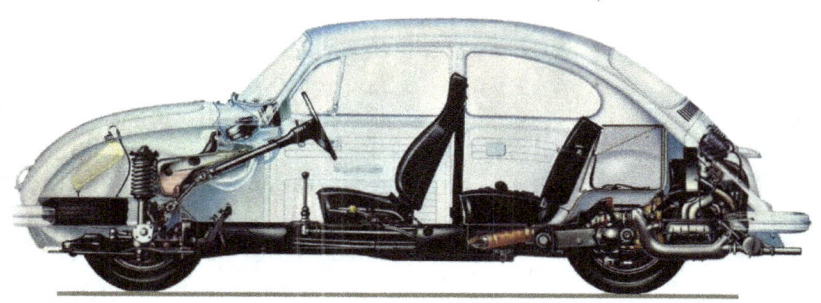

Especially in the era of conversion vehicles, a kind of standard procedure developed when a Beetle was to be turned into an individually designed dream car. Countless building instructions were produced. At that time, every kit supplier included building instructions with his kit to enable a hobby craftsman to realise the dream of a self-built car. The following pages will show you what is important in such a project. What possibilities the Volkswagen chassis has to offer the car hobbyist and what should best be done by a professional.

Searching for a Good Basis

Above: X-ray image of the VW-Beetle.
Below: typical rust spots marked in yellow.

When buying a Beetle, you should primarily look at the body, but when looking for a good basis for the conversion, your interest shifts purely to the parts that are to be reused later. In this respect, it is helpful to know the places where rust typically develops very well on the Beetle. The sill moulding, for example, is often a problem area that cannot be seen directly. It is often necessary to lift up the carpet in the interior to be able to guess the condition of the vehicle. A careful look under the running boards also gives an indication of

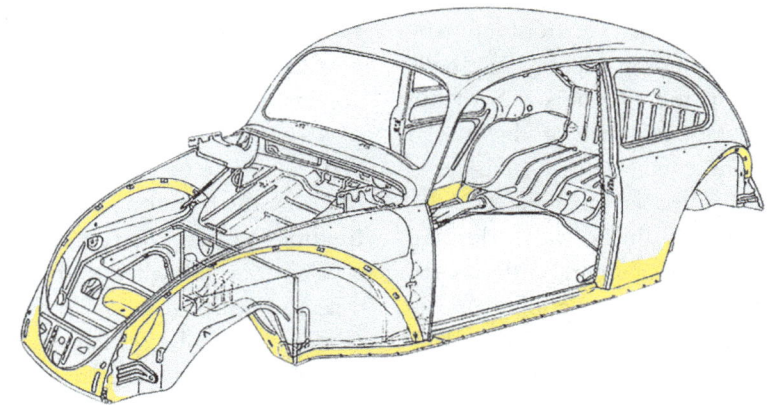

the overall condition of the Beetle. The Beetle also likes to rust in the area of the heating ducts and the

17

History of the Automobile

battery. Concentrating on the floor assembly, the front frame head and the entire floor panel should be checked very carefully by tapping. Even if thick underbody protection has been applied, the sound or resistance when tapping with a screwdriver, for example, can give an indication of rust-through. Unprofessional repairs can often also be considered as destruction of the substance.

Rolling chassis after lifting off the body.

By pressing the belt pulley back and forth, you can detect any axial play of the crankshaft or damage to the front main bearing. When starting the engine, it should start spontaneously after a few revolutions. If the starter slips, this can be very expensive. After long periods of standing, oil may have collected in the cylinders due to the long standing time. If the smoke remains even when the engine is warm, there is most likely a defect. Often this is valve damage on the 3rd cylinder, as this is directly under the air cooling and is not cooled sufficiently. The valves therefore overheat and suffer damage.

Removing the VW body

The body of the Beetle is relatively easy to separate from the floor assembly. Due to slight differences between the various years of manufacture of the Beetles, the position of individual parts may differ from the general instructions, but the basic procedure is as follows: Start by disconnecting the battery, draining the fuel tank and removing it. All electrical connections must be disconnected. Then disconnect the steering column from the Hardy washer on the steering gear and pull it out into the interior. The connecting hose between the brake fluid reservoir and the master brake cylinder must also be disconnected. The front seats and the rear bench seat are removed together with the backrest. The carpets in the front footwell and the coverings stuck to the floor panels of the frame must also be removed. Along both sides under the doors, at the front bulkhead and at the bridge under the rear seat, the VW body is connected to the floor assembly with a total of 28 screws (spanner size M 17). Two further fastening screws are accessible from the boot, the last two screws can be reached through the wheel cut-out above the shock absorber suspension when the rear wheels are removed. After removing all screws, the body can be lifted upwards from the floor assembly with three helpers. Between the body and the chassis is a rubber seal which should not be damaged when removing the body. This seal will be reused later when the new body is fitted.

The following parts should still be removed from the VW body: Bulbs, regulators, interior lighting, switches, wiring harnesses, windscreen wipers with linkage and motor, instruments, locks, locking wedges, mirrors, hinges, handles, crank apparatus, fittings and small parts. These parts can be reused in the construction of many kit cars and help save money.

Preparing the Chassis

Topic number one is always rust control. Often the seat rails and jack mounts have to be removed before the kit can be assembled. On chassis from August 1967 onwards, the gear lever can be rotated. To avoid negative effects, experts recommend removing the gear lever and replacing it with one of an older type. For this to be possible, the old shift linkage must be pulled out to the front and a slot sawn in the ball mount with the hacksaw. The camber of the rear wheels can be shifted negatively by one degree to compensate for the weight saving of the new body. If you plan to widen the track with spacers, wider wheels or on chassis with double-jointed axles, the original camber is retained. Often chassis stiffeners have to be fitted to ensure the torsional rigidity of the vehicle.

Shortening the chassis

Many kit cars will only fit on a shortened floor assembly. Depen-

INTRODUCTION

ding on the kit manufacturer's specifications, between 25 and 40 cm must be removed. When shortening, always make sure that a section about 2 cm longer is cut out of the floor panel, because afterwards the resulting parts are overlapped and welded together again. First, the gearshift linkage is separated from the gearbox at the end of the frame tunnel. Then the sheet metal plate at the front for fixing the gear lever can be removed and the linkage can be pulled forward out of the frame tunnel. Now the pedals can be removed, the cables loosened at the rear and pulled out to the front. The handbrake lever must also be removed and the two handbrake cables pulled out to the rear. The two cables for the heater are also pulled out of the frame tunnel. Along the tunnel 144 cm can be measured to the front on both sides and a mark made (148 cm applies to 1302/1303). Another mark is made 25 cm in front of each of the first marks. Then measure about 6 cm forward on the outer edges and make a mark. The second mark is again to be placed 25 cm further forward in each case. This determines the segment to be cut out of the floor assembly. Manufacturers of small series made templates in the 70s to be able to shorten the chassis as quickly as possible. It is recommended not to cut through the floor panel completely, so that the whole construction is still halfway stable during cutting in the area of the frame tunnel. This is important because the cutting of the frame tunnel has to be done very carefully in order not to damage

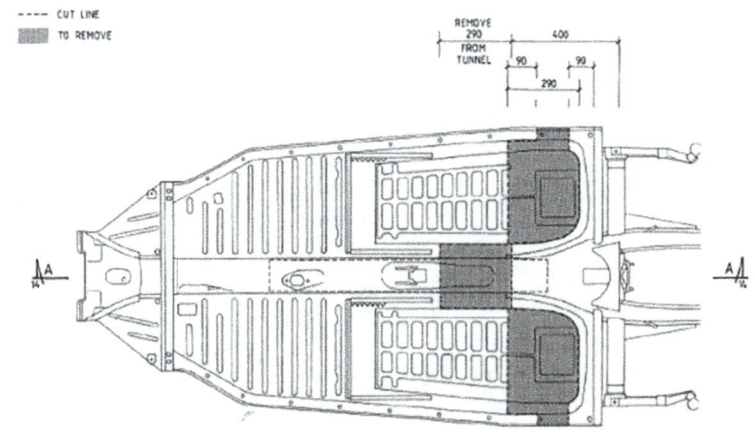

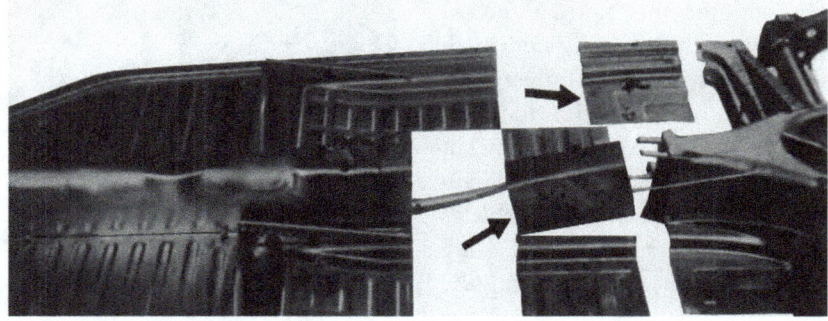

Left: the areas marked in dark are cut out when the chassis is shortened. Right: the cut-out sheets before the individual parts are welded together.

At the top of the frame tunnel, a rectangle measuring 38 x 9 cm must be cut out so that there is later access to the inside of the frame tunnel. On the sides of the frame tunnel we measure 10 cm backwards and 5 cm downwards to be able to cut out another rectangle on the left and right. Once the segment has been cut out of the floor assembly, the two remaining parts can be welded together again with an overlap of 5 to 6 cm. Before the welding machine is used, exact measurements must be taken. The parts are set up and fixed so that the symmetry of the vehicle is still upright later. There should be a side length of about 150 cm on both sides.

The guide tubes for the heater control and the handbrake cables must be shortened. Shorter cables, which were usually included in the

The main components before assembly.

kit, should be pulled in here later. A 25 cm long piece is also cut out of the linkage for the gearstick and then welded together again.

Lowering the Seats (optional)

For tall drivers but also for certain kit cars the seats have been lowered. For this purpose the floor plate has to be cut along the rails for the seats. At the end of the running rail, the floor panel is also cut crosswise to the direction of travel. Then the segment with the running rails can be carefully pressed down up to 15 cm. Now two sheet metal wedges can be cut to size and welded in vertically on the left and right. On some vehicles the wedges were laminated using GRP. This way, when pushing the seat back, it can be pushed down at the same time and additional headroom can be gained.

Mounting of a Tubular Frame and Camber Modification

After removing the spring strut hub cap, the spring strut is detached from the rear brake anchor plate and pulled from the torsion bar after the spring strut has been drawn in its original position with the torsion bar. The torsion bar is reinstalled twisted upwards by one pitch each on the inside and outside of the torsion bar. The top fixing screws of the spring strut cover are screwed back in together with the screws of the anchor plate. This creates about 10% negative camber. Then the tubular frame supplied with the kit can be slid under the chassis. This is done so that the open fork points to the rear. The frame is lifted and screwed into the lower holes of the spring strut cover with the two lugs using two hexagonal bolts M6x85mm each and enclosing spacer washers. At the front, four bolts M10x65mm are provisionally fitted in the slotted holes and the square tube of the frame. The two square tubes on the outside of the frame on the left and right are drilled all the way through with a 9mm ~ drill at the fixing holes in the floor panel (5 holes on each side).

If the body needs to be extremely flat, the floor panel below the seats can be lowered.

Preparing the GRP Body

Many operations are easier to carry out when the body is not yet assembled. For example, sawing out the holes for the instruments, the side air vents, the engine air ducts, fitting the headlights, tail lights, number plate lights, windscreen wiper system. If necessary, sound insulation can be fitted around the engine compartment. When drilling fibreglass, always choose the lowest possible speed. Drilling should also always be done on the smooth side so that any material that breaks out cannot cause any visible damage. Measuring points and markings should always be made with a pencil. Marker pens can permanently alter the surface. A simple hand saw is sufficient for cutting GRP. When using a jigsaw, ensure that the finest possible cutting blade suitable for metal is used. The surface should be protected from scratching with tape along the planned cutting line. After cutting, the cutting line can be smoothed or optimised with a file. When joining metal to GRP or GRP to GRP, large shims should always be used so that when mechanical loads are applied, the forces can act on as large an area as possible. If GRP parts are laminated to metal, the metal must be roughened well beforehand so that optimum adhesion can be achieved.

Putting on the body

The tubular frame is placed underneath again. The four front fastening screws of the frame are removed again. The body is now placed on the chassis, aligned and screwed to the floor assembly through the pre-drilled holes. Using a 9mm ~ drill bit, the body mounting holes must be drilled through the sides under the door boxes and in the flange of the rear storage area. Use a ll mm drill to drill four holes in the front partition.

After the VW rubber sealant has been applied to the floor assembly with Teroson or VW Sealing Compound and the underside of the mounting flanges has also been coated with the sealing compound used previously, the new body can finally be bolted to the floor panel.

During this operation, make sure that body shims with a diameter of at least 10 mm are inserted between the head of the bolts and the nuts.

Electrical System

The original VW wiring harness from the VW 15oo is often used for the wiring itself. As polyester has no electrical conductivity, special care must be taken that all devices not only receive power supply, but that an additional earth wire is also laid.

Heating System

The basic principle of the Volkswagen's heating system is also used in many kit cars. Commercially available heating hoses with a diameter of 55mm run from the heat exchanger to the adjustment controls. From there, these hoses continue under the door sills to the front of the dashboard, where they end in two adjustable nozzles for defrosting the windscreen. The heating of the interior is done by two short heating hoses, which lead from the heat exchanger to the regulator flaps in the transverse sheet metal wall behind the driver's seat.

Fitting the Steering Column

After removing the steering wheel, the VW steering column is disassembled to such an extent that it can be pulled out of the jacket tube. To do this, the circlip and the following brass washer must be removed from the head of the steering column. After the flange for fixing the Hardy washer has been removed, the steering column can be pulled out of the jacket tube. The steering column, often supplied by the manufacturer of the kit vehicle and fitted with a maintenance-free intermediate joint, is reinstalled in the VW jacket tube in the reverse order. The mounting flange for the Hardy disc, which has been removed from the Volkswagen steering column, is refitted exactly as on the old steering column.

A hole of 45 mm is drilled in the front partition wall for the jacket tube to pass through. The steering column is pushed through the partition from the interior and screwed to the steering gear with the Hardy disc. Two 8 mm holes are drilled through the underside of the dashboard to fix the jacket pipe. A cut-out of 8o x 25 mm is also made in the underside of the dashboard at the height of the connection box for the indicator switch and the ignition lock. The outer casing can now be screwed in place. Again, make sure that body shims are placed underneath.

Fuel Tank

The fuel tank is inserted into the opening provided for this purpose in the inner casing and the height of the filler neck is marked. The filler pipe must now be shortened accordingly. Then the four mounting holes for the tank can be marked and drilled on the interior panelling. The two front body mounting plates are inserted and screwed to the suspension points on the front axle on one side and to the body itself on the other side. Again, large body washers must be used. The mounting of the plates on the front axle is done with the original VW rubber elements and screws.

The brake fluid reservoir is bolted to the front of the inner casing using the VW fastening tape. A 12mm ~ hole is drilled in the partition and the reservoir is connected to the master cylinder with the brake fluid hose.

The fuel tank can now be finally installed and screwed on. A 12mm ~ hole must be drilled in the front partition for the stopcock, into which a rubber seal is inserted. The stopcock is fitted and the tank connected to the fuel line leading to the engine.

Instruments

The installation of the instruments, switches and indicator lights leaves many possibilities for the application of own ideas. The original VW instruments can be fitted. Of course, it is always possible to fit additional instruments such as rev counter, oil pressure gauge, oil thermometer or similar instruments. Please note, however, that when taking over instruments from other vehicle brands, it will be necessary to calibrate the instruments to the new conditions if the display is to correspond to the facts.

Bonnet Cover

Often a wooden block was and still is glued into the bodywork in such a way that the hinges for the car's hood can be mounted on it. The bonnet is placed on top and the position of the fixing holes for the hinge tab is marked. At this point, a wooden block for each hinge part must also be laminated in with fibreglass mats. Then the hinges are attached.

Before this, the canopy must be aligned. To do this, place the lid in the opening of the main part so that the gaps are the same size all around. Now transfer the hinge fixing holes to the previously glued wooden block and pre-drill them with a 2.5rnrn drill. Wooden screws connect the canopy to the hinge part. Three holes are drilled on each side of the canopy flange, in which canopy spacers, for example from the Ford 12m or 15m, are fixed. These spacers allow precise adjustment of the bonnet in relation to the main body part. A Bowden cable provides the connection from the bonnet lock to the passenger compartment.

Gluing in the Windows

If windscreens are used that come from production vehicles, the appropriate seals are available for fitting the windscreens into the thoroughly cleaned windscreen frames. Newer windscreens are now only glued in place. The sealant needed for bonding is often supplied with the standard kit.

First, the respective windscreen is fitted into the body. The distances from the pane to the body are determined, and small wooden blocks are cut to the appropriate thickness.

The discs as well as the body are covered with adhesive tape and the glued areas are coated with sealant on both sides. The discs must now be pressed into the body flange until they are flush with the surface of the body. Now the previously cut wooden blocks are pressed into the still soft rubber to hold the disc in the required position. After the sealing material has hardened, the wooden pieces are removed and the resulting opening is closed with sealing compound. Now the adhesive strip can also be removed. The adhesive mass that has come out at the gluing points is cut off with a knife or razor blade.

Painting

Most body parts are almost flawless on the outside. Nevertheless, there are small material weaknesses and mould seams that have to be sanded down and then brought into line with the contour using a body putty (drawing spatula). The surface of most body parts consists of a particularly tough and scratch-resistant gel-coat. All GRP parts should nevertheless be sanded with water-based sandpaper (400 grit) before painting to create a good bond with the paint. To remove dirt and grease, the entire body should be washed with trichloroethyl (Tri). Painting should be done in a dust-free environment - ideally in a heated box. After application, the paint can be baked at a temperature of up to 65 degrees C.

GRP Care and Repair

Depending on the finish of a GRP component, care and repair can be carried out. Body parts with a gel-coat finish should be cleaned regularly and coated with a protective layer of wax. GRP parts that have been pigmented throughout can also be treated in this way. For painted parts, there are polishes and wax preparations that will keep the surface looking radiantly fresh for many years.

For deep scratches or unevenness, new material must be applied. For the repair of gel-coat surfaces, gel-coat powder in the corresponding colour shade and a catalyst are required. For touch-up work on GRP parts with continuous pigmentation, things become similarly difficult. It is assumed that synthetic resin, to which the same proportionate amount of colour pigments has been mixed, and a catalyst are available. It is relatively easy to remove craters and irregularities on GRP parts that have a painted surface. Here, the surface can be smoothed with filler. By means of colour analysis, the recipe of the surrounding paint can be calculated and the desired amount of paint can be remixed. The fact that usually neither gel-coat nor synthetic resin with the right amount of colour pigments is available explains the fact that most kit vehicles have now received at least one coat of paint.

Repairing GRP parts can be very costly. In most cases, more or less small structural insecurities develop over the years, which manifest themselves in the form of small cracks on the surface. These cracks can extend through the entire cross-section of the part due to mechanical stress. In this case, the problem must be treated from both sides. With a suitable tool, one begins to widen the crack. In doing so, one should proceed with the angle grinder only up to the core material in a V-shape along the crack. The final fine sanding

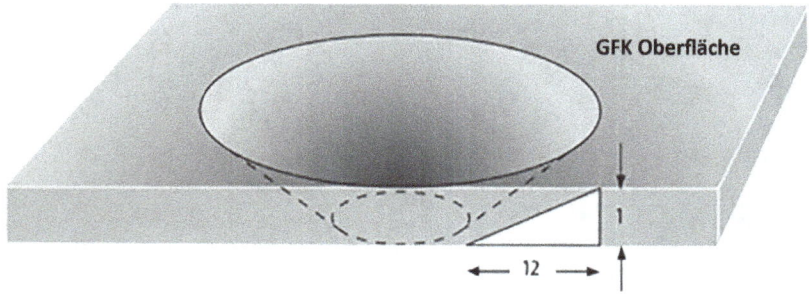

When repairing GRP, the damaged laminate is sanded at a ratio of 1:2.

should always be done by hand.

The correct mixing ratio of resin and hardener (usually 4:1) is important for successful work with epoxy. It must be meticulously observed. Resin and hardener are available in canisters of different sizes with a dosing pump. One stroke of resin plus one stroke of hardener - and the mixture is correct. Otherwise, follow the three golden rules for processing: measure exactly, stir slowly, mix thoroughly. Epoxy resins and even more so their hardeners are toxic. Health protection rules must be followed urgently. So: Only go to work wearing protective goggles and gloves. Contact of resin and hardener with eyes or skin causes irritation. A dust mask must be worn when adding fillers and when sanding. Elaborate extraction systems, on the other hand, are not necessary. Although epoxy also evaporates, no solvents are released, such as the harmful styrene in polyester.

Sources
With the kind support of family Schneider and Volkswagen AG.

The unshortened chassis of the VW-Beetle with lowered seat recesses and 4-cylinder in-line engine in the mid-engine configuration ready to accommodate the Mantacars body.

CARS of the 1980s

Kitcars at the Summit

The 1980s is generally regarded as the decade of the most powerful cars. One notable example was the Porsche 959, which was the fastest road-registered car of its time. The legendary Ferrari F40, the last creation of company founder Enzo Ferrari, also set new standards. On the other hand, the development of „fuel-efficient" cars was driven by the ever-increasing price of petrol and an increasingly heated environmental debate. Kit cars were able to strike a balance between an exciting sports car and moderate fuel consumption. Against a backdrop of high accident rates worldwide, the call for greater safety became louder and louder. Tighter legislation pushed the kit car industry further and further into a shrinking niche. Small manufacturers in particular cannot afford the crash tests that have become mandatory. Only the highest quality and most elaborate kit cars are approved for road use. The price of these cars at the end of the 1980s was comparable to that of series production.
Reproductions of classic 1960s Porsches and Ferraris were typical of this period. Examples include the Aspen 550 RSK, Beck Replicas, Charmonix, Cintra 959, Classic Roadster, Corbet Countach, CTC Panzer, Pulsar 911 and many more.

The Rawlson 250LM is a remarkably authentic replica of the Ferrari 250LM. The car on display has been restored in 2018 to its current state and is impressive in every way.

CARS OF THE 1980s

AC Sportcar (PT)

In the early 1980s, A. Dornhai Automóveis Lda. of Figueira da Foz developed a gullwing sports car similar to the MBC Charger that had been launched in England years earlier. Marketing of the AC Sportcar began in 1982. The car was built on the undercarriage of a VW-Beetle. Customers could bring in their used Beetles. The conversion was completed within a few weeks. The standard version was powered by a 1.5-litre Volkswagen boxer engine. The 1.2-litre, 1.3-litre and 1.6-litre engines from the Volkswagen range were available as options. Deceleration was provided by disc brakes at the front and the typical Volkswagen drum brakes at the rear. The rectangular headlights could be hidden behind a flap under the bonnet. The GRP body was mounted on a tubular steel frame and bolted to the floor pan. The gullwing doors were standard. A soft top was also available as an option for the convertible version. The plan was to build 24 cars in the first year of production. The AC sports car was to be built to order. At that time it was expected that 5 cars per month would be ordered. It is no longer possible to say exactly how many AC Sportcars were actually built. However, it can be assumed that less than 10 cars were built by 1985. Production of the AC Sportcar ceased in 1985.

Available from 1972, the AC Sportcar could be ordered with gullwing doors or as a convertible with a soft top.

Technical Details
AC Sportcar
Engine: VW engine
Power: 34 - 50 hp
Length: 3920 mm; Width: 1620 mm; Hight: 1220 mm; Wheelbase: 2.400 mm
Weight: -

Sources:
O Automóvel AC Sport Car, Turbo (magazine) issue 8 from 1982.
http://rodasdeviriato.blogspot.co.at/2009/10/ac-sportcar-na-revista-turbo-1982.html
http://rodasdeviriato.blogspot.co.at/2008/04/ac-sport-car.html
http://rodasdeviriato.blogspot.co.at/2010/10/ac-sport-car-por-recuperar.html

Akamine   (BR)

A new edition of the Malzoni GTM was launched in São Paulo (SP) in 1987. The car was built on the platform of the VW Brasilia, which had to be shortened by 30cm.

Akamine Convertible
A convertible version of the Akamine was presented to the public at the 1989 Motor Show. The car was offered as a kit and as a turnkey version.

The convertible version of the Akamine was presented at the São Paulo Motor Show in 1989.

CARS OF THE 1980s

Akamine Buggy

Also in 1989, a buggy was introduced that could be bolted to the floor of a VW-Beetle. Both a hardtop and a softtop were available for the Akamine buggy. There was also a choice of two different bonnets.

The 1962 Albar Jet looked very professional back then.

Sources:
www.lexicarbrasil.com.br/akamine/
Officina Mecanica (magazine), issue 11 from 1987.

Almenara Buggy   (BR)

In the early 1980s, Anuar Chequer, a mechanical engineer from Itaúna, developed a buggy he called the Almenara. The design was completed in 1983. The following year, 1984, the first unit of the newly created buggy was built.

The first prototype was made from wood in 8 months with the help of Antonio Lacerda. The body was made in Anuar Chequer's workshop. Most of the cars were assembled in Belo Horizonte. The car itself could be described as both a buggy and a kit car. The entrance - without a door - is clearly in the style of a buggy. The rear is more like a sporty speedster. The front end is a very unique creation, lacking bumpers in the classic sense, but on closer inspection resembling the Colani GT.

There were two chassis options for the body, both from Volkswagen. The buggy was a Monoquoc design made from fibreglass and built on the floor pan of a VW-Beetle. Most of these air-cooled Almenaras were fitted with an air-cooled 1,500 or 1,600 cc boxer engine.

The second, slightly longer version was built on the floorpan of a VW 1600 TL from 1971 onwards. The water-cooled Almenara was fitted with a 1.5 or 1.6 litre engine from the VW Passat. In this version the rear end was slightly longer to make room for the radiator.

In addition to the speedometer

and fuel gauge there was an optional rev counter on the dashboard. Alloy wheels were also available at extra cost. The headlights were from the Brasilia or Passat. The air intakes at the front were mainly for visual reasons. The car offered space for 2 + 1 persons. In the back the third person had to sit on an emergency seat.

Between 1984 and 1988, 17 units were sold. Over the years the Almenara underwent a number of improvements. However, the basic design always remained the same. In comparison to the first car, the following productions used different seat upholstery, Telmo wing mirrors, different rear lights and wheels.

Sources:
www.diariodojequi.com.br/
http://brasilforadeserie.blogspot.com/2011/03/almenara.html?utm_source=BP_recent
www.lexicarbrasil.com.br/

CARS OF THE 198

Alto (UK)

Peerhouse Cars, based in Farnham, Surrey, started production in 1983. Production ceased in 984. Cardo Engineering tried in vain to continue production in 1988. In total about three cars were produced. The body of the Alto is very similar to that of the Avante GT.

> **Sources**:
> Chris Rees, Peter Filby, Classic Kit Cars, p. 13.
> George Nick Georgano, The Beaulieu Encyclopedia of the Automobile. Volume 1: A–F, Chicago 2001, p. 41.
> Steve Hole: A–Z of Kit Cars. The definitive encyclopaedia of the UK's kit-car industry since 1949. Sparkford 2012, p. 24.

Alto from Peerhouse Cars from 1984.

The kit could be bolted onto a VW-Beetle platform. Alternatively, a spaceframe chassis with an Alfa Romeo engine in the middle of the car was planned. Power was provided by either air-cooled Volkswagen Boxer engines or water-cooled VW Golf engines. A mid-engine version with Alfa components was also available.

American Fibre Craft - AFC (US)

American Fibre Craft Inc. was founded in February 1979 by Robert S. Mueller. The company was based in Cupertino, California. The company's main products were the Aquila and Stiletto. American Fibre Craft also offered various adapters that allowed Mazda and Porsche (Porsche 911) engines to be fitted to a Beetle transmission. A Porsche engine with a 5-speed Porsche gearbox was also fitted to the company's own kits on request. This often resulted in kit cars with no less than 270 bhp, which was easier to get on the road in America than in Europe.

AFC Aquila (1980-1981)

Robert (Bob) Mueller developed the first Aquila in 1979, based on the chassis of a VW. The Aquila prototype was built in Bob Mueller's garage in Santa Clara. In terms of style, he based his creation on a BMW show car called the Turbo. There is also an undeniable stylistic affinity with the BMW M1.

The Aquila kit went into production in 1981. The Aquila was one of those kits that could not be assembled in a matter of days or weeks. However, with a little effort, an experienced hobbyist could build a very nice car.

CARS OF THE 1980s

Above and previous page: Around 50 kits for the Aquila were sold. Most of the vehicles were equipped with VW engines. Some customers installed engines from Porsche or Mazda.

The interior of the Aquila is very well laid out. The armrest in the doors doubles as a glove box. The profile of the armrest merges seamlessly into the dashboard when the doors are closed. The centre console extends almost all the way behind the seats and features an armrest with storage space underneath and space for additional engine monitoring instruments. The light switch controls the automatically extending headlamps. Air inlets are located at the front of the bonnet to supply the car's fresh air system. A semi-automatic air conditioning system was available as an option. In order to keep the car as low as possible and still provide sufficient headroom, the rear floor halves of the Beetle were replaced by specially lowered sloping floor panels. Once the floor panels were welded in, the position of the gear lever and pedals had to be changed. A ‚builder's kit' contained all the materials needed for the conversion, including additional wiring, fans and exhaust system.

Adapters to fit a Mazda engine were supplied by Kennedy Engineered Products at the customer's request. This required significant modifications to the cooling system. The company also supplied an adapter for the Porsche 911 engine. In 1982, an electrically powered Aquila with a power output of 20 bhp was produced.

It is estimated that around 50 kits were sold. The existence of the cars with body numbers 44, 112, 143 and 144 is certain. A modified Aquila was completed in Quebec - the body number is unknown. A yellow car was offered for sale in Texas. A white car is also for sale as a project in America. Only about half a dozen cars were actually built, due to the high level of expertise required. One of them is in Detroit and can be seen regularly at car shows.

Technical Details
AFC Aquila
Engine: VW, Mazda, Porsche
Power: 34 - 100 hp
Length: 4170 mm; Width: 1880 mm; Hight: 1090 mm; Wheelbase: 2.400 mm
Weight: 870 kg (empty)

AFC Stiletto

The Stiletto is a further development of the Aqila. Bob Mueller tried to improve the car in detail. However, his efforts are unlikely to have progressed beyond the prototype stage. No finished car is known for a long time.

The prototype of the Stiletto. It never went into series production.

Sources:
www.vwkitcars.com/aquila-kit-car-by-american-fibre-craft/
www.kitcarmag.com/tech-faq/26104/index.html
www.evalbum.com/3379
Harold W. Pace, The Big Guide to Kit & Specialty Cars, Castle Rock 2010, p. 80.
Kit Car (magazine), issue 3 from 1998, Air-Cooled All Stars
http://priceofhistoys.com/aquila-vw-kit-car/

CARS OF THE 1980s

Angelmar (AT)

Between 1980 and 1994, Mr Angelmar from Klosterneuburg built three cars based on VW-Beetles and resembling various Ferrari models. The bodywork of the sports cars is made of GRP and is extremely carefully crafted, considering that the builder is a self-taught car mechanic.

The second car weighs around 820kg dry and is powered by a 1.5 litre VW Boxer engine producing 60 bhp. The third car has a Porsche Super 90 engine and four disc brakes. The dashboard is very similar to that of the Porsche 911, with some of the switches coming from the VW-Beetle 1302/1303 or VW Type 3.

Sources:
Austro-Classic (magazine), issue 2 from 2005.
Auto Revue (magazine), issue November 1986.
www.motorclassic.at/php/main_site/modell.php?markeAktuell=Angelmar&typAktuell=Angelmar%201500

The Angelmar II is very well made and is in a car museum in Lower Austria.

Aspen 550 RSK (US)

In the mid-1980s, a company based in Fontana, California, produced the Aspen 550 RSK Spyder. This was a mixture of various Porsche variants from the 1950s with references to the Porsche 550 Spyder. Initially the Aspen was only available as a finished car. Only later were kits sold that could be bolted to the undercarriage of a VW-Beetle. The first Aspens were fitted with air-cooled engines. Later the car was also available with water-cooled engines. In 1985 a mid-engined version was produced, using a Porsche 914 power unit.

Sources:
Harold W. Pace, Kit & Specialty Cars, American classics from the past and present, Anaheim, 2. Ausgabe, 2002, p. 119.

The Aspen 550 RSK is a mixture of several Porsche variants.

Aumann (DE)

Peter Aumann founded Aumann-Kunststoff-Fertigung GmbH in Rheine in February 1985. Shortly afterwards he started to develop kits for cars. On 23 August 1989, Aumann-Kit-Cars-GmbH was entered in the Commercial Register of the Rheine District Court. Cancellations were made on 11 April 1992, 25 June 1999 and 1 December 1999. 1992 was probably the end of the production of Aumann kits. From 1986, Aumann offered a kit for converting a VW-Beetle into a van with a side-hinged rear door. Shortly afterwards, the Speedster and Spyder kits were added to the range.

CARS OF THE 1980s

Aumann Van (1986-1992)

The kit for converting a VW-Beetle into a van was created in 1986. It could be a kind of licence production of a Vandetta. The kit was laminated behind the driver and passenger doors after the roof and most of the rear structure had been removed from the Beetle.

Aumann Speedster (1987-1992)

In 1987, Peter Aumann introduced the conversion kit for a VW Speedster. This was primarily a modification of the rear of the car, resulting in a two-seater convertible in the tradition of the Hebmüller cabriolet. Aumann's Speedster is characterised by the air vents above the bonnet, positioned between the bonnet hinges.

Aumann Spyder (1987-1992)

The kit for the Spyder is very similar to that for the Speedster. Similar to the Porsche 550, the contours of the integrated headrests of the rear seats behind the driver and passenger were modelled. For both the Spyder and the Speedster,

Aumann offered widened inner fenders and special GRP running boards.

Sources:
http://de.wikipedia.org/wiki/Aumann_Kit-Cars
Harald Linz, Halwart Schrader: Die Internationale Automobil-Enzyklopädie. München 2008.
www.moskopp.com/vw-pkw/aumann-speedster
www.allcarindex.com/
www.cruisenewsonline.com

From top to bottom: the Aumann delivery van (orange), the Speedster (dark green) and the Spyder (drawing).

Avante (UK)

Melvyn Kay, Terry Sands and Paul de Roma of Avante Cars Ltd, based in Stoke-on-Trent, Staffordshire, launched their latest product, the Avante MK, at the 1981 Kenilworth Motor Show. The car was manufactured by Clewlows Motors in Stoke. It sits on a Beetle chassis and looks very similar to the GT40 from the front and the Ferrari Dino from the rear. In 1987, Top Hat Coachworks of Blackpool, Lancashire, took over the moulds and production rights. Today we can only speculate whether any significant numbers were produced.

Avante MK (1981-1982)

Unlike previous cars in this category, the car had normal doors, cranked side windows and enough room for an average European - even up. The body was mounted on its own steel frame and bolted to the Beetle's chassis. Parts of the body that needed extra strength were reinforced with sheet steel.

Technical Details
Avante MK
Engine: VW
Power: 34 - 50 hp
Length: 4010 mm; Width: 1600 mm; Hight: 1170 mm; Wheelbase: 2.400 mm
Weight: 840 kg (empty)

CARS OF THE 1980s

On the road, the Avante represented a successful compromise between sporty design and practical handling. All stages of completion were offered, from pure kit to finished car. In addition to the classic boxer engine in all its variants, engines from the Golf, Scirocco, Lancia, Lotus Twin Cam and Porsche 914 were also fitted. The Avante MK's lighting system is particularly attractive. The headlights can be uncovered by means of a folding mechanism. This changes both the angle of the headlights and the position of the louvres for optimum light output. The complete interior was available as an option on the Avante. It is estimated that a total of around 50 cars or kits were sold between 1981 and 1983.

Avante MK II (1982 - 1986)

The Avante Mk II was introduced towards the end of 1982. The Mark II was slightly higher and also longer than its predecessor. The fuel tank is located at the front of the Mark II so that the original 2-seater could become a 2+2 coupé. The small rear window is heated. Relatively small triangular windows have been added to the sides behind the doors, which also give the driver a larger field of vision diagonally to the rear. In the Avante Mk II, the rear window can also be heated. Unfortunately, only a few vehicles or kits were delivered before Avante Cars Ltd. ceased trading. Collectors' circles believe that around 10 kits were produced. Only a short time later, the „Alto" appeared on the market, which utilised the technology of the Alfasud and was also produced until 1986.

Above: the Avante MK with a very elaborate design. Below: the very spacious Avante MK II from 1982.

Technical Details
Avante MK II
Engine: VW
Power: 34 - 50 hp
Length: 4220 mm; Width: 1750 mm; Hight: 1210 mm; Wheelbase: 2.400 mm
Weight: 1080 kg (empty)

Sources:
www.allinoneweb.co.uk/avante-home.html
www.priceofhistoys.com/category/avante/
Kit Car (magazine), issue Dec. 1982.

BCW Model 52   (US)

British Coach Works Ltd. of Arnold, Pennsylvania sold kits and finished cars between 1980 and 1985. The body of the Model 52 is an imitation of a 1952 MG TD. The range was supplemented by appropriate accessories.
BCW went to great lengths to make their Model 52 as authentic as possible. A real 1952 MG TD was used as a model for the development of the kit. Many original TD parts are used. Most of the chrome and trim (bumpers, lights, grille, etc.) can still be ordered from Moss Motors. The TD accessories fit perfectly.
The 1952 MG TD replica was

CARS OF THE 1980s

available between 1980 and 1985 in the rear-engined version on a Volkswagen chassis with an air-cooled flat-six engine. The front-wheel-drive version was fitted with a Chevette engine and mounted on a specially designed subframe.

The MG radiator grille, the long flowing fenders, the low-slung doors and the rear-mounted spare wheel cover give the car a distinctly British look. The typical two-tone colour scheme also gives the car an authentic appearance. British Coach Works focused on quality. The gap dimensions fit surprisingly well. Even the details are beautiful with pinstripes that combine both two-tone colours. The soft top also has a high quality finish. The side windows can be zipped in if required.

The interior also looks very authentic. The seats appear to be correctly upholstered. The curved dashboard in real wood and the arrangement of the instruments correspond to the original. A little unusual for a kit car is the well-functioning heater, which makes

it possible to drive in colder weather.

Because the body is made of GRP, the finished car is considerably lighter than the 1952 MG TD. The air-cooled boxer engine from the VW-Beetle also provides surprisingly good acceleration. This makes the replica much sportier than the original.

British Coach Works launched the replica of a MG TD 1952 in 1980.

Sources:
http://davidsclassiccars.com
https://classiccars.com/

Beck Replicas (US)

Chuck Beck, president of Atlanta-based Beck Development Corporation, became known for his custom racing products. His company quickly became even better known for the classic car replicas he added to his line. With Chuck Beck's replicas, you can always tell that he is not just copying, but improving, while never losing sight of the original idea behind the solution. Only Beck and Envemo have the official „factory authorisation" from Ferry Porsche and Helmuth Bott to use the original design. All other manufacturers of Porsche replicas must deviate from the original at least to a certain extent, or risk an injunction.

Beck Spyder

Chuck Beck's first replica was built in 1982 and was based on the Porsche 550 Spyder. Based on the floorpan of a VW-Beetle and powered by a VW Type 1 Boxer engine, the car could be offered at a fraction of the price of the original. Around 200 Beck Spyders

CARS OF THE 1980s

were sold.

Only Beck and Envemo were allowed to create exact replicas.

The Beck 904 is five inch longer than the original.

Beck 904

Chuck Beck's third major project was dedicated to the Porsche 904/908. Ferdinand Porsche designed the Porsche 904 in 1963,

Technical Details
Beck 904
Engine: VW
Power: 34 - 50 hp
Length: 4190 mm; Width: 1630 mm; Hight: 1070 mm; Wheelbase: 2.310 mm
Weight: 660 kg (empty)

which was also marketed as the Porsche Carrera GTS road car. Three prototypes were built and tested. These were the first production cars with a Porsche fibreglass body. Changes and improvements made during the tests led to the development of the Porsche 908, which was officially presented to the public in November 1963. Between 1963 and 1965, around 100 units were produced in order to obtain homologation.

The Porsche 904 also inspired kit car developers because of its spectacular shape and rarity. Chuck Beck did not create an exact copy, but a very good kit. The Beck 904 was very close to the original. While the Porsche 904 was designed for competition, the Beck kit was designed for street use. So that a driver of „normal" stature could drive the car, he stretched the wheelbase by 5 inches compared to the original. This widening of the body allowed the driver and passenger to get in and out of the car comfortably, as well as providing a relatively comfortable seating position, without significantly changing the overall height of the car.

Sources:
http://www.beckspeedster.com/

Beep Netuno (BR)

Beep Parts Industry and Trade Ltda Mooca, based in São Paulo SP, was founded in 1979 by Claudio Labate. The aim of the company was to produce GRP body parts for the car accessory trade. Between 1983 and 1988, the company also produced a replica of a Corvette Stingray based on the Beetle. The car was designed by Claudio Labate himself. He had already put one of the first Baja Bugs into production in Brazil in 1977. The Beep Netuno consisted of a plastic bodyshell that could be screwed onto the undamaged floor pan of a Beetle. The kit was designed for the late 1.6 litre Bee-

Beep Netuno convertible with softtop from 1983.

tles and the more modern McPherson strut suspension. Disc brakes were usually fitted to all wheels. Inside there was a choice of leather upholstery or vintage cloth. Equipped with two carburettors, the 1,600 cc engine produced 65 bhp with slight modifications. Considering the car's low weight, subjectively it was quite a fun car to drive. The kit was available as a 2-seater coupé and as a convertible (Netuno C) with a rubberised fabric roof. Less than 10 kits were sold.

Labate

In 1991, Claudio Labate began building neo-classic cars, which were largely free interpretations of various cars from the 1920s and 1930s. This resulted in at least four models bearing his name: the Labate 1903 (with a VW Boxer engine at the rear), the Labate 1922 (Chevrolet Opala engine), the Labate 1929 and 1934 limousines (Ford V8 engine). For a long time, the Labate neo-classics were hired out for weddings or receptions.

Labate neoclassic launched in 1991.

Sources:
www.forumfuscabrasil.com/index.php?topic=17420.390
www.allcarindex.com/auto-car-model/Brazil-Beep-Netuno-C/
www.lexicarbrasil.com.br/netuno/

Belfusca (BR)

Santina Veículos, a Rio de Janeiro-based car manufacturer, was founded in 1985. The Belfusca was launched in the same year. It was a buggy with a striking shape that could be driven all year round with a hardtop. Two years later, Santina introduced the Beljippe, a pick-up with the angular shapes that became increasingly popular in the 1980s. Both vehicles were available as kits and as turnkey vehicles. The rights to produce the Belfusca were later transferred to Duna.

Belfusca Buggy

The Belfusca Buggy has a rounded front line with a striking appearance. The four rectangular headlights at the ends of the body make the car appear wider than it actually is. A hard top was available as an option to ensure that the car was equipped for all weathers. The soft top was made from red and white striped canvas.

Top: The Belfusca Buggy
Below: Beljippe from 1987.

Beljippe

In 1987, Santina presented the Belijpe, a very functional car with room for four people. The roof is attached to the windscreen frame, the roll bar, the door and a brace between the windscreen and the roll bar. Without the roof, the result is the appearance of a Targa. The roof construction consists of the two front side panels and the cover for the rear row of seats and the luggage compartment. The four rectangular headlights are taken from the Belfusca.

Sources:
www.lexicarbrasil.com.br/

CARS OF THE 1980s

Bernardi (CA)

The Bernardi is a further development of the Cimbria SS.

A variant of the Cimbria SS was also offered in Canada in the mid-1980s. However, very few cars (allegedly less than 10 until 1989) were built under the Bernardi designation. Whether this was a licensed production or a more or less tolerated copy is not known today.

Fortvac Automobiles in Quebec marketed the Bernardi for some time. The car was stretched a bit and some fundamental changes were made. For example, the entire rear of the car could be opened and the engine was placed in the front of the car. The Pantera-style rear wing is one of the optional extras. Contrary to the tradition with kit cars, the DOT (Department of Transportation) in Canada was able to give the car a general approval with a certificate.

The Bernardi was built on a special chassis optimised for a V8 engine. According to the manual, the brake system was taken from the Corvette. As a fully-fledged car, it was a sort of halfway house between the Cimbria and the Viper 2000. The high price and the not too well-known name of the manufacturer were probably the main reasons why the car did not become a bestseller.

Apparently there are still a red, a white and a black Bernardi. The black Bernardi was also the model for the Bernardi brochures. The white Bernardi is owned by a collector. Unfortunately nothing is known about the whereabouts of the red Bernardi. There is also a rumour that copies of the Bernardi were made in America by Blakely Auto Works.

Sources:
www.nationalsterling.org/About.html
www.sterlingkitcars.com/history_pages/cimbria/history_module_cm.html
Harold W. Pace, KIT CAR, The Car Builder's Authority, 2. Edition, 2000, p. 87f.

Blasi Cross (BR)

The brothers Alfredo and Waldomiro Blasi, together with Felipe Nicollielo, built the first auto cross monoposto to be raced in Brazil in 1981. This set a new trend in rallying that lasted for several years. The car was first used on a track in 1983.

The design of the exhaust is interesting, pointing upwards at an angle of almost 50 degrees and rising high above the car. Optimised for use on bumpy tracks, the rear wheels are kept as close to the ground as possible by two shock absorbers. The entire structure is made up of a tubular steel frame that closes around the driver like a driver's cage. The body panels are made of relatively thin GRP to keep the overall weight as low as possible. The development was sponsored by CBP, a helmet manufacturer who later produced replicas of the Porsche Super 90.

The car had only one door on the left side. The roof could be easily removed by the driver as an emergency exit. The seating position took some getting used to. Taller drivers definitely had problems with the lack of headroom and legroom.

Like the early Formula Vee cars, the interior of the car didn't have much to offer. The 4-cylinder boxer engine of 1584 cc was fed by the usual Brazilian mixture of alcohol and petrol via two 40-bar-

CARS OF THE 1980s

rel twin carburettors. A rear wing, also unprecedented in this class, improved traction.

After a few years, however, enthusiasm for the Cross Monoposto waned and the cars disappeared from the track. The car shown here still exists today. It is privately owned by one of its creators.

Sources:
http://www.pumaclassic.com.br/

Blasi Cross from 1983.

Büffel Koupe (US)

The Büffel Koupe is still being built today.

Burly Industries, based in Mendon, Utah, developed the Büffel Koupe in the late 1980s. This was a conversion of a VW-Beetle into a 4-seater coupe with a notchback and split rear window. The Koupe is very similar to the Stoll Coupé and the Hebmüller Coupé. The front of the car is modelled on the front of a 1932 Ford Deuce Coupé. The design and moulds for the kit were developed by Bill Siddens in Indiana. The first Büffel Koupe was bolted to the floor pan of a 1968 VW-Beetle by Burly Burlile. The May 1989 issue of Hot VWs and VW Trends magazine featured the Büffel Koupe. In the 1990s the rights to the kit and the moulds were transferred to BGW Spectre. An almost identical kit is still offered today by BGW Spectre under the name Club Coupe.
The existence of at least one Büffel Koupe, assembled by a hobby mechanic from Mexico City, is certain. The car has a rain gutter running laterally above the doors from the windscreen to the middle of the rear wings. According to Burly Burlile, such a rain gutter was never part of his kit.

Sources:
VW Trends (magazine), April 1989.
Hot VW's (magazine), April 1989
Popular Mechanics (magazine), Feb. 1991.
Popular Mechanic (magazine), issue June 1989, p. 55.
VolksWorld (magazine), May 1989.
www.volksrods.com/forum/showthread.php?t=23473&page=3
www.bgwspectre.com/rodcoupes.html

CapCar (US)

A kit car-style sports car was probably built in America in the 1980s, based on expensive models from Lamborghini, for example. The GRP body was built on a VW Beetle platform. The name „CAPCAR" was embedded in the integrated bumper at the front of the car. With a few simple steps, the sports coupé could be converted into a convertible.
A CAPCAR convertible was offered for sale in California (Kew Gardens) in 2022. The platform was a 1969 VW-Beetle, which is why the car's documents show 1969 as the year of manufacture.

CARS OF THE 1980s

The car is powered by a boxer engine from a VW bus in mid-engine configuration with twin carburettors. The 4-speed gearbox comes from the donor car. The car is registered as a 1969 Triumph Custom Convertible Volkswagen.

Previous page and right: Cap-Car convertible with flipping doors.

Sources:
https://dailyturismo.com/car-car-1969-volkswagen-triumph-kit-car/

CBP (BR)

CBP Indústria, Comércio e Exportação, based in São Paulo (SP), began its involvement in the automotive industry in the early 1980s. CBP was previously known as a helmet manufacturer. Under the leadership of João Perfeito, the company entered the automotive industry with kits for autocross and baja competitions. The vehicles were offered both as components and as complete kits. In 1984, a replica of the Porsche 356 C Super was created, which was also available as a convertible. This was CBP's first step towards specialising in the reproduction of Porsche vehicles. The following year, a replica of the Porsche 550 Spyder was launched. This was followed shortly after by a replica of the 1973 Porsche 911 Turbo. In the 1990s, the company was sued by Porsche for unauthorised use of the brand name and for producing a copy of the Porsche 911. This happened at a time when the Porsche 911 was still on the market in Germany. From 1987 CBP also offered a replica of an MG MGA. Also in 1987, a commercial vehicle with a VW Boxer engine and plastic bodywork was launched. After João Perfeito's sudden death in 1994, a management buy-out was attempted. This failed and the production of kits and finished replicas was discontinued.

CBP Baja Bug
(1983 - 1994)

João Perfeito, a mechanical engineer, began his career in the automotive industry by developing VW Beetle conversions. In the style of the American model, he created an interpretation of the Baja Bug, which was offered as a kit and in the form of converted vehicles.

CBP Baja Bug from 1986.

Speedster Replica
(1984 - 1994)

The replica of the 1964 Porsche 356 C Super was built on the chassis and mechanics of the VW Brasilia. Manufactured by CBP, the car was powered by an air-cooled PS 65 flat-six engine. The moulds for the kit originally came from Envemo. The same moulds were later given to Charmonix.

Speedster replica from 1988.

CBP 550 Spyder
(1985 - 1994)

In 1985 the replica of the Porsche 550 Spyder was launched. The cars produced by CBP were fitted with a 1.6-litre Volkswagen boxer engine, as used in the VW Brasilia.

CARS OF THE 1980s

As an alternative to the air-cooled Boxer engine, the water-cooled AP engine with a capacity of up to 2.2 litres was also offered. The CBP 550 Spyder was delivered with disc brakes front and rear.

911 Turbo Replica (1986 - 1994)

At the São Paulo Motor Show, the Envemo stand featured the body of what was supposed to be a Porsche 911. A real Porsche 911 was also on display. The production of replicas of the Porsche 911 had been announced, and the demand was there, but no manufacturer had yet been found. During the exhibition, talks were also held with CBP, among others. João Perfeito made a deal with the developer of the replica and started production in 1987. CBP engineers mounted the body on a Volkswagen chassis and fitted disc brakes to the front axle. Within a short space of time, all the components had been developed or suppliers had been found to produce complete vehicles. As it was almost impossible to import vehicle parts due to high import duties and complicated regulations, parts from local series production were mainly used. For example, Alfredo and Waldomiro Blasi decided to use the mechanics of the Fiat 147 for the front suspension. João Perfeito found a strong partner in Newton Masteguin to ensure that the cost of the replica did not get out of hand. The former CEO of Puma do Brasil had gone into business for himself with Chamonix and was now supplying CBP with much-needed components. The cars produced by CBP were offered with either the 1.6-litre boxer engine from the VW Brasilia or a water-cooled AP engine with a displacement of up to 2.2 litres.

Above: CBP 550 Spyder replica from 1987.
Below: The 911 Turbo replica with VW technology.

EJ1 (1987 - 1994)

In 1987, a small car was created that was available as a pickup and in a 4-seater version. The EJ1 was a modification of the Formigão pickup originally developed by Renha. CBP bought the production rights and moulds. The project was later sold to Menon. The resumption of production failed. The EJ1 was built on the shortened underbody of a VW-Beetle. The rear is very reminiscent of the Kübelwagen. The rear hatch gives access to both the engine and the storage space inside the car. The car has similarities to the Puma Mini designed by Anisio Campos in the 1970s, but was far ahead of its time. The vehicle is powered by a VW Boxer engine, depending on the donor vehicle.

The EJ1 is basically a Formigão modified by CBP.

MGA (1987 - 1994)

In 1987 the replica of an MG MGA was added to the CBP range. These cars were also designed to be built on a VW Brasilia platform. The cars produced by CBP were fitted with 1.6 litre VW Boxer engines with twin Solex Brosol carburettors, as used in the VW Brasilia. The 2-seater convertible had an elegant velvet or leather interior.

CARS OF THE 1980s

CBP developed a replica of the MGA based on the chassis of a VW Brasilia; the picture was taken from a sales broshure from 1987.

Sources:
www.geocities.ws/motorcity/downs/5756/c.html
www.lexicarbrasil.com.br/cbp/
http://flaviogomes.grandepremio.uol.com.br/2008/11/xerox-2/comment-page-1/

Chalon (US)

The Chalon is a body kit that transformed a Porsche 924 into a Porsche 911 mixed with elements of the Porsche 959.

Mitcom Inc, based in North Hollywood, California, was a manufacturer of body styling accessories in the late 1970s and into the 1980s. With their help, customers could make their 924s look better. They could slant a 911 or turn it into a 959. The body modifications were made from GRP and offered in the form of conversion kits. The Chalon kit is a notable example.

The conversion kit for the Porsche 914 was marketed under the name Chalon. The conversion made the car slightly longer. The B-pillar was given a curved cover. All four fenders were widened and given different characteristics. The rear fenders had to be cut out for the conversion to bring them back into line with the doors. The wheels designed for the conversion would not fit into the original wheel arches. The bumpers are reminiscent of the Porsche 911.

This conversion probably won a few fans in the 1980s. Depending on the craftsman's skills, the 17 GRP parts, which often only fit approximately, could be made into a high-quality Chalon conversion. In most cases the work was outsourced to Profil. The basis was often a car that had been involved in an accident and needed to be repaired anyway. In any case, it is rather rare for a Porsche to form the basis of a kit car. This makes the Chalon a historically interesting example of its type.

Sources:
https://barnfinds.com/chalon-body-kit-1970-porsche-914-6/
Sales brochure of Mitcom from 1981.

Chamonix (BR)

The company Chamonix Ind. e Com. Ltda. was founded in 1985 in Jarinu (SP) by Milton Masteguin, the former CEO of „Puma Indústria de Veículos S.A.". Together with his son Newton and Chuck Beck, Milton Masteguin started the production of Porsche replicas in 1987. Most of the cars were exported to the USA (under the Beck name), Japan, Europe, Latin America and the Middle East. Approximately 70% of sales were made in Japan. In Germany, the Chamonix 550 was assembled by Gehrke Classic Cars in Ketsch and the Bavarian company Scheib and sold as a complete vehicle or as a kit. The focus on export meant that more attention had to be paid to quality than in Brazil. The bodies were made using the hand lay-up method. This allowed for a consistently high quality surface finish on the GRP components. The Chamonix cars are recognised worldwide as Porsche replicas with outstanding workmanship. The Chamonix 550 Spyder was named the world's best replica in its category by the German magazine auto motor und sport and the American magazine Road & Track.

The first Chamonix model was the 550 Spyder in 1987, originally designed by Chuck Beck. The Super 90 Convertible was introduced in 1988. Production of the 550S Spyder began in 1992. Barely a year later, in 1993, the Speedster 356 was offered with 62 and 120 bhp engines. Through a collaboration with João Perfeito of CBP, Chamonix obtained a licence to build the Porsche Super 90. In 2000, Chamonix entered the racing scene for the first time with the 356 R and 550 R models. The 550 R was powered by a 1.8-litre VW engine with a turbocharger that produced 300 bhp. Milton Masteguin was unable to achieve his goal of creating a 365 Cup.

At the same time as building the Porsche replicas, Chamonix also offered services to third parties. A prototype was built for Autolatina. A rally version was also developed for Fiat and the moulds and tools were built. Around 1,500 cars were built over a period of more than 20 years. Due to the economic crisis that began in 2010, exports to Japan and America were stopped. Production then ceased completely. Milton Masteguin died on 15 August 2012, but Milton's son Newton took over the factory in Jarinu shortly afterwards and resumed production on a smaller scale. In 2020 Athos Cars was founded under the management of Newton Masteguin. The replicas are still marketed under the name „Athos".

550 Spyder (1987 -)

Chuck Beck designed the body and frame of the Porsche 550 Spyder replica. The Chamonix 550 Spyder uses a 3" tubular frame. All Type 1, Type 4 and air-cooled Porsche engines can be installed in the mid-engine layout. Access to the engine is provided by folding up the entire rear of the vehicle.

The Porsche 550 Spyder replica is visually and technically very close to the original.

The use of VW and Porsche components means that spare parts are readily available. Details such as Heating, air conditioning, vanity mirror, power steering, navigation system, electric seats, car radio and the like are not available in this vehicle. The driving characteristics are not far removed from those experienced by Hans Herrmann or Graf Berghe von Trips on the racetracks of the 1950s and should not be falsified by modern technology. Disc brakes were fitted front and rear. The standard air-cooled Volkswagen flat-twin engines had electronic fuel injection and produced 65 bhp. From 2001, Chamonix also offered an optional 1.9-litre engine with twin Weber carburettors or fuel injection, producing 115 bhp for the Speedster and Spyder models.

550 Spyder S (1992 -)

Visually, the „S" model is very similar to the Chamonix 550 Spyder. Only the chassis has been com-

The Porsche 550 Spyder replica with roll bar for driver and front passenger from 2005.

CARS OF THE 1980s

pletely redesigned. Power comes from a 2-litre, 125 bhp, water-cooled AP engine from the VW Santana, with multipoint fuel injection and a 5-speed gearbox. The rear suspension comes from Dion and consists of oscillating trailing arms and coil springs. Disc brakes on all four wheels ensure the best possible deceleration of the car, which weighs only 680 kg and has a top speed of 230 km/h. With this configuration, the car accelerates from 0 to 100 km/h in 6.5 seconds. The Chamonix 550 Spyder S can be recognised by the front grille, which is necessary for the water cooler. There are also chrome roll bars behind the driver and passenger.

A small special edition of the Chamonix 550 Spyder S was launched in 2008. These cars were painted orange and the roll bars and rims were coated in grey graphite. The 1.8-litre AP engine with twin carburettors from the VW Gol produces 103 bhp in the petrol version. The alcohol-fuelled version for Brazil delivers 106 hp on the road.

Super 90 Convertible Replica (1988 - 1996)

In 1988, Chamonix launched the

Super 90 Cabriolet, a replica of the 1964 Porsche 356 C. CBP took over the production rights, moulds and tools used to build the cars. The Chamonix Super 90 is very similar to the Spyder in all its technical characteristics. The GRP body, the tubular frame, the mechanical components such as the VW Boxer 1.600 engine with 54 bhp (later 65 bhp) and the front disc brakes. A few Super 90 convertibles were also delivered with the 1.9-litre 120 bhp engine. Unlike the Spyder models, the engine was mounted at the rear. The car had side windows and a soft top. Less than 30

Porsche 550 Spyder S replica special edition from 2008.

cars were built until 1995 when production was discontinued.

Speedster Replica (1993 - 2010)

The replica of the 1954 Porsche 356 Speedster is almost identical to the replica developed by Chuck Beck. The collaboration between Milton Masteguin and Chuck Beck resulted in Chamonix ob-

**Red: Super 90 Convertible
Black: Speedster from 2007.**

taining the licence to produce the Speedster and at the same time taking over production of the Beck Speedster for Beck. The Chamonix Speedster has the same action as the Chamonix Super 90.

Sources:
www.gehrke-classic-cars.com
http://de.wikipedia.org/
www.automobilly.com/auto-wiki/chamonix/550
http://revistaautoesporte.globo.com/Revista/Autoesporte/0,,EMI89227-15846,00.html
http://revendachamonix.blogspot.co.at/

Cheda   (BR)

The Volkswagen dealership Mari Auto SA was founded in São Paulo in the early 1960s. In 1982, the company designed its first car, which was sold under the brand name Cheda. The Cheda CB is an elegant two-seater convertible with a wedge-shaped profile. The Cheda MB buggy and the Cheda MC convertible were presented to the public at the 13th Motor Show in São Paulo in 1984. Two new cars were also presented at the 1986 Motor Show. The Cheda MB Selva and the Cheda MB Endurance, presented in 1986, can be seen as further developments of the Cheda MB Buggy. After the

CARS OF THE 1980s

economic pressures of the early 1990s became almost unbearable for most small car manufacturers, Mari Auto SA was also forced to withdraw from car production. The rights to the Cheda models were probably sold to BRM in 1990, along with the moulds and tools.

Cheda CB (1982 - 1984)

The Cheda CB was built on a VW-Beetle platform that had been shortened by 30 cm. The GRP body is still very angular, although at this time the trend among car designers was towards more generous curves. Initially, the headlights were covered by Plexiglas caps. As these were banned, they had to be removed shortly after launch. Striking are the side air intakes behind the driver and passenger doors, also seen on the Puma AM. The door buckles are from the Alfa. The hood disappears almost completely into the body. The bonnet has a rear spoiler made of black-painted hard plastic. Chrome has been largely omitted. A VW boxer engine with a capacity of 1.6 litres and two carburettors, as used in the VW Brasilia, was installed in the rear of the car.

Cheda MB Buggy (1984 - 1986)

The Cheda MB Buggy was first introduced in November 1984. It was a 2 seater buggy with a very individual design. The car was designed by Mario Bellato Jr, who anticipated some of the design elements of the Griffon. The front of the car in particular looks very harmonious. The proportions are well balanced and well suited for use on Brazilian roads. The GRP body was built on a shortened VW Beetle chassis. A relatively spacious tool box is located under the rear seat. The most important instruments are mounted on the dashboard so that the engine status is always easy to read. Most Cheda MB buggies were delivered in two colours. The underbody and front spoiler were often painted in a contrasting colour to the rest of the bodywork.

From top to bottom: Cheda CB from 1982; MB Buggy from 1985; MC Convertible from 1984.

Cheda MC Convertible (1984 - 1986)

The Cheda MC is the direct successor to the Cheda CB. Launched in 1984, the car was largely identical to its predecessor. The front end of the car was significantly changed in order to gain approval for markets outside Brazil. New features included the rectangular twin headlights from the VW Passat and the marker lights above the bumpers. The side air intakes are now accentuated by black hard plastic covers. The car has an adjustable steering wheel, electric windows, sports seats and sound system.

CARS OF THE 1980s

MB Selva (1986 ?)

In 1986 Mari Auto launched two new models. Both buggies were further developments of the Cheda buggy. The Cheda MB Selva was designed for off-road use. Compared to the previous model, the front of the car was slightly modernised. The buggy got new bumpers, more ground clearance and wider tyres. A whole range of accessories was added. A spare wheel could be bolted to the bonnet as an option. A larger fuel tank, a cable winch, headlight shields, rear lights, a reversing light, additional headlights and a sports exhaust system were available as options.

MB Endurance (1986-?)

The MB Endurance was first offered for sale in 1986. This evolution of the Cheda MB Buggy looked both elegant and futuristic. It was to be powered by a 1.8-litre W-box engine with electronic fuel injection and 94 bhp (Type 4 engine). An adjustable suspension was also planned. The market prospects were not so good at that time. As a result, the Cheda MB Endurance never went into production.

Above: The MB Selva was designed for off-road use.
Below: The MB Endurance is particularly characterised by its futuristic styling elements.

Sources:
www.lexicarbrasil.com.br/cheda/
Motor 3 (magazine), issue 42 from December 1983.
Especial Fusca & Cia (magazine), Guia Histórico Esportivos de Fibra, issue 2015, p. 21.

Chimo (CA)

Customotive Inc. of Quebec introduced the Chimo kit in the early 1980s. This was one of the few GRP bodyshells still produced using the hand lay-up method. This made the tubular steel frame and body relatively light and less susceptible to stress cracking. The kit could be bolted to an unmodified Volkswagen chassis. In addition to the technology, the door handles, windscreen wiper mechanism and body locking mechanisms could be reused from the donor car. The side windows on the kit can be lowered, which was not a common feature on the kit car scene at the time. The windscreen from the GM Chevette fits into the prefabricated frame. All other windows are custom made and are included in the kit.

The standard kit included the one-piece bodyshell, pre-assembled doors, all glazing including gaskets, headlights and rear lights, steering column mounting brackets, a fuel tank conversion kit, steering column and dashboard. The many extras available from Customotive included tinted windows, an interior kit with seats, emergency rear seat, side panels and headliner, a set of instruments, a wiring harness with all the necessary connections and fuses and a defroster kit. The Deluxe kit included most of the extras listed above and was available for just under £5,000. At

CARS OF THE 1980s

least 5 Chimos are thought to have survived the test of time.

The interior was available in vinyl or vinyl/cloth. The GRP body was supplied in a white finish; although painting was recommended, the manufacturer felt it was not essential. A sunroof, rear window louvres and centre console were available as options. At least in the advertisements it is said that 80 hours of work are needed to complete a basic kit.

Sources:
www.cardomain.com/ride/2674468/1980-volkswagen-thing/
Sales brochure of Customotive Inc., 2719 Diab, St. Laurent, Quebec, H4S 1E7
http://priceofhistoys.com/chimo-vw-kit-car-body-for-sale-on-ebay/
www.evalbum.com/1554
www.evalbum.com/3112
www.montrealracing.com/forums/showthread.php?782670-What-is-that-car
www.kitcarmagazine.com/Classifieds/Item-Details.asp?id=725

The Chimo impresses with its good workmanship and unusual design.

Cintra 959   (BR)

In 1988, Aniso Campos became the patron of a design school. One of the students in the first class was André Cintra, who had already worked on the Porsche 959 at the age of 15. His masterpiece is a 1985 Beetle that incorporates many elements of the Porsche 959. First, sketches were made to anticipate the future proportions. Then came the first 1:1 prototypes for the new components. It took André Cintra almost a year and several attempts to get the moulds right. The Mexico Beetle was rebuilt step by step as the individual components were finalised. The first step was to remove the front fenders and the boot lid so that the GRP front of the car could be adapted to the existing conditions.

Anisio Campos supported the development of the Cintra 959.

The rear of the car is made up of two side panels which are laminated together after being bolted to the body. Apart from that, the technology of the Beetle can be largely reused. In keeping with the Beetle's new look, the wheels were of course based on the Por-

CARS OF THE 1980s

sche rims. Inside, the Cintra used Recaro leather seats. At least three units of the Cintra 959 were delivered with a turbocharged 1.8 litre engine.

Production of the kit and the market it could serve seemed promising. With the support of Anisio Campos, the kit was developed to production stage and offered under licence on the Brazilian market. The kit for the Cintra 959 essentially contains the three GRP parts needed for the conversion and a construction manual with instructions on which parts fit which car. The rear lights, for example, come from the Porsche 911.

Sources:
http://brasilforadeserie.blogspot.com/2011/03/cintra-959.html

Classic Roadsters (US)

The Duchess MG TD comes very close to the original.

Classic Roadsters was founded by Gary Rutherford in Fargo, North Dakota. In the 1980s, Classic Roadsters was the largest supplier of kit cars after CMC. In 1991 Rutherford sold the company. It took the new owner only 2 years to drive the company into bankruptcy in 1993. Rutherford bought it back. The new name of the company was „Cobra and Austin-Healey Replicas". In 2000, a Hummer replica called Badlands was released. The kit can be bolted onto a truck chassis.

Owners of kit vehicles have consistently given positive feedback on the workmanship and fit of the parts supplied by Classic Roadster. This is one of the recipes for success that has secured Gary Rutherford a significant market share in the kit car sector.

Duchess MG TD

In 1989 the Duchess, an MG-TD replica, was launched. The kit could be bolted onto a VW floorpan or a Chevy Chevette chassis. Compared to the original, the wheelbase is slightly longer to allow for a more comfortable interior. Many parts of the kit are simple copies of original MG parts. Another large part of the components are standard parts from the Chevy Chevette. The spare parts situation is correspondingly good.

Saxon Austin Healy 3000

The Saxon is very similar to the Sebring MX, which is also available from Classic Roadster. It is a relatively detailed replica of the 1962 Austin Healey 3000 sports car. The kit was not only available for V6 or V8 Ford engines, but also in a cheaper version that fitted on a Beetle floor pan. A number of parts from the Chevy Chevette could be used for the body of the CR Saxon. Later kits used many chassis components from the Pinto and Mustang II. One of the most significant differences between the Saxon and the Austin Healey: the Saxon had side wind deflectors and crank adjustable side windows.

The Saxon Austin Healy 3000 ialso very close to the original from 1962.

Sources:
Harold W. Pace, The Big Guide to Kit & Specialty Cars, Castle Rock 2010, p. 89f.
www.gtsca.com

CARS OF THE 1980s

Corbett Countach 5000S (US)

Adrian Corbett, founder of Corbett Motor Cars, developed the Countach 5000S, a replica of the Lamborghini Countach, in Santa Barbara, California, in the early 1980s. The basic version of the kit, designed to be mounted on a Beetle chassis, was available for around $3,900 at the time. The extended kit included all windows, sports seats and interior trim for $7,000.

The Countach kits can be divided into two groups. The less expensive ones were mounted on a Fiero chassis, while the more accurate but also more expensive variants required the Fiero chassis to be lengthened to the same wheelbase as the original. The Countach 5000S was the only VW based Countach kit from Corbett.

Countach 5000S replica from 1983.

Sources:
http://priceofhistoys.com/2008/06/07/corbett-vw-based-lamborghini-countach-kit/
www.kitcarmag.com/thehistoryof/0511kc_lamborghini_cars_history/viewall.html

Corsair (US)

Corsair Products in Ontario, California offered a range of kit cars between 1980 and 1984. Corsair Sales in Madison, South Dakota was also a distributor. Each kit was based on a VW-Beetle chassis with a GRP body bolted on.

MG TD (1983-85)

The Corsair MG TD is a replica of a 1952 MG TD. The kit, which was designed to be mounted on a VW Beetle chassis, was also offered under licence by CMC in Miami (Florida) and Fiberfab, among others. The cars built by Corsair were mainly equipped with the 1.6 litre VW Boxer engine. The GRP body has a white gelcoat finish. The doors are hinged at the rear, just like the original. The burl wood dashboard has a very high quality look. The 2-seater cabriolet has ample luggage space behind the one-piece bench seat for the driver and passenger. A soft top provides protection from the ele-

CMC and Fiberfab licenced the MG TD replica as well.

47

CARS OF THE 1980s

ments. Seat belts, wind deflectors, side curtains and a Persian rug were available as options.

Stripper (1980-84)

For Corsair, Chuck Berry designed a buggy with a detachable body called the Stripper. The body of the Corsair Stripper was made of fibreglass. For road use, the Stripper could only be driven with the body on. Away from official roads, the body can be removed in a few simple steps and the off-road fun can begin. The car is also occasionally offered under the name „Holiday Buggy". Around 150 Strippers were produced between 1980 and 1984.

Stripper Buggy from 1980.

Sources:
Harold W. Pace, The Big Guide to Kit & Specialty Cars, Castle Rock 2010, p. 89f.
www.gtsca.com

Countess (UK)

Dave Forsyth founded Kingfisher Mouldings Inc. in 1982 in Wigan, Greater Manchester. He started by producing cars and kits. The first and best selling model was the Countess. The kit was designed by Paul Lawrenson. It is similar to the Lamborghini Countach and represents a trend in the 1980s for replicas of famous road-legal sports cars. Initially, the chassis and four-cylinder boxer engine were taken from the VW-Beetle. From 1983, a tubular steel frame was available as an option to accommodate the Austin Maxi's four-cylinder engine. The quality of the kit and the changing conditions for kit cars were the decisive factors that led to the end of production in 1986. A total of 73 cars were built..

The Countess was launched in 1982.

Sources:
George Nick Georgano: The Beaulieu Encyclopedia of the Automobile. Volume 2: G–O. Fitzroy Dearborn Publishers, Chicago 2001, p. 825.

Steve Hole: A–Z of Kit Cars. The definitive encyclopaedia of the UK's kit-car industry since 1949, Sparkford 2012, p. 137–138.
Chris Rees, Peter Filby, Classic Kit Cars – A Comprehensive Buyer´s Guide to every Kit Car Produced between 1953 and 1985.

Covin (UK)

Tim Cook and Nick Vincent wanted to bridge the gap between a stylish GT with the comfort of a production car and the low price of a kit car. They founded Covin Performance Mouldings and developed replicas of various Porsche models. The kits were launched in the early 1980s under the

CARS OF THE 1980s

Covin name. The name „Covin" is made up of the first letters of the two designers' surnames CO (Cook) and VIN (Vincent). Early Covin models were built on the shortened chssis of a VW-Beetle and had a Beetle engine. Later Covin Porsches were fitted with a newly developed chassis, the Type 3 chassis. Some Covins were equipped with Porsche 911 engines. In addition to the Porsche 911 replica, Covin Performance Mouldings also sold some Porsche 356 Speedster replicas. The Covin 911 is available in 3 body styles, all based on the Turbo model. The company was sued by Porsche for trademark infringement and lost the case. Covin registered a copyright and a patent for the 2-layer moulding process. As a result, no other kit car manufacturer could produce better replicas. Covin Performance Mouldings was sold to DAX Cars in the 1990s and later to GPC. Finally, the rights to Covin were transferred to a company in Galway, Ireland, without any further kit production.

911 Flatnose

Flatnose is the name given to the 911 with a flat front end and folding headlights. The kit was available in convertible and coupé versions.

911 Turbo

The Covin 911 Turbo is a relatively faithful replica of the Porsche 911 Turbo, which was available as a coupé and convertible, as a kit or as a turnkey vehicle.

Speedster

A particularly successful replica of the Porsche 356 A convertible was also in the Covin range for a short

From top to bottom: white 911 Flatnose; blue 911 Turbo; white SApeedster .

time. The car looks very authentic. However, only a few of the Speedster replicas were sold.

Sources:
www.covin.co.uk/
http://en.wikipedia.org/wiki/Covin_(automobile)
www.madabout-kitcars.com/pictures/325/3982/Covin+Performance+Mouldings_Covin+Speedster
Mike Lawrence, A to Z of Sports Cars, 1945-1990, 1993.
www.allcarindex.com/

CARS OF THE 1980s

Crosby (US)

Jim Crosby founded Crosby Metal Products in 1982 in Ontario, California. Between 1982 and 1990 he produced kits and complete vehicles based on the Beetle and a tubular steel frame he developed. His first creation was an Indy car-style recreational vehicle. This was followed by the Crosby Can-AM. The Crosby Manta follows in the tradition of the many Ford GT 40 replicas.

Crosby Formel Fun (1+1)

The Crosby 1 + 1 was designed by John Griffith. The car had two back-to-back seats and a protruding front. The appearance of the Crosby Formula Fun 1+1 is very reminiscent of the Indy cars of the 1970s. The Crosby Formula Fun (1+1) was equipped with a Porsche 5-speed gearbox.

Crosby Manta

The Crosby Manta is one of the

Above: The Manta was modelled on the Ford GT40 and launched in 1982.
Right: The 1+1 Formula Fun has two seats arranged one behind the other.

many replicas of the Ford GT 40, with a GRP body mounted on an unshortened VW chassis. There was also a version of the Manta assembly with a tubular steel frame and the option of a V8 engine. It can be assumed that the Crosby Manta was produced under licence. The shapes are the same as the Manta Montage from Manta Cars.

Sources:
Harold W. Pace, Kit & Specialty Cars, American classics from the past and present, Anaheim 2002, p. 129.
Kit Car (magazine), March 1985.
www.autotitre.com/forum/Discussions-generales/Rarete-only-le-retour-38539p342.htm

Crusader (UK)

Clive Clark founded Excalibur in 1985 in West Looe, Cornwall. He was involved in the manufacture of boats and kit vehicles. He later took over the distribution of the AED Bonito, which was based on the Fiberfab kit. This became the kit for the Excalibur Bonito. Between 1985 and 1996, 32 kits and kit vehicles were produced.

Crusader (1984 – 1996)

The first in-house design was created in 1984. The prototype was based on the VW-Beetle chassis. At the time, the motoring press reported on a new robust frame chassis and the development of an exceptional body made from GRP. Test reports on the new car were promising. The car was available as a turnkey kit. Initially the Excalibur Crusader was offered as a kit to be mounted on a VW-Beetle chassis. Later the kits were mainly equipped with Ford technology. In April 1985 the Volkswagen kit cost £1,925. The finished car was available for £2,775. The kits were offered in different levels of completion, so there was something for every budget. The luxury version of the kit contained almost all the components needed to build the car. A total of 32 were produced. The Crusader is similar to the Bonito, but combines many of the stylistic elements of a sports car that was already a classic at the time. The production models had a special steel frame. The body was made of GRP. Initially, only a 2+2 coupé was offered. In 1992 an open version was added to the range. Parts such as the suspension and gearbox were taken from the Ford Cortina.

Volkswagen four-cylinder engines were available from 1300 cc. The six-cylinder engines up to 2900 cc were supplied by Ford. From 1992 the Rover V8 engine was also available. Excalibur Cars ceased trading at the end of 1996.

CARS OF THE 1980s

Sources:
Peter Tuthill, Cornwall´s Motor Industry, The story of the many fascinating motor vehicles manufactured in Cornwall from 1981 to date, 2007, p. 56ff.
http://forum.britishv8.org/read.php?12,16401
George Nick Georgano: The Beaulieu Encyclopedia of the Automobile. Volume 1: A–F, Chicago 2001, p. 513.
Steve Hole: A–Z of Kit Cars. The definitive encyclopaedia of the UK's kit-car industry since 1949. Sparkford 2012, p. 90.

CTC Panzer   (US)

California Touring Coach became known in 1982 as a supplier of kits for replicas of the Porsche 935. In 1982 two versions of the Porsche 935 were introduced to the public. One kit was largely based on the standard model and the other on the racing version, the 935 RSR. Marketed under the Panzer name, the kits could be bolted onto the chassis of a VW-Beetle. The engine compartment accommodates a VW boxer engine and a Porsche power unit. The kit consists of the one-piece body, boot lid, engine cover, doors, front and rear bodywork and an extra rear wing for the RSR version. The glazing, headlights, rear lights and much of the interior could be taken from the Porsche, depending on the manufacturer's financial resources.

Porsche 935 replica called Panzer from 1982.

Sources:
Harold W. Pace, Kit & Specialty Cars, American classics from the past and present, Anaheim 2002, p. 124.

CWA Targa   (BR)

Carwag Indústria, Comércio e Exportação Ltda, based in Rio de Janeiro (RJ), was founded in 1980. The young company's product range included a Targa, which was marketed under the name CWA. The GRP body could be bolted onto the shortened chassis of a VW-Beetle. The quality of the kit was extremely high compared to what was available in Brazil at the time. This can be seen in the fact that rain stays outside the windscreen without any special precautions. The bumpers are reinforced with rubber strips. The dashboard is padded to protect the occupants. The car has electronically adjustable sports seats with integrated headrests. Magnesium rims were standard. A car radio with cassette deck and metallic paint were also available as options. Despite the high quality of the CWA Targa,

CARS OF THE 1980s

production of the car was discontinued in 1983 after only three years.

Sources:
With kind support of Joao Scharinger from www.lexicarbrasil.com.br/cwa/

Dacon (BR)

The São Paulo Volkswagen dealer Dacon (Distribuidora de Automóveis, Caminhões e Ônibus Nacionais) was taken over by Paulo de Aguiar Goulart in the mid-1960s. As early as 1964, he imported Porsche engines for installation in Karmann Ghia cars. After 19 successful conversions, Chico Landis persuaded him to enter one of these modified Karmann Ghia cars in the 1,000 Miles of Guanabara. This led to the formation of the Dacon team, which competed successfully in various competitions. After this foray into racing, Dacon produced a series of modified Volkswagen cars. Of particular note was the Dacon SP2, which could be described as an unofficial prototype for the SP3. Unfortunately, Volkswagen abandoned the project at an early stage and did not take up the proposal. Paulo Goulart then concentrated on the Passat, which had been on the market since 1978. Dacon produced modified versions with two and four doors, which were later given the designations Dacon 820, 821 and 822. In 1981, Dacon offered three derivatives of the VW Gol: a convertible, a „Targa" and the station wagon F. The „Targa" version was given the designation Dacon 827. The collaboration with Anísio Campos continued in 1981. The first independent creation was the Mini Dacon 828. This development was inspired by the collaboration on the Mini Puma.

The prototype of the Dacon 828 was presented in 1981, but in October 1982, Dacon had to file for bankruptcy. The economic recession had pushed up the cost of building the new headquarters and sales had collapsed.

In 1984, Paulo Goulart set up a new company called PAG to manufacture his cars. PAG stands for Projects d'Avant Garde. The acronym is also the initials of his name. That same year he launched the PAG Dacon, a smaller version of the Porsche 928, whose rear end had already inspired the Mini Dacon. The car, also designed by Anísio Campos, seats four and uses the mechanicals of the VW Gol GT 1.8, with a four-speed gearbox, front-wheel drive and disc brakes on the front wheels. The design is based on the original Gol monobloc structure, including the front windscreen and door skeleton. The headlights came from the Passat and the rear lights from the estate (as on the Dacon 828). The 2.1 litre engine developed 99 bhp. The finish was luxurious and clean, as usual with Dacon products.

Karmann Porsche (1967)

Paulo de Aguiar Goulart founded Escuderia Dacon in 1966. Four Karmann-Ghia / Porsches were prepared for racing: two with a 120 bhp 1.6 litre engine and two with a 200 bhp 2.0 litre engine. The brakes and suspension were modified to cope with the increased engine power. Some of the bodywork was replaced with fi-

Scuderia Dacon successfully entered four Porsche Karmanns in competitions.

breglass components, but the original Karmann style was largely retained. With drivers Emerson and Wilson Fittipaldi, José Carlos Pace, Chico Lameirão, Anísio

CARS OF THE 1980s

Campos and Carol Figueiredo, the Dacon team won half of the ten competitions they entered in 1967. At the time, there were plans to build a Karmann Ghia mid-engined Porsche six-cylinder with 250 bhp, disc brakes on all four wheels and a fibreglass body. The project was abandoned, although Anísio Campos had already started building the moulds. Around the same time, Dacon became the official Porsche dealer for Brazil.

Dacon SP3 (1976)

Dacon's experience with the Karmann Ghia Porsches led to the modification of other cars, mainly based on the Beetle or the VW Brasilia. The construction of a prototype of the VW SP-3 in 1976 with the water-cooled engine of the Passat TS is interesting. This project had already been abandoned by Volkswagen in 1976. The engine was placed at the rear and the radiator at the front instead of the spare wheel. However, this reduced the volume of the boot. The compression ratio was increased to 8.5:1 and the power increased to around 100 bhp (SAE). This allowed the car to reach a top speed of 180 km/h. The transmission, suspension and brakes (discs at the front, drums at the rear) were the same as on the SP2, but adapted to the higher power and reinforced. Bodywork modifications were carried out by Karmann do Brasil. The car was fitted with the Passat's instruments, seats, steering wheel and leather interior, air conditioning and electric windows. The body was slightly modified to accommodate the new mechanicals. The air intakes for engine cooling were made more discreet, the side windows enlarged and the shoulders and side mouldings re-

Porsche Karmann with mid engined Porsche six cylinder.

moved. A wide black radiator grille sits above the front bumper. Volkswagen do Brasil decided not to continue the project. Dacon then offered to convert the car into an SP3. However, due to the extremely high price, demand was very limited.

with a need for a personalised appearance. The vehicle was luxuriously equipped and offered the same comfort as the large luxury cars of the time. The Dacon 828 was intended as a typical second car for daily use in Brazil's congested cities. Above all, the

Prototype of the SP3 with VW Passat TS engine.

Dacon 828 (1982 - 1985)

The Dacon 828, just 2.65 metres long, became famous for its revolutionary design. Anísio Campos and Paulo Goulart also played a key role in its development and manufacture at Puma Veiculos S.A. This innovative project was aimed at a high-income public

car was designed to be very easy to park without sacrificing luxury and comfort. The idea was excellent, but not well received. This is probably because when you are successful, you want to show it. People who can afford high-priced luxury cars want an expensive

CARS OF THE 1980s

car to be perceived as such. The concept didn't work at the time. It was not until the 1990s that the idea of the compact car was successfully taken up by Daihatsu, among others. The success of the Daihatsu Cuore was not based on the design, but on the good price/performance ratio.

The Dacon 828 was powered by a 2-cylinder BMW engine with 650 or 800 cc. The Dacon was also available with a 1.3 litre and a 1.6 litre engine. Weighing only 360 kg, the car had a top speed of 120 km/h. It offered space for 2 persons plus one person on the emergency seat. Many of the mechanical components came from Volkswagen. The body was made of GRP and sat on a VW-Beetle platform shortened by 78 cm. The headlights and radiator grille are from the Passat. The windscreen wiper is recessed under the edge of the bonnet. The one-piece seats are actually modified rear seats from the VW 1600, and the spare tyre is positioned vertically behind the right-hand seat. In the lower rear corner of the wide doors there is a cut-out to strengthen the structure of the car and reduce the risk of side impact. In the first series, the Dacon 828 was fitted with 10-inch wheels. Later the cars were fitted with 13 inch wheels. The car was positioned as a „luxury toy" for buyers who were not affected by the crisis. In March 1983 only the Dacon 828 S (luxury version) with a 1.6 litre engine was delivered. The car was reviewed by the press and described as stable, agile and with a surprisingly spacious interior. The first 11 bodies were built by Puma Veiculos S.A. Dacon in Santana do Parnaíba (SP) then took over production completely. A total of 48 Dacon 828s were built before production was finally discontinued in 1985.

Dacon 828 of the first series.

Anisio Campos, creator of the Dacon 828.

Sources:
Puma – Typen und Geschichte, Paderbron 2011, 1 edition, p. 121f.
www.lexicarbrasil.com.br/dacon/
www.gptotal.com.br/2005/Colunas/Pandini/20060322.html

D´Norbert (BR)

In 1982, an interesting offer for drivers of Volkswagen Passat and SP2 was created in São Paulo. The company D'Norbert developed a conversion kit that gave the SP2 a new design. The most important changes to the SP2 were the rectangular headlights and taillights from the Fiat 147, a black-painted fake radiator grille, the removal of the side mouldings and the side air vents behind the rear wheel arches. The interior was lined with velvet and imitation leather. Of historical interest is the two-piece bumper, which bears a striking resemblance to the bumpers of Volkswagen's main competitor in Brazil in the sector the SP2 is intended to cover. The development of the SP was commissioned by Volkswagen following the surprising success of the Puma do Brasil.

D´Norbert offered a conversion kit for the Passat and the SP2 in the early 1980s.

Sources:
www.lexicarbrasil.com.br/dnorbert/
Motor3 (magazine), issue 1982.

CARS OF THE 1980s

DRB Sabre (AU)

In the late 1980s, Dennis Bedford developed a kit that could be bolted to the undercarriage of a VW Type 3. New regulations for home-built and kit cars had recently been introduced in Queensland. Front and rear bumpers were now mandatory. This meant the definitive end for most kit cars, as most designs could no longer work with bumpers.

Sabre MK I

Dennis Bedford solved the problem elegantly by placing the bumpers inside the car and covering them with the GRP bodyshell. To improve the comfort of getting in and out of the car, the doors were often lowered. This meant that the roof also had to be modified. Once the body was finished, the car could be painted. The finished DRB Sabre has similarities to the Ferrari 250 LM at the front and the Ford GT40 at the rear and was sold well over 100 times in the 1990s. The DRB Sabre was available as a coupé and a roadster.

Sabre MK II

The DRB Sabre has been technically upgraded to optimise production and visually given a gentle facelift. The most obvious change was the bonnet, which on the MK II had two parallel rows of air vents. For customers who wanted more power, a Subaru turbocharged engine could be fitted at the front.

In the Sabre MK-I (red), the bumpers are integrated into the bodywork.
After a facelift, there are only two rows of air intakes on the bonnet; the white car is from 1994.

Sources:
KIT CAR AUSTRALIA (magazine), issue 7 from 1986, p. 76.

Dukat Coupé (CH)

In the early 1980s, Mr Dukat developed the coupé named after him with a plastic body. The 2+2-seater coupé with sleeping eyes from the Porsche 982 was also to be mass-produced. There were even prices. CHF 15,000 for the kit and CHF 25,000 for the finished model. A Targa version was also announced.

The Dukat was to be built by ex-racing driver Jürg Weinem in Horgen on Lake Zurich. This did not happen, although the advance publicity in the Auto Revue (issue 26 of 23 June 1983) was considerable. The article reported interest from Switzerland and strong demand from Germany. It is still not entirely clear why the prototype was never built. In any case, the prototype has survived to this day. In 2015, a report on the Dukat was published in the German

CARS OF THE 1980s

Prototype of the Dukat from 1983.

Sources:
https://www.zwischengas.com/de/blog/2019/11/27/

Eagle (US)

Barry Goldstein founded Eagle Manufacturing Inc. in 1978 in San Jose, California. He started out working with art objects and sculptures. This more artistic approach brought him closer to automotive design. Goldstein's first automotive project was a replica of a Ferrari Dino 246 GTS, initially sold among friends. In 1980, he took the project public under the name Eagle GT1. Impressed by a test drive with a Porsche 914, the kit for the Dino was adapted in 1981 so that it could be built on the undercarriage of a Porsche 914. A total of 6 versions of the Eagle GT were produced in just 3 years. One set of moulds went to John Graham in Bellflower, who marketed the Dino replica on his own account under the name Karma. After Graham had another set of moulds made by Wayne Jacobson, he passed them on to the Lyle company, who then started production of the Magnum. Eagle went on to produce replicas of a Ferrari 250 GTO, a Porsche Speedster and an AC Cobra. With just under 100 employees, Goldstein produced between 35 and 40 cars a year. After only seven 250 GTOs, the moulds were sold to Alpha Design & Engineering in 1983. Production at Eagle ceased in 1984 after Ferrari became more vigilant about protecting its design and took legal action against all replica manufacturers. The moulds were sold to Bob Warren and Michael Dell of Wardell Production in Campbell. In 1985 this adventure also came to an end due to increased pressure from Ferrari.

Eagle GT1 und GT2

The Eagle is basically available in GT1, GT2 and GT versions. There were up to 6 different versions, as the design was constantly being optimised, and there was a Targa version as well as a Coupé. While the first GT1 and GT2 models are clearly recognisable as Beetle con-

The Eagle GT was too similar to the Ferrari Dino, so Enzo Ferrari obtained a court order to stop production.

versions, the later GT models look very professional on the road with chrome bumpers from a '67 Corvette, the windscreen from a TR7 (including hardtop) and tyre sizes that fill the wheel arches. Thanks to Porsche technology, the newer GT models are also technically well equipped. In the Porsche version, the engine is usually placed in a mid-engine configuration. Volkswagen, Porsche and Corvair engines were used. After Enco Ferrari took legal action against Eagle and ordered the company to destroy the moulds for the Dino replica, production was discontinued at the end of 1984.

Sources:
www.eaglegt.com/index.php?section=eaglegt1
Kit Car Guide 1983
Kit Car Monthly (magazine), issue 1981.
Dune Buggies and Hot (magazine), issue 3 from 1982.

CARS OF THE 1980s

Eagle SS (UK)

Eagle Cars Limited was originally founded in 1981 by Allen Breeze. The company was based in Lancing, West Sussex. Tim Dutton Wooley and Alan Breeze bought the moulds and rights to the Cimbria from Joe Palumbo shortly before the company was formed. Some rather cosmetic changes to the design led to the development of the Eagle SS, which remained in the range from 1982 to 1988. Almost coincidentally, the successor to the Nova was also launched in South Africa under the name Eagle. In 1988 the company's headquarters were relocated near Storrington. Rob Budd bought the company in 1989 and moved the headquarters to Walberton, West Sussex. Eagle Cars Limited officially ceased trading in 1998, although production ceased much earlier.

The first product launched was a Jeep CJ6 replica, the Eagle RV. The Eagle RV found around 100 customers over the course of the company's history. Immediately after the launch of the RV, the Eagle SS was introduced in 1982. Eagle cars were exported to countries such as Poland, France, Germany, Sweden, Norway and Spain. About 50% of the Eagle SS is based on Volkswagen technology. In 1998 the design of the Range Rover based Eage RV was sold to Robert May. The RV based on Ford technology went to Jordan Developments. Neither company achieved significant sales.

In 2005, the rights to the Eagle SS were reactivated by Tim Naylor of TEAC Sports Cars and the old moulds were prepared to resume body production. The plan was to build a mid-engined car based on the Toyota MR2. The Eagle SS MK IV was unveiled to the public at Stoneleigh in 2006. Unfortunately, there was not enough interest in the new model to put it into production. The prototype was later sold on eBay to Wexford and the company went out of business in late 2008.

Eagle SS (1982 – 1988)

The Eagle SS was advertised in England as a spin-off of the Cimbria SS, which had sold very successfully in America. There is a certain irony in the fact that a replica of a successful British car, because it was so successful in

The Eagle SS was launched in 1982 as a spinn-off of the Cimbria SS that was already very successful in America.

America, was being promoted as a great new car in England, when the Nova MK 2 was already well established in the British market. Compared to the original, the Eagle SS had round headlamps, which pointed upwards when not in use, to match the contours of the body. The headlamps were borrowed from the Porsche 928. A licence to use the same technology was also available from Porsche. The front end and the bonnet were also slightly redesigned. The side air intakes were made more discreet and moved to the rear. The Eagle SS had an internal roll cage, opening side windows, a relatively long front end and a rear hatch with louvres to improve airflow into the engine compartment. Later models of the Eagle SS were optionally available with a front engine. These cars were mainly based on components from the Ford Cortina. The front-engined cars are easily recognised by the distinctive curve of the bonnet. The Eagle SS was sold approximately 680 times. The rights to the Eagle body are still in private hands. The

Technical Details
Eagle SS
Engine: VW
Power: 70 - 100 hp
Length: 4240 mm; Width: 1780 mm; Hight: 1040 mm; Wheelbase: 2.400 mm
Weight: 750 kg (empty)

moulds used to make the body panels are said to still exist.

CARS OF THE 1980s

Eagle SS MK II

The Eagle SS MK II is an evolution of the basic model. The front end has been significantly shortened and now consists of two parts. The folding headlights were replaced by two smaller magnifying headlights on the left and right. The side profile of the front end was hardly changed by this measure.

passenger compartment. Seatbelts and a roll bar ensured safety. A Raid sports steering wheel provides an unobstructed view of the instrumentation.

Due to registration regulations in most European countries, an Eberspächer independent heater was often fitted at the front of the car to ventilate the windscreen. The side windows were enlarged to improve all-round visibility.

The MK II was designed as standard for the installation of a 1.6 litre Beetle engine with approximately 65 bhp (55 bhp registered). The large engine compartment provides ample room for the installation of a more powerful Beetle engine, a Type 4 or, using an adapter, a Porsche or Alpha engine. The MK II is also available in a Ford Cortina engine version based on a specially developed tubular steel frame. For the Ford version, the bonnet was raised at the front to make room for the engine. On later models the front ribs were removed and the boot lid was completely smooth. For better weight distribution the plastic fuel tank was placed in the front together with the battery.

Eagle SS MK-II (yellow) has two small twin headlights; the Eagle SS MK-III with gullwing doors.

The entire interior was covered in leather or carpet. The driver and front passenger were seated in Cobra bucket seats, but were not allowed to be much taller than 1.8 metres due to the design of the

Sources:
www.motor-talk.de/marktplatz/eagle-ss-mark-ii-show-auto-der-superlative-t2541855.html
www.sterlingkitcars.com/history_pages/cimbria/history_module_cm.html
www.madabout-kitcars.com/kitcar/kitcar_details.php?74
http://eaglekitcars.proboards.com/index.cgi?board=EagleSS
www.koon-design.de/eagle-ssspecial.html
www.bluefrog.plus.com
http://sterling-nova-defi-france-lille7.webnode.fr/a-propos-de-nous/
Erwin, Daryl. „History: A brief history of the Eagle Kit Car range 1981 - 1998". Eagle Owners Club. Archived from the original on 2010-10-06.
www.eagleownersclub.org.uk/history%20page.htm.

Bellu, René, ed. (September, 1989). Salon: Toutes les Voitures du Monde 89/90 (Paris: l'Auto Journal) (issue 15 & 16): p. 343.
Auto Katalog 1983. Stuttgart 1982. p. 86.
www.sterlingkitcars.com
www.madabout-kitcars.com/kitcar/kitcar_details.php?74. Retrieved 2011-10-06.
Negyesi, Pal. „British Specialty Cars - Eagle". KTUD Online Automotive Archive.

www.team.net/www/ktud/eagle.html. Retrieved 2010-10-06.
Harald Linz, Halwart Schrader: Die Internationale Automobil-Enzyklopädie. München 2008, chapter Eagle.
George Nick Georgano: The Beaulieu Encyclopedia of the Automobile. Volume 1: A–F., Chicago 2001, p. 478.
Steve Hole: A–Z of Kit Cars. The definitive encyclopaedia of the UK's kit-car industry since 1949. Sparkford 2012, p. 81–82.

CARS OF THE 1980s

Eagle SS MK III

The Eagle SS MK III was slightly taller, allowing drivers over 5ft tall to sit comfortably in the passenger compartment. This model was also available in VW and Ford versions. The headlights could be folded up again, similar to the MK I. The side windows were slightly larger than the MK II. The Eagle SS MK III was sold until at least 1998. The Eagle SS MK IV was only built with Ford Cortina technology.

Eagle SS (UK)

The Cimbria SS returned to the UK in 1981 as the Eagle SS. Tim Dutton Wooley, owner of Dutton Kit Car, and his cousin Alan Breeze bought the rights to the Cimbria replica and launched their version of the car under the name **Eagle SS**.

Alan Breeze became the head of the new „Eagle Cars" and the company paid a one-off flat fee to replicate the Cimbria in the UK and EU. For this fee he also received a complete Cimbria car from which to make a new set of moulds. The development of the Eagle SS was aided by a close working relationship with his cousin Tim Dutton's already established company, Dutton Kit Car.

The company changed hands and locations several times during this period. Subsequent owners included test rider Robb Budd in 1989 and Tim Naylor of TEAC Sports Cars. Naylor sold the Eagle SS tools in 2012 to an undisclosed buyer in the UK, whose whereabouts are unknown.

Approximately 340 of each version were sold on a VW basis. A further 340 of the last two versions were produced and sold on a Ford basis. Approximately 180 Eagle SS are registered with the Eagle Owner's Club (as of 2022).

Eagle SS (1981 – 1983)

The British version of the Cimbria was fitted with pop-up headlights in the style of the Porsche 928 and was initially offered as a kit to be fitted to the floor pan of a VW-Beetle. The only modification required to the VW donor chassis was the lowering of the steering gear. It was estimated that the car could be built in about 130 hours using basic tools and moderate skill. Visually the original Eagle SS is almost identical to the Cimbria except for the headlights.

Eagle SS MK II (1983 - 1997)

The newer Eagle SS was offered with a Ford Cortina front engine. A bespoke chassis was also developed for this newer version. Both the VW and Ford based MK2 versions also received an integral roll cage, a shorter removable front bumper and longer side windows (hinged from the A-pillar) for extra ventilation.

The Cimbria SS returned back to UK as the Eagle SS and is different in many details to the American version.

The second version of the Eagle SS with some improvements.

At the end of the 1980s a 2+2 version with a targa roof was designed and put into production. By now the car had evolved to the point where it was almost unrecognisable as a Nova derivative. Production of the Eagle SS ended in 1998.

Sources:
Phil Fenton, The Nova/Sterling/Eureka Kit Car, 2007, p. 27f.
https://nvautomotive.ca/extremely-rare-1981-eagle-ss/
https://rarecomponentcars.blogspot.com/2021/07/the-eagle-ss-game-of-telephone.html

CARS OF THE 1980s

EMIS (BR)

In 1980, the founder of Emis, Eduardo Miranda Santos, focused his energy on a buggy based on the VW-Beetle. Development was completed in 1981. Emis buggies were available from 1981 to 1986. Since 2010, the Emis buggy has been available again with a hardtop or as an open version, although the company now trades under the new name of Emisul. Shortly after the buggy's launch, a small car was created and EMIS continued to produce it until 1987. The opening up of the car market forced EMIS to withdraw from the market.

EMIS Buggy (1981 – 1986)

The Emis Buggy was developed in the tradition of the Meyers Manx. There was a fully open version and a closed version with hardtop and gullwing doors. Sales were very successful. Within a short time, Emis buggies were populating the beaches and cities of Brazil.

The EMIS buggy was available with a soft top or hard top.

ART EMIS (- 1987)

As a second mainstay, Eduardo Miranda Santos teamed up with dentist and hobby car designer Alfredo Soares Veiga to produce a Volkswagen-based compact car. The result of this collaboration was launched under the name Art Emis. The car had a simply designed body with many details reminiscent of the Dacon 828. With this creation, Santos wanted to appeal primarily to the clientele

The ARTEMIS The ARTEMIS is a small car with surprisingly good driving characteristics.

living in Brazil's large cities. Today, motorsport enthusiasts in Brazil like to refer to the car as the Brazilian Smart of the 1980s.

The car was designed by dentist and hobbyist Alfredo Soares Veiga, who says the Dacon 828 was a major source of inspiration. He says: „It was in the early 1980s when Nelson Piquet first appeared in the Formula 1 paddock at the Rio de Janeiro circuit in a Mini Dacon and I was allowed to get behind the wheel. That's when the idea of developing a similar car was born. After a development period of just under 9 months, the plans were ready and he could start looking for a company to take on the project. He chose Emis, a company that had already made a name for itself in the 1980s as a traditional manufacturer of prams and other special vehicles.

The Art Emis gained regional fame when it was featured in the 1986 novel „Cambalacho Rede Globo".

With a length of 3100 mm, the Art Emis only offered space for two passengers and a small trunk behind the seats. Some cars also had small rear seats. The chassis is a proprietary design consisting of two steel sections in a tubular Y-shape. The body is made of fibreglass, as was common for small production cars at the time. The windscreen, doors and side windows are from the Chevette. The dashboard is similar to that of the Gol. The brake system was taken from the VW-Beetle 1600, while the indicators and headlights were from the VW Brasilia.

A test report in Quatro Rodas magazine praised the Art Emis' straight-line stability, saying that it was the best in its class. Even at high cornering speeds, the car is relatively slow to reach its limits. The VW boxer engine is equipped with two carburettors. The extended gear ratio of the gearbox corresponds to that of the SP2. This resulted in a reduced noise level. The low overall weight of the car ensured very good performance data and excellent driving pleasure. Fuel consumption was also significantly lower than that of the Beetle.

A total of 153 cars were produced. A total of 130 Art Emis were sold. A further 23 were offered after the factory moved to Porto Alegre in Rio Grande do Sul. Production ceased in 1987.

Sources:
http://brasilforadeserie.blogspot.com/2011/03/emis-art.html
http://planetabuggy.com.br/classicos/emis/index.htm
www.emisul.com/
www.bbbarcos.com/
Quatro Rodas (magazine), issue 7 from 1986.

Enseada (BR)

Enseda Veículos Especiais was founded in São Paulo (SP) in 1987. A range of buggies and replicas were offered until the end of the 1990s. The best-known model is the 1952 MG TD replica, a continuation of the MP Lafer, which had been very successful since 1974. Also very successful were the buggies first introduced in 1988, which were also sold by Pantera at the same time. The company survived the shock of the sudden opening of the car market in the early 1990s. Although demand fell, the company survived for a long time by diversifying. From 1992, for example, replicas of the Porsche 550 and Porsche 911 were added to the range. The Buggy was given a much more modern look.

The replica of the MG TD corresponds to the early version of the MP Lafer.

Enseada MG TD

The Enseada MG TD kit corresponds to the early versions of the MP Lafer. The company probably bought the moulds and production rights. At first glance it is very difficult to tell the difference between the early MP Lafer and the Enseada MG TD. Enseada used wood panelling and painted plywood for the interior with great attention to detail. The kit could be built on the unshortened platform of almost any Volkswagen. The chrome radiator grille with vertical louvres is characteristic of the early MP Lafer. The chromed bumpers can also be found on the Enseada MG TD.

Mini Buggy

At the end of 1988, the company launched two buggy models. The Enseada Plus with a standard wheelbase for four people and the Mini Buggy with an extremely short wheelbase, similar to the Pantera buggy, for two people. The buggies were fitted with round headlights in front of the wings and rectangular tail lights. A multi-piece soft top was available as an option.

CARS OF THE 1980s

The buggy was available in a short and a long version.

Top to bottom: The Tupy Buggy is a two-seater; the Porsche 911 replica, the Porsche 505 replica.

Tupy Buggy

In 1990, the Buggy Plus received a facelift which resulted in the Enseada Tupy. Rectangular lights were fitted to the front and rear. The buggy got a slightly modified side guidance. The spare tyre disappeared from the front bonnet.

911

In 1992, Enseada added the Porsche 911 replica to its range. The kit could be screwed onto the unshortened floor pan of a VW-Beetle.

505

Enseada also bought the rights to produce a replica of a Porsche 505 in 1992. The kit was designed to be mounted on a VW-Beetle chassis. Air-cooled VW boxer engines and Porsche engines were used.

Sources:
http://www.lexicarbrasil.com.br/enseada/
With kind support of João F. Scharinger.

Fibrario (BR)

Paulo Renha of FibraRio Comércio e Indústria Ltda. in Rio de Janeiro (RJ) presented a buggy in 1982 and a Ferrari Dino replica in 1983. Renha was already well known for designing the Renha tricycle and other vehicles. His foray into the kit car scene lasted only until 1986, when he had to close his company due to insufficient sales.

Dimo GT (1984 - 1986)

Paulo Renha has always been a big fan of the Ferrari Dino 246 GT, launched in 1966 in honour of Enzo Ferrari's late son. With the Dimo GT, Renha has created a very authentic replica of this classic car. A special double Y tubular chassis with independent suspension, McPherson struts and disc brakes on all four wheels has been developed. Originally, the car was fitted with a 1.6 TS engine from the VW Passat, mounted in front of the rear axle. Later, the 1.8-litre Santana engine with 99 bhp was fitted. The GRP body and interior are faithfully reproduced by Renha. Like the original, the aluminium instrument panel features a speedometer, rev counter, water temperature gauge, oil pressure gauge, oil temperature gauge, real-time clock, fuel gauge and ammeter. This effort to be faithful to the original also resulted in a respectable price for the car. Even customers such as Nelson Piquet were unable to significantly boost sales of the Dino replica. As a result, the Dino GT was also marketed by L'AutoCraft for several years.

Terral (1982-1986)

The Fibrario Dune Buggy is designed by Eddie Moyna. The kit consists of a one-piece GRP body, windscreen frame and slightly curved windscreen. The Terral uses a double Y tubular frame, similar to that developed for the Dimo GT. With a wheelbase of 1,950 mm and an overall length of 3,130 mm, the vehicle offers space for a maximum of 2 people. The chassis was not derived from the Beetle, as was the case with most buggies at the time. The rear wheels were fitted with coil springs, resulting in an atypical negative camber. The square headlights were taken from a 1982 Chevette. The Fibrario Terral was powered by a 1.6 litre boxer engine from Volkswagen, which gave the very light 480 kg car a very sporty feel.

Terral 4 (1982-1986)

Shortly after the Terral buggy was launched, the Terral 4 was brought to market. This is a 50 cm longer version of the Fibrario Terral, which offers space for a maximum of 4 people. There is no roll bar on this vehicle. The soft top is pulled over a classic soft top frame. Side panels can also be attached using press studs and a zip. A colourful decorative strip was available as an option. Optional extras included fog lights and safety glass with a green glass bar as sun protection.

Top to bottom: Dimo GT very close to he original; Terral Buggy equipped with a 1.6 litre VW engine; Terral 4 similar to the Terral, but for four pssengers.

Sources:
www.lexicarbrasil.com.br/fibrario/
Quatro Rodas (magazine), issue 287 June 1984, p. 68ff.
http://autoentusiastas.com.br/2014/11/10-melhores-brasileiros-parte-ii-replicas-2/
http://autoentusiastas.com.br/2014/11/10-melhores-brasileiros-parte-iv-bugues/
http://veiculos.mercadolivre.com.br/buggy/poodle-rio-de-janeiro

CARS OF THE 1980s

Fiera (BR)

In 1989, a small manufacturer called Fibrax was established in Erechim (RS), initially producing a dune buggy called Bargus. The company's capacity was geared towards the production of 2 units per month. In 1991, the Fiera was created, a 2-seater sports car built on the platform of a VW 1600. The design of the car was based on the Corvette. The Fiera has gullwing doors. The interior of the sports car is covered in velvet. For a short time, the company also offered a van with a crew cab.

Sources:
www.lexicarbrasil.com.br/fibrax/
Jornal do Brasil (magazine), issue 3 from 1991.

Fiera sports car based on a VW 1600 platform.

Fyber (BR)

Fyber Indústria e Comércio Ltda. was for many years one of the largest buggy manufacturers in the Northeast of Brazil. The company was founded in 1974 by brothers Agliberto and Rogério Farias in Fortaleza (CE). The original aim of the company was to manufacture products in GRP. In 1981, the company entered the buggy business with the launch of the Duna buggy. In addition to the classic buggy, a creative amphibious vehicle was created that is still unrivalled in Brazilian domestic production. Powered by a 65 hp air-cooled Volkswagen engine in the rear, the car had a tubular chassis covered in fibreglass, making it one of the first designs not based on the original Volkswagen platform.

In 1991, the company was transformed into a joint stock company and renamed Fyber Indústria de Veículos S.A. In 1992, the Brisa commercial vehicle was launched in pickup and ambulance versions. The Brisa had front-wheel drive. The engine was a 67 hp Fiat Fiorino. In 1992, Fyber bought a plot of land in Horizonte, a town near Fortaleza, where it planned to build a plant for the production of 150 light trucks per month, with a payload capacity of one to three tonnes. The following year, however, Fyber's course began to change radically: Rogério Farias left the company and remained as a partner at the Horizonte site, where two years later he founded Troller and began producing his highly successful Jeep.

In 1995, Fyber Comércio de Veículos S/A was declared bankrupt, leaving employees, suppliers and the consortium of hundreds of partners with debts of around US$20 million, who have still not received their money. In 1996/1997, the bankruptcy assets of Fyber Comércio de Veículos S/A were auctioned off and several people bought the moulds for the buggy production. By this time, the licence for the Fyber brand had probably expired or lapsed. By 1995, it is estimated that around 12,000 vehicles had been produced.

In 1996, the former Fyber dealer Peixoto Veículos from Fortaleza resumed the production of vehicles. In 1999, Nil Araújo reported that Fiberstar Indústria e Comércio de Veículos Especiais Ltda had succeeded in regaining the Fyber homologation granted by the National Ministry of Transport (Denatran). In 2002, Fyber Indústria e Comércio Ltda, the owner of the Fyber word mark for agricultural equipment, attempted to register the Fyber mark for motor vehicles, but was unsuccessful.

In 2003, Hiderlandson Peixoto, the owner of Peixoto Veículos Ltda, attempted to homologate the Fyber 2000 trademark with Denatran, also without success, as it already belonged to Fiberstar Indústria e Comércio de Veículos Especiais Ltda. Peixoto was then forced to develop a new brand of buggy and register the „Fyber 2000W". Until then, Fiberstar had only produced the Fyber 2000 in small quantities because one of the partners was afraid that the creditors of Fyber Comércio de Veículos S/A would come to collect their debts. Because of this fear, the company developed another model under the name Cauype. Following the withdrawal of this partner in 2017, Nil Araújo of Fiberstar decided to return to manufacturing buggies under the names Fyber 2000 and FyberStar. In August 2019, the German company Axxola, led by Dirk Wittenborg, bought Fyber Indústria e Comércio Ltda, with the assumption that the original Fyber brand and homologation would be maintained. In July 2019, Fyber Fabricação de Veículos Automotores Eireli was founded. The tools and moulds were then purchased from Peixoto Veículos in order to produce the buggy again in its own industrial facilities in Paracuru (CE). Due to the coronavirus pandemic, vehicle production did not begin until 2021. In 2022, increased investment will be made to increase production capacity to up to 1,000 vehicles per year. A new factory will be built on newly acquired land.

By 2022, around 2,000 Fyber buggies could be used by professional guides in Ceará. Some of them are more than 20 years old and offer unforgettable moments to about 1 million tourists every year. At the same time, Axxola offers two versions of the vehicle: The Fyber Boxer, powered by a 1.6-litre, 53 hp, air-cooled Volkswagen Boxer engine, and the Fyber AP, powered by a 1.8-litre, 112 hp, liquid-cooled Volkswagen in-line engine.

However, the dispute over the Fyber name would lead to new developments. In November 2019, Fyber Indústria e Comércio, the successor to Fyber Star, announced plans to build the „largest buggy factory of today" in São Gonçalo do Amarante (CE), next to the port of Pecém, where four new models would be produced „alongside the traditional Fyber 2000 and Star". On this occasion, concept images of the new Star

were unveiled - a beautiful project by designer Du Oliveira, with angled diamond-shaped headlights and a curved windscreen.

Mobilised by the article, Axxola challenged the competitor's use of the trademark in court, which was upheld by the court of first instance in November 2020. Fyber Indústria e Comércio appealed the decision.

In 2022, Fyber Indústria e Comércio resumed production of the traditional 2000 and Star models, always with Volkswagen engines: 1600 Boxer or AP 1.8, EA 111 1.6.

Duna Buggy (1982 - 19995)

Designed by Milton Nunes, the Duna Buggy is available in two versions. The „terrestrial" version, which is road legal, and the Duna Anfibio, which can even float. The road version lacks the propeller, the front winch and the additional headlights on the roof. The exhaust system was modified and the air intakes for engine cooling, which were otherwise only hinted at, were open. By 1984, some 180 cars had been built, including seven floatable Duna models.

The Duna Buggy was sold 180 times in 1984.

Duna Anfibio (1982 – 1995)

The Anfibio's hull consists of five watertight GRP chambers. Two bilge pumps and rubberised canvas bellows were used to seal the chambers and reduce water ingress. These were coupled to each of the four axles. Propulsion in the water was provided by an electrically driven propeller, coupled to the rear socket and activated by an electromagnetic clutch from the control panel. The vehicle had an adjustable front axle, disc brakes on all four wheels and full instrumentation on the dashboard. With such a configuration, the Duna's could navigate calm waterways and shallow flooded areas at speeds of up to 10 knots.

CARS OF THE 1980s

The Duna Anfibio is equal to the Buggy with some extra features.

Fyber 2000 (1984 – 1992)

In 1984, a new model - the Fyber 2000 - was launched with a short front end and square headlights. The new model seemed to be inspired by the Gurgel X-12 with its angular lines, rectangular headlights and monobloc body. The tubular chassis was fully integrated into the body and was a completely new development, eliminating the need for a Beetle floor pan. The rear suspension used coil springs, also similar to the Gurgel X-12. The Fyber 2000 set a precedent and became the prototype of the „north-east style" in the buggy scene.

The Fyber 2000 was launched in 1984.

Fyber Star (1992 – 1995)

In 1992, the Fyber Star appeared as the successor to the Fyber 2000 with almost no external changes and was a completely new car. The engine also had zero kilometres on the clock. There was a choice of twin or single carburettors. Standard equipment included exclusive wheels, a digital instrument panel, an on-board computer, seats with headrests, a sunshade and special metallic paintwork.

Jipe Fyber 3000 (1988 – 1995)

The small 3000 was launched in 1988 with the same concept as the Buggy (tubular frame, GRP body, air-cooled VW engine in the rear) but with a semi-closed body, all-round bumpers and two Jeep-style doors. Nearly 90 were produced until 1995.

The Jipe Fyber 3000 has a semi-closed body.

Fyber 2000 von Peixoto Veículos (1996 -1997)

Peixoto Veículos, a car dealer and Fyber distributor from Fortaleza, bought part of the bankruptcy assets and restarted production of buggies with the Fyber logo. A small series was planned, with an average of ten vehicles per month. The Fyber 2000 model already had a water-cooled VW AP-1800 engine with 102 bhp installed in the rear. The Fyber 2000 is easily recognised by the round headlights in the still square frame. Also characteristic are the three mouldings on the sides of the buggy, which converge at the front. The Fyber 2000 was available in two versions: with and without a snorkel-style exhaust.

The Fyber 2000 was sold by Peixoto Veículos after the bankruptcy of Fyber Comércio.

Fyber 2000W (1997 – 1998)

Just one year later, the buggy underwent a slight facelift and was renamed the Fyber 2000W. The tapered sides disappeared. The box-shaped bulge can be used as an entry aid. Disc brakes were fitted at the front.

The Fyber 2000W was launched after a slight facelift in 1997.

Fyber Star (1999 -)

Production of the Fyber Star was continued in 1999 by Fyber Star Indústria e Comércio de Veículos. The cars were assembled in Eusébio (CE). The plan was to resume production in small numbers and to continue using the Fyber brand.

CARS OF THE 1980s

The technology remained unchanged. The Fyber Star was available with a variety of options, such as the soft top (rigid, with or without fabric cover), the finish (black or body-coloured windscreen frame) and accessories.

Prototype of the new Fyber Star.

Fyber Boxer (2021 -)

The 2000 model has been reissued by Axxola with virtually unchanged technology. The Fyber Boxer is equipped with an air-cooled Volkswagen Boxer engine with a capacity of 1.6 litres and 53 bhp. The car has torsion bar suspension at the front, coil springs at the rear, disc brakes at the front and drum brakes at the rear. The new rear lights and the relatively open engine compartment are striking features.

Fyber X (2020 -)

The Fyber X is the largely unchanged interpretation of the Fyber 2000, with optional features including a running board, usually painted in the same colour as the car. The front bumper has been updated and the new rear lights are also used on this model.

Fyber AP (2020 -)

The Fyber AP was developed by Axxola using the moulds from the 2000 model. The front of the car has been completely redesigned, with air grilles behind which the radiator is located. The rear of the car has new modern tail lights. The liquid-cooled engine is supplied by Volkswagen, has a capacity of 1.8 litres and produces 112 bhp. The car has torsion bar suspension at the front, coil springs at the rear, disc brakes at the front and drum brakes at the rear. An interesting feature is the front grille, which is most effective in cooling the engine at the front. The new rear lights and the relatively open engine compartment are noticeable.

Right: Fyber AP based on the moulds of the Fyber 2000.

Sources:
https://www.lexicarbrasil.com.br/
www.fyber.com.br
https://diariodonordeste.verdes-mares.com.br/
https://www.azulnews.com.br/single-post/fyber-recebe-investimento-para-ampliar-produ%C3%A7%C3%A3o-de-buggies-no-cear%C3%A1
https://www.opovo.com.br/

The Fyber Boxer launched by Axxola.

The Fyber X is the nearly unchanged successor of the Fyber 2000.

Garra (BR)

SPJ Indústria e Comércio Ltda. of Rio de Janeiro launched a two-door car in 1988 using Volkswagen engineering. The rear lights were taken from the VW Passat. The car was powered by an air-cooled Volkswagen boxer engine. Magnesium rims, electric windows, a radio with cassette deck and fog lamps were available as options. The GRP-bodied car had room for four passengers. Only a few of the Garra were produced before the manufacturer, SPJ, went out of business due to lack of funds.

Sources:
https://formulatotal.wordpress.com/2014/10/20/spj-garra/
www.lexicarbrasil.com.br/garra/

Advertisement for the Garra from 1987.

CARS OF THE 1980s

Griffon LB   (BR)

In 1974, students from the Escola de Engenharia de São Carlos (SP) developed a sports car as a practical final project for the Mechanical Engineering Department of the Institute of Aeronautical Engineering. The students were supervised by Dr Dawilson Lucato and Mário Bellato Jr. Lucato is an aeronautical engineer and has completed numerous courses and specialisations at various institutions, including outside Brazil. He has also worked as a rapporteur for the safety section of the Brazilian Transport Code and has done a lot of work in this area.

The Griffon LB is the result of a final project by students at the Escola de Engenharia de São Carlos.

His final thesis was to present the basic functions of the vehicle and an attempt to build it. The project seemed so promising that two prototypes were developed for series production. It took almost seven years to build the two prototypes. Experience gained from the realisation of an aircraft was directly incorporated into the project. The car was even tested in a wind tunnel. The results led to further optimisation of the vehicle.

The so-called Griffon LB uses a number of design elements borrowed from aircraft concepts. The car also has a lot to offer in terms of driving performance and ergonomics. The vehicle was built on the VW Brasilia platform, which is very popular in Brazil, with a 1.6-litre boxer engine in the rear. Alternatively, the second vehicle was designed and tested with different engines in a mid-engine configuration. The result is a vehicle with a Cd value of 0.35, a GRP body and ergonomic controls. Unlike comparable vehicles, the Griffon LB has efficient ventilation, very good interior soundproofing, retractable headlights, electric windows and interior adjustable door mirrors. With a weight of 860 kg, the car was not very dynamic to drive due to the choice of engine. A top speed of 140 km/h is documented.

Remarkable is the extremely thin A-pillar, which means that the car has almost no blind spot at the front. The fact that the rear window is almost vertical means that there are hardly any reflections. A remarkable aerodynamic detail can be found at the front of the car. The protruding trailing edge means that the air forced upwards creates less turbulence above the car. This has a positive effect on road handling and the noise level in the Griffon is only half that of the VW Passat. Likewise

The Griffon LB was unveiled to the motoring public at the 12th Geneva Motor Show in 1981. The following year the rights to the Griffon LB and the tools were put up for sale. Even an in-depth article on the Griffon LB by Expedito Marazzi in the June issue of Motor 3 failed to attract a buyer. So the project was shelved. It was not until the early 1990s that the designer of the Cheda Buggy and the Ventura took up the project again. He planned to produce the Griffon LB at his factory in São José do Rio Preto (SP) with a mid-engined version of the Chevrolet Monza. Due to his untimely death in 1996 at the age of 42, the project was finally abandoned.

Sources:
www.carroantigo.com/portugues/conteudo/curio_carros_conceito_nac_5.htm
Lindeberg de Manezes Jr., Motor 3 (magazine), issue June 1982.
www.lexicarbrasil.com.br/griffon/

CARS OF THE 1980s

Gringo   (BR)

In Rio de Janeiro (RJ), Spiller Mattei Indústria e Comércio de Fiberglass Ltda. built a small-series car in the style of a neo-classic, based on an unmodified VW-Beetle platform. The Gringo was sold as a turnkey kit in the early 1980s. In many details, the car is identical to the Citroën 15 CV Traction Avant Cabriolet offered after 1934 or the 11CV Coupé. In this case, it cannot be called a replica, as the designers created an independent vehicle inspired by the Citroën 15 CV by omitting the doors and many other design choices. As the vehicle's centre of gravity is relatively low, it is almost impossible to make the Gringo roll over. However, Spiller Mattei promised a new Gringo to anyone who managed it. In total, Spiller Mattei probably produced around 30 of the Gringo.

Sources:
Sales brochure from 1981.
www.classicmagazine.com.br/2012/03/fora-de-serie.html
http://fuscaclassic.blogspot.co.at/2011/01/vw-replica-11cv.html
www.lexicarbrasil.com.br/gringo/

The Gringo is a neo-classic with a rear view that resembles a Citreon.

Jornada   (BR)

The company NBM Indústria e Comércio LTDA, based in Rio de Janeiro, developed the prototype of a vehicle that would go into production some time later. The Jornada was unveiled at the 13th São Automobile in São Paulo in 1984. A year later, the company was renamed NDM Indústria e Comércio LTDA. Together with several sales partners, the coupé based on VW technology was offered on the market until 1988. In 1986, NDM launched another model called the Spirit. This model was equipped with a water-cooled VW AP 800 engine.

Jornada Convertible

The NBM Jornada was designed by Paulo Rhena. It is one of the first small-series cars on the Brazilian market to use Volkswagen mechanicals, but the turnkey version was built on a chassis developed in-house. Traditionally, the engine is located at the rear. The L version was offered as a convertible with a soft top. The LS version was fitted with a two-piece hardtop, which could be removed in a few easy steps, an electric antenna, electric windows, carpets and alloy wheels from the Ford Escort. The 4-seater was delivered with leather upholstery. The dashboard features a central instrument panel and open storage compartments. The Jornada was available as a kit and as a turnkey version. The Jornada was powered by an air-cooled VW Boxer engine with a displacement of 1,600 cc. A hardtop was available as an option. The headlights and rear lights were taken from the Chevrolet Chevette. The dashboard is fully upholstered and

CARS OF THE 1980s

has five round instruments developed for the Jornada.

Sources:
Sales brochure from 1986.
http://autosclassicos.blogspot.co.at/2011/10/fora-de-serie-jornada.html

The Jornada LS is equipped with a two piece hard top.

Karma (UK)

In 1982, Perry Automotive brought to England the replica of the Ferrari Dino that Custom Classics had developed in California to be built on a Beetle platform. The moulds were taken from the car to produce a version of the American model for the British and European markets. In 1983 the project was taken over by Roger Woolley, founder of RW Kitcars LTD of Newport Lodge, Northfields Close, Melton Mowbray, Leicestershire. Initially the kit was only available to be fitted to a Beetle undercarriage. The call for more power was heard relatively quickly. The result was a chassis suitable for a mid-engine design. This version mainly used technology from the Ford Granada and Ford Cortina. Around 1100 kits were sold. In the 1980s Roger Wooley also produced several trike choppers with VW boxer engines. There were also 32 Countach-like cars called Taurus.

Karma 2-PLUS

The Karma is a road-legal car with proportions that are very similar to those of the Dino. The air intakes, rear window, doors and rear lights were all modified in detail. The kit was offered in two basic versions: For customers who wanted more power, there was a separate chassis that allowed the installation of V8, V6, V4 and 4-cylinder inline engines with water cooling. Alternatively, the Karma kit can be bolted onto the bare VW-Beetle chassis. In this case all type I, II, III, IV, Porsche 914 and Corvair V6 engines can be used. An unusual feature of the car is the generous luggage space. Even tall drivers will find plenty of room and headroom, something that sports cars of this type rarely offer.

The design has gone through three iterations. The first generation kits had a rear window. The dashboard had a dent on the driver's side where the instruments were mounted. The second generation kits have a modified rear window which was easier to produce. The solution developed for the mid-engined version may have prevailed here. The third generation kits have an extra frame for the front hinged windows. The kits were offered with coloured gelcoat surfaces or without gelcoat ready for a classic paint job. For an extra charge, RW Kitcars offered

Karma 2 Plus Dino replica.

pre-assembled wiring harnesses, wheels, instruments and similar accessories.

More than 1,000 units of the RW Karma Dino were sold. Some of the figures are slightly distorted, as more or less high quality copies of the kit were offered.

Sources:
http://karma.tribbeck.com/about.html
www.classic-kitcars.com/classic-kitcar-details.php?82
Mike Lawrence, A to Z of Sports Cars, 1945-1990, 1996.
http://car-from-uk.com/sale.php?id=116710

CARS OF THE 1980s

Kaylor (US)

Roy Kaylor, founder of Kaylor Energy Products, based in Alameda, California, has over 30 years experience in electrical engineering. He has pioneered many fields including microwave, medical electronics, electrochemistry, automotive, aircraft, aerodynamic design including rocketry. He achieved national fame in America as a manufacturer of conversion kits. Over time, more than a thousand conversion kits for Volkswagen-based vehicles were produced. For the electric drive, Kaylor used parts from Radio Shack, which were also used successfully on the Mars Explorer spacecraft. Kaylor Energy Products operated from 1980 to 2009.

**Top & Middle: Invader GT-V.
Right: Dino GT**

Invader GT-V

The Invader GT originated with Bruce Weeks and his company Autokit. Kalyor Energy Products bought the rights to the Invader and marketed it under the name Invader GT. The kit is based on the fifth generation of the Invader GT, which is why it is sometimes referred to as the Invader GT V. Over time, the Invader was manufactured under licence in some countries. After Kaylor Energy Products went bankrupt, the Invader GT moulds were purchased by Kelmark-Kaylor Engineering of Chicago.

Dino GT

Kaylor's replica of the Ferrari 246 Dino is based on the VW-Beetle and Porsche 914 platforms. The electric conversion kit includes a 30hp shunt motor to protect the engine from over-revving. The core of the kit is the motor, adapter plate and cooling system, which can be easily installed with four screws. Key control instruments,

including relays and control electronics, are also supplied.

Sources:
www.kaylor-kit.4t.com
www.autopasion18.com/HISTORIA-INVADER.htm

Kestrel / Briton (UK)

In 1984/1985 Peter Iredale developed a neo-classic called Krestel for Protoflight, a company of the ISS Car Corporation, based in Gillingham, Dorset. In 1985 the project was sold to Dovetail Plastics of Lambourn, Berkshire. In 1988 the rights to Krestel were sold to FES of Beith, Ayrshire (Scotland). The company attempted to market the kit under the name Briton. However, as the market could not be created, FES had to realise after a few months that the project had failed. Between 1989 and 1990, Cartell, based in Haydock, Meyreside, held the rights to the Briton. There is only speculation about the production figures, but it can be assumed that only a few cars were built between 1984 and 1990, apart from the prototypes. As it became increasingly difficult to get such kit cars on the road

CARS OF THE 1980s

Kestrel and Briton built this neo-classic roadster.

Sources:
Chris Rees, Peter Filby, Classic Kit Cars – A Comprehensive Buyer´s Guide to every Kit Car Produced between 1953 and 1985, p. 60.

in the late 1980s, this neo-classic always remained an exotic. From the outside, the car is certainly impressive. Even the doors consist of two shells, which indicates good workmanship.

Kitcar Centre / KCC   (ZA)

Kit Car Centre Pty, based in Boksburg, produced kit cars for the South African market between 1982 and 2003. The first model was designed by Rudi Malan and was a dune buggy called the Salamander. The rights to the Salamander were later transferred to Universal Products. Over the years Kitcar Centre has produced the KCC 356 Speedster Classic, the KCC Cobra V8, the KCC 550 Spyder, the KCC Badger Jeep and the KCC Razzo Barchetta. These are mainly replicas that could be built on the undercarriage of a Volkswagen. In 1997, Kit Car Centre launched the Hayden Dart brand and introduced a replica of the first African car under this label. In 2003 the company ran into financial difficulties and filed for bankruptcy. This marked the end of the production of KCC vehicles and the Hayden Dart brand. KCC and Hayden Dart were sold in South Africa and Egypt. The rights to the KCC vehicles were sold to a company called Backdraft. The new owner restarted a small production of Cobra vehicles a few years ago, mainly for export. The company sold twelve cars in 2000 and 2001 and only six in 2002. For 2003, 20 complete vehicles and 40 kits have been delivered.

Salamander

The Salamander was designed by Rudi Malan and largely followed the tradition of the Dune Buggy. The GRP body could be bolted onto an undamaged VW-Beetle chassis. The 2+2 seater buggy has a roll bar and roof and side panels that can be easily removed with a zip. As the kit was relatively inexpensive, around 200 of the Salamanders were sold within a short time.

356 Speedster Sebring

In 1982, a replica of a Porsche 718 RSK appeared that could be bolted onto the chassis of a VW-Beetle. This model found about 1200 buyers until 1991. The KCC 356 Speedster Classic was supplied as a kit and as a finished car with 52 or 58 bhp. The plastic body matches the original down to the last detail. Kitcar Centre was a little more liberal with the technology. The frames were made from steel tubing. The engines were South African VW boxers. In addition to the air-cooled four-cylinder boxer engines, VW Golf, VW Jetta, Toyota and Mazda Wankel engines were also used.

550 Spyder

The KCC 550 Spyder is a licence production of the now legendary Porsche 550 Spyder. This replica was mainly delivered as a finished vehicle with a Volkswagen Boxer engine with 52 or 58 bhp. The

**Top to bottom: Salamander Buggy from 1982.
356 Speedster Sebring - replica.
550 Spyder replica.**

KCC 550 Spyder is identical to the original right down to the last detail. Only the technology in the cars supplied by Kitcar Centre is more modern.

718 RSK

The KCC 718 RSK is a replica of the Porsche 718 RSK. The kit includes the front end, rear end, bodyshell with neck supports, doors and bonnet. The engine compart-

CARS OF THE 1980s

ment can accommodate VW boxer engines, air-cooled Porsche engines and other engines.

Badger Jeep

In the late 1990s, Kitcar Centre bought the rights to a Jeep-inspired vehicle called the Veep from Fibreglass Designs (originally Kango Cars). The plastic body was mounted on a VW-Beetle undercarriage and the vehicle was largely completed with Volkswagen components.

The moulds of the Badger Jeep are originally from Kango Cars.

Sources:
http://de.wikipedia.org/wiki/Kit_Car_Center
Autokatalog 1980 bis 2002 (Vereinigte Motor-Verlage GmbH & Co. KG, Stuttgart)
www.universal-products.co.za/replicacars/Salamander.html

Marian Suman-Hreblay: Automobile Manufacturers Worldwide Registry. McFarland Books, Jefferson, North Carolina, USA, 2000, p. 161.

www.aircooledvwsa.co.za/viewtopic.php?f=23&t=2456&start=450
George Nick Georgano: The Beaulieu Encyclopedia of the Automobile. Volume 2: G–O, Chicago 2001, p. 829.

Lalande (UK)

In the summer of 1983 the moulds for the Centron II were stored at the Alternative Autos factory in Threemilestone outside Truro. A deal was soon struck with John Gilbert of G.V. Plastics, based in St Columb Major, Cornwall. Together with the moulds, G.V. Plastics received a black-painted Centron II in return for painting other Centron IIs that had already been completed. This car was unveiled to the public under the name Lalande at the Wheels West Car & Hot Rod Show in August 1983. At this event the car won the award for the best painted car. The black

The Lalande based on the moulds of the Centron II.

finish was airbrushed with snakes and spaceships. A few years later the car was given a rather mediocre red livery.

The design of the Lalande is based on the GP Centron 2. The GRP body sits on the unabridged platform of a VW-Beetle. The car has room for a driver and passenger. The brochure describes the Lalande as a 2+2 seater GT. The kit cost £2,530 at the time and consisted of the one-piece body, doors and lids, fuel tank, wiring harness, top-mounted roof console and battery box. The doors and lids were factory-matched to the body. In total 13 colours were available. Many parts of the interior were also made from GRP. The seats available for the kit were upholstered in leather as standard and could be ordered in many colours. There were many accessories for the Lalande. The front tyres were 175/70/13. The rear tyres were 205/70/13. The kerb weight of the finished Lalande was about 670 kg. Compared to the Centron II, the Lalande's rear windscreen is

Sources:
Sales brochure for the Lalande
Peter Tuthill, Cornwall's Motor Industry, The story of the many fascinating motor vehicles manufactured in Cornwall from 1981 to date, 2007, p. 92f.
www.worthpoint.com
http://anarchadia.blogspot.com/

CARS OF THE 1980s

flat and considerably larger. Only two Lalande were sold between 1983 and 1986. In 1986 MDB, based in Tredegar, Wales, took over the moulds and rights to the kit. With only minor modifications, the kit was marketed under the name Sapphire.

L´Autocraft (BR)

L'Auto Craft Montadora de Veiculos Ltda, based in Barra do Pirai (RJ), bought the moulds and rights to the cars from L'Automobile in 1983. L'AutoCraft produced the Alfa Romeo P3 replica, the Bugatti T-35 replica and the Ventura or Ventura II under a new brand name. L'AutoCraft also produced a replica of a Ferrari Dino powered by a Volkswagen Boxer engine for Fibrario. A buggy called Terral was also produced for Fibrario. In 1986, Fibrario was bought out and the rights to the Dino replica and the Terral were transferred in full to L'AutoCraft.

Top: Alfa P3 replica from 1984.
Above: Bugatti 35B replica from 1986.

Alfa P3

The production rights and moulds were supplied by LÁutomobile. This is a replica of an Alfa Romeo P3 sports car, which was offered both as a kit and as a turnkey vehicle. Compared to the American model, the Brazilian version has a hood, doors and bumpers. As the Volkswagen boxer engine is mounted at the rear, air intakes had to be fitted at the rear to cool the engine compartment. The front grille is only there for visual reasons. In the front there is a large storage compartment for luggage. A lot of attention has also been paid to details in the interior. A wooden steering wheel with four spokes, original-style instrumentation and individual small windscreens look very authentic. Even the rivets have been incorporated into the moulds for the GRP parts.

Bugatti 35B

The replica of the Bugatti T-35 was also designed to be mounted on the floor pan of a VW Brasilia. Due to the arrangement of the engine, some changes had to be made to the original. The instrumentation is very faithful to the original. When designing the body moulds, the rivets on the original were also reproduced due to the manufacturing method. The cars were only delivered in the turnkey version. The LC Bugatti T-35 was also not available as a kit from LÁutoCraft.

Ventura RS/SLE (1984-1989)

The Ventura RS is very similar to the Ventura SLE. However, the air-cooled boxer engine was replaced by a 1.6-litre liquid-cooled engine from the Brazilian VW Passat. The RS was available with a 1.6-litre and a 1.8-litre engine. The 1.6-litre version was discontinued from 1986. With the more

CARS OF THE 1980s

powerful engine the Ventura had 85 bhp. The top speed was 185 km/h. A few were exported to America and Germany. In most cases, it was dealers who had had good experiences selling the Puma do Brasil that added the Ventura to their range.

In the Ventura SLE the engine was mounted transversely. With the fuel tank moved to the front, there was little room for luggage.

Ventura RS II (1984 - 1988)

In 1984 the Ventura was updated. The front of the car, including the bumper, was redesigned by the designers at L'Automobile. The Ventura RS II had a 2.0 litre engine but was not very successful. In 1988 the design of the car was once again fundamentally revised. Production of the Ventura III was discontinued in the same year. In addition to the coupé, a convertible version was added to the range. Only a few convertibles were completed before production was finally discontinued.

Ventura IIIa (1988)

In 1988 the design of the car was once again fundamentally revised. Production of the Ventura IIIa ceased in the same year. In addition to the coupé, a convertible version was added to the range. Only a few convertibles were completed before production was finally discontinued.

Ventura IIIa convertible from 1988.

Ventura LC (1988)

Another prototype of the Ventura was built for the XV Motor Show in São Paulo. The inspiration was the American Pontiac, which also had no bumpers, front-wheel drive and a two-litre engine from the VW Santana. The car never went into production. Instead, it became the basis for the development of the Sabre, which used components from the Chevrolet Opala 4.1.

Top: Ventura RS with twin headlights.
Left: Ventura RS II with rectangular headlights

Tander Buggy

After Tander-Car Industria e Comercio de Veiculos Ltda. of Itaim-Bibi, Sao Paulo, went out of business in 1983, L'AutoCraft took over the moulds and rights to the Tander Buggy. This is a dune buggy developed by Tander in 1976. The Tander Buggy was only sold as a kit.

LC Tander Buggy from 1985.

Ventura LC prototype from 1988.

CARS OF THE 1980s

Sources:
http://fuscaclassic.blogspot.co.at/2010/10/vw-alfa-romeo-8c-1933-replica.html

http://bestcars.uol.com.br/classicos/glaspac-2.htm
http://planetabuggy.forumeiros.com/t6151-mais-um-glaspac-tander
www.lexicarbrasil.com.br/

Thomas Braun, Puma – Typen und Geschichte, 1. Auflage 2010, p.175f
http://wj2d.100megsdns.com/ventura.html
Hot VWs (magazine), Nov. 1980

Lejin (ZA)

In 2022, a homemade car turned up in South Africa which, according to the owner, was built on the undercarriage of a right-hand drive VW-Beetle. Judging by the appearance of the body, Mr Lejin probably built this car in the late 1980s or early 1990s.

The two-seater convertible has a very cleanly designed body made of GRP. The conclusion is obvious that Mr Lejin intended to market his development in the kit car scene. The kit does not appear in any of the well-known kit car catalogues. It is possible that this prototype is all that is left.

The windscreen is glued into the frame. A wiper covers the entire field of vision. The somewhat unconventional looking roof construction can be removed in a few easy steps and stowed in the rear boot. The car is powered by

a liquid-cooled 1.8-litre VW Golf engine.

Sources:
With kind support of the members of the facebook groupe „Rare Component Cars Group".

Beetle floor pan with 1800 Golf engine.

LeMazone (UK)

Mike Parkington founded LeMazone in 1984 in Leigh, Lancashire. He started by producing cars and kit cars. Over time, the Comet, Can-Am and Pulsar were created using Volkswagen technology. Production ceased in 1987.

Comet (1984 – 1987)

The LeMazone Comet is a further development of the SN 1, with some of the edges of the body softened to improve the design. The compact notchback coupé had a GRP body bolted to the floor of a VW-Beetle. Only one car was built between 1984 and 1987.

The Comet is based on the SN 1 and was launched in 1984.

Can-Am (1985 -1987)

In 1985 LeMazone began production of the LeMazone Can-Am. This is a dune buggy originally developed by Beaujangle Sales in the early 1970s. It is based on the shortened chassis of a VW-Beetle. The one-piece GRP body is mounted on top. The silhouette of the LeMazone Can-Am is vaguely reminiscent of a racing car as seen in the Can-Am Cup. The kit cost 150 pounds. A hardtop with gullwing doors was available for an extra charge. Six cars were built between 1985 and 1987.

CARS OF THE 1980s

The Can AM Buggy was taken over from Beaujangle.

Pulsar (1984 -1985)

In 1985 LeMazone took over the production rights to the Pulsar kit developed by Amplas between 1984 and 1985. A ladder frame formed the basis of the Porsche replica. Many parts such as the front axle, steering and air-cooled four-cylinder boxer engine were taken from the VW-Beetle. The windscreen was taken from the Citroën GS. The Pulsar was one of the less successful replicas of the Porsche 911, but it was nevertheless exported to Germany, where two examples were registered at the end of the 1980s.

The Pulsar kit was taken over from Amplas in 1984.

Sources:
George Nick Georgano (Chefredakteur): The Beaulieu Encyclopedia of the Automobile. Volume 2: G–O, Chicago 2001, p. 889.
Steve Hole: A–Z of Kit Cars. The definitive encyclopaedia of the UK's kit-car industry since 1949, Sparkford 2012, p. 37, 145, 201 und 234.
Chris Rees, Peter Filby, Classic Kit Cars, p. 63.

Letherbarrow   (ZA)

A young designer called Roy Letherbarrow developed the kit for a caravan built on the platform of a VW Type 2. The one-piece body includes a GRP floor. The doors are hinged. According to a Letherbarrow customer, the GRP aspects of the kit are very well done. What was not done in a mature way were the locks and strike plates. There were many small details that an ambitious builder had to take into his own hands in order to get the Letherbarrow approved. A total of 13 bodies were built by the end of 1989.

The Letherbarrow caravan is sitting on a VW Type 2 platform.

Sources:
www.woodworkforums.com/showthread.php?t=14089

LN-33   (US)

David & Nancy Gray designed and built a neo-classic model based on the 1933 Duesenberg SSJ. Both the VW-Beetle saloon and a Beetle convertible were considered as donor vehicles. The kit cost $4895 in 1984. The finished Neoclassic, including the donor Beetle and necessary parts, cost around $10,000 at the time.

The LN-33 is a replica of the 1933 Duesenberg SSJ, and includes a steel frame to extend the front of the Beetle chassis by 76cm. Once the kit was bolted to the Beetle's floor assembly, the original Beetle doors could be used. Large parts of the body of a Beetle converti-

CARS OF THE 1980s

The LN-33 is a neoclassic roadster with similarities to the Duesenberg SSJ from 1933.

Cruella Deville's vehicle from the Disney film „101 Dalmatians".

ble can be used. The original soft top had to be slightly modified for the conversion. The front of the car and the fenders are made from GRP.

The kit was produced in Florida between 1984 and 1987 and the original manufacturer was sold to Neithken Associates in Fishersville, Va. About 40 units of the LN-33 were sold. Approximately 30 have survived to this day. One LN-33 was sold to Disney and was driven by Cruella Deville in the film „101 Dalmatians".

Sources:
Popular Mechnics (magazine). issue 11 from 1978, p. 172.
http://m.ebay.ca/itm/370774565971

London Roadster (US)

London Motors Corporation, based in Dearborn, Michigan, set out to produce a faithful replica of the 1952 MG TD. The aim was to develop a kit that would be attractive to the hobbyist. For fans of British nostalgia with more budget and less time, the finished roadster was delivered. The company was probably active in the 1980s.

The London Roadster was built on a custom tubular steel frame to achieve the most faithful dimensions and proportions possible. High quality materials were used and many parts were sourced from the Moss Motors spares store. At the rear of the car is an air-cooled boxer engine from a VW-Beetle. The gearbox was also sourced from a VW-Beetle.

Sources:
https://www.classicautomall.com
http://smclassiccars.com

The London Roadster is a replica of a MG TD from 1952.

CARS OF THE 1980s

Mac Laren (BR)

The „Mac Laren" shipyard was founded in 1938 in Niterói (RJ). In 1984, the company tried to utilise its spare machinery capacity in the shipbuilding sector. Due to a steady decline in orders in this sector, it became necessary to diversify. Mac Laren quickly acquired the rights to build the Julia saloon from Dankar. A subsidiary, Mac Laren Açofibras, was set up to handle the new business. Some 50 units were sold in the first year. A total of around 100 Mac Laren Julia were produced.

Julia (1984)

The car was offered to the market as a turnkey vehicle. In addition to the patents and production rights, the moulds and tools for the body were also bought from Dankar. Components such as the headlights from the Passat, the rear window from the Fiat 147 (but with the windscreen), the rear lights from the Opel and various controls such as the door handles from the Alfa Romeo 2300 TI were bought on the open market. The wheels came from the Passat Dacon, the grille between the headlights from the Chevrolet Chevette. At the end of 1984 the Mac Laren Julia was fitted with twin headlamps and new rear lights, as used on the Passat at the time. A large sunroof, a sports steering wheel and a centre console were added as options. Inside, care was taken to ensure that the comfort features of the VW Passat were retained as far as possible. The side windows at the rear of the car could also be rolled down. Although the car was sold under the brand name Julia, there are some examples in Brazil where the designation „Julie" can be found in the vehicle documents. As the Mac Laren Julia with twin headlights often has an Audi emblem on the radiator grille, the car is very difficult to identify on Brazilian roads. The car was sold with either a new or reconditioned 1.6-litre boxer engine and a six-month factory warranty.

Mac Laren acquired the rights to build the Julia from Dankar in 1984.

Apollo (1984)

Mac Laren also began developing a mini-van in 1984. The prototype was built with a GRP body and a VW Boxer engine in the rear. The base was donated by the VW Brasilia. The glazing and dashboard were also taken from the donor car. The Mac Laren Apollo has a large sunroof. The plan was to sell it as a turnkey car and as a kit. The Mac Laren company withdrew from the car business before the series production could start.

Prototype of a minican with GRP body based on the platform of a VW Brasilia in 1984.

Sources:
www.lexicarbrasil.com.br/mac-laren/
www.essevaleumafoto.com/2011/06/vw-mac-laren-passat-julia-1983.html
www.fotolog.com/80s_cars/8114081/

CARS OF THE 1980s

Marauder (US)

Wiegert studied at the Centre for Creative Studies in Michigan before working for General Motors and other companies. In 1980 he founded Marauder & Co, based in Potomac, Illinois. Over the years he has created a number of replicas of famous sports cars and his own interpretations, both for road use and competition. The Marauder & Co range also included a number of kits suitable for building vehicles on a Volkswagen chassis. These included a Dune Buggy for the general market. On the other hand, the focus was definitely on replicas of well-known names such as Lola, Ferrari, Lamborgini and the like. Between 1980 and 2007, Marauder produced a number of very high quality sports cars, always with the aim of combining the appeal of racing cars with the greatest possible comfort and practicality. Marauder cars were always designed so that two adults could be reasonably comfortable in the Recaro seats. The cars could be fitted with air conditioning. A 5-speed synchromesh gearbox and plenty of power were what customers wanted for a long time, until the regulations for road traffic approval left little room for creativity.

MK I Deserter (1980 -)

The Marauder GT MK I is a licensed version of the Deserter Buggy. The kit has been added to the range to serve the local market with dune buggy kits.

MK II Chevron (1986-)

Randy Berry bought the body of a Chevron B-16 with the designation DBE16-35 (body number 35 and thus one of the last original bodies ever produced) and had it shipped from Spain (Barcelona) to America. There the Chevron B-16 served as a model for the Marauder GT MK II. The MK II kit was available in two versions. One version was designed to be mounted on a VW Type 3 chassis. The other version had a tubular steel frame and everything needed to mount a mid-engine. In both versions the front and rear of the car could be folded up and removed. The MK II was fitted with a roll cage. In addition to the body, the kit included the windscreen, windows, doors, wiper motor, instruments, headlights, rear lights and pre-installed heating pipes with fan. The complete kit also included seats and wiring harness. The GRP body was reinforced with aluminium struts and steel beams to prevent the body from twisting and at all points where the components could be bolted together. For the body on a VW Type 3 chassis, an additional frame was used to provide a strong connection between the body and chassis. The front and rear structural frames had to be welded or bolted to the floor assembly.

MK III Lola

The MK III occupies a special place among the Marauder replicas that were also available to be mounted on a Volkswagen chassis. This is a replica of a 1967 Lola T70, which won the world championship title in the CanAm series. Eric Broadley, the founder of Lola, brought in Franco Sbarro in 1968 to turn the racing car into a road car. A very authentic replica of the Lola was available from Marauder as a kit or as a turnkey car.

The Marauder GT MK I is basically a Deserter Buggy.

The MK II is the replica of a Chevron B-16.

The MK III is the replica of a Lola T70 from 1967.

Sources:
www.flat4.org/forum/viewtopic.php?f=3&t=1218&start=60
The complete Guide to kit cars, auto parts & accessories
Mike Lawrence, A to Z of Sports Cars, 1945-1990, p. 204.
Popular Mechanics (Magazin), Ausgabe Dez. 1981, p. 86ff.
http://tentenths.com/forum/showthread.php?t=88516&page=7

Marauder (AU)

DRB Sportscars of Melbourne released a Ferrari Dino 246 replica in 1981. Founder and manufacturer was Denis R. Bedford (hence DRB). In 1988, after less than five Marauders had been completed, production was moved to Southport in Queensland. Shortly afterwards the moulds and tooling for the Marauder were sold to Adelaide. Ken Knolder produced a few Marauders before going out of business. Geoff Tan then bought the moulds for the Marauder. Geoff was a high school teacher and the moulds were used to train students in the use of composite materials. Geoff passed away and the moulds were bought by Norm Clements. Norm Clements ran the polymer courses at the Murray Bridge High School Skill Centre and used the Marauder moulds as part of his courses. The moulds were stored at the school until 2012. Norm was no longer interested in them. So the moulds went to Tasmania where a private individual is building his own Marauder. Assuming a maximum of one finished unit per year, it is likely that no more than 35 Marauders were ever produced.

With the original VW Boxer engine, it was even possible to obtain a Queensland registration. The GRP body was built over a steel frame and could be bolted to a VW Type 3 chassis. The tubular steel construction included a roll cage and side impact protection around the door surround. The VW Type 3 chassis was largely retained at the front. In addition to the VW boxer engine, the Marauder could also be fitted with a Mazda 13B rotary engine. The Marauder was available in various versions, from a kit to a pre-assembled version to a turnkey solution. A steel frame had to be bolted to the Volkswagen floor assembly before the GRP body could be fitted. The finished vehicles were customised according to the customer's requirements. The standard version includes an overhauled engine, dashboard from a BMW 323i, sports seats and wide tyres on aluminium rims. Prices start at $3,500 and are relatively open at the top. Delivery is promised within four weeks of the order being placed. For a completely finished vehicle with a Wankel engine, a waiting period of around 12 months had to be accepted.

Body of the Dino replica called Marauder from 1981.

Sources:
www.flat4.org/forum/viewtopic.php?f=3&t=1218&start=60
The complete Guide to kit cars, auto parts & accessories
http://paulsweb.info/marauder/index.html
Marauder, Sports Car World (magazine), issue 02 from 1990.

Mikada (AU)

The Mikada kit could be bolted to the floor pan of a VW Type 3. An advertisement from early 1986 offered the moulds for the construction of a Mikada body for sale. Two years earlier, the same supplier had offered the prototype for the Mikada. This vehicle is advertised as a convertible with a valid registration. The kit was actually designed with gullwing doors. In this respect, the car on offer may well be the first convertible to have been developed using the original moulds.

Dandy Volks of Dandenong and Purvis must have worked closely together at the time. There is evidence that they helped each other with spare parts. It also appears that Dandy Volks was the distributor for the Mikada kit at least in 1984. It was not until November 1984 that the first advertisement appeared, offering to make the moulds for the convertible prototype and the moulds and tools for the coupé. The person behind the telephone number 720 4448

CARS OF THE 1980s

is probably a private individual. It was this person who probably drove the project forward for almost three years. During this time no significant quantities were produced or sold. Two Mikada are documented. A white car appeared in 2020 and a turquoise Mikada became known in the VW scene a year later.

Sources:
With kind support of Rick Perceval (automotive historian)
With kind support of Mick Hargreaves

This Mikada has surfaced in 2021; still waiting for restoration.

Mulholland (US)

Creative Car Craft, based in St Harbor City, California, coined the so-called Mulholland Look in the early 1980s with its unconventional conversions for VW-Beetles. The story of the look actually began as a joke when some companies, looking for new business for their GRP products, began to think of imaginative ways to make a VW-Beetle look like an expensive sports car. Many companies rejected this approach for fear of making a fool of themselves with these products. Although some Beetle modifications were created, they disappeared into the garages of the manufacturers for safety's sake. Only one company from Florida took the idea further and ventured into the public eye with their creations. Probably at one of the then popular BugJams, Creative Car Craft presented simple modifications such as GRP wings and started a trend that encouraged other companies to bring their ideas to market. New headlights, bumpers, running boards, tail lights and fenders revitalised the scene.

Creative Car Craft's range included wings with internal and exter-

CARS OF THE 1980s

nal extensions, with standard and special lighting. Rectangular headlamps were particularly popular at the time. Rear lights also tended to be rectangular. The all-round bodywork with laminated bumpers and rear fenders in the style of the Porsche 911 was also popular. The chassis was usually customised as well. The typical Mulholland Beetle had wheel spacers, wide tyres and was lowered.

Sources:
www.creativecarcraft.com/frontend.htm
www.volkszone.com/VZi/archive/index.php?t-893314.html

Orion (BR)

The Orion Buggy, also known as the ‚Corvette Gaucho' due to its similarities, was created in Porto Alegre (RS). On a smaller scale, but with similar proportions, the American model is clearly recognisable. The Orion Buggy is a kit that was offered in Brazil in the 1980s. The GRP bodyshell is mounted on a 32 cm shortened VW Beetle chassis. The cabriolet can seat two people. The four headlights are taken from the Passat. The rear lights were borrowed from the Gol and the windscreen from the Fiat 147.

Orion I

The first version of the Orion Buggy has two doors with sliding side windows. The air intakes, which supply fresh air to the engine compartment, are located above the door latch. The front of the car looks like a „small" Corvette.

Buggy I

The second attempt simplified the model. The convertible became a buggy without doors. A GRP hardtop was available as an option. The hardtop consists of several parts, so that only the driver and passenger are protected from the sun or light rain. The beading on the sides of the car was retouched. The air intakes behind the driver and passenger also had to be removed. This made the car and the kit much cheaper to produce.

Buggy II

Another facelift brought the Buggy more in line with contemporary tastes. The closeness to the Corvette was less obvious. A styling element was added to the side, sug-

Top: Orion I two-seater.
Middle: Buggy I with two doors and Targa top.
Bottom: Buggy II with roll bar.

gesting air intakes. The rear bumpers are more pronounced. There

CARS OF THE 1980s

was only a soft top that could be stretched over the roll bar.

Orion II

The fourth version of the Orion was a closed car in which all similarities to the Corvette had finally been eliminated. For the first time a water-cooled engine was installed at the front of the car. Air intakes were required above and below the front bumper to provide sufficient cooling air. Only two headlights were fitted at the front. The front of the car had to be completely redesigned to accommodate the engine. The car has doors again. The roof can be removed. At the rear, the rectangular tail lights were replaced by four tail lights.

Orion III

The latest version of the Orion is again rear-engined and has a more Corvette-like design. The front of the car is dominated by four round headlights borrowed from the Ford Focus. At the front, there are triangular turn signals at the side edges. At the rear, the four tail lights from the previous model have been retained. The rear of the car has been completely redesigned. The engine compartment is supplied with fresh air via side air intakes and louvres on the engine cover. The rear windscreen is positioned almost vertically behind the driver and passenger to make access to the engine as practical as possible. On some of the latest Orion vehicles, the roof is made of Plexiglas.

Orion II coupé with water-cooled VW engine.

Orion III with twin headlights and sun roof.

Sources:
http://www.lexicarbrasil.com.br/orion/
With kind support of João F. Scharinger.

Ostermann GR-C   (DE)

Between November 1987 and 1990 the company „Speedster Ostermann" offered the kit for the reproduction of a Karmann Ghia convertible under the name „GR-California" or „GR-C". A total of about 100 kits were sold. A total of about 100 GR-California kits were sold. At that time 65 kits went to the Netherlands. Approximately 75 kits were registered. The GR-California differs from its predecessor in a number of distinctive features. The GR-C had no trunk lid and therefore no trunk. The rear fenders are wider to accommodate the wide tyres (225mm). The entire body is lowered so that the doors end at the sill. The heating duct of the Beetle chassis is located directly under the door sill. With the entire body lowered to the floor panel, recesses had to be made in the bonnet to make room for the engine. These changes made the GR-C distinctive and gave it a sportier look. The seats and door panels were often upholstered in beige artificial leather with beige carpets. The dashboard, steering wheel and gear lever were veneered in mahogany. A K&N air filter was fitted due to the cramped engine compartment. The exhaust system is registered as 91 phon.

Sources:
www.gr-california.de
www.ostermann-cabrios.de/
Ostermann sales brochure from 1990.

The Ostermann GR C (California) is a replica of the Karmann Ghia convertible close to the original but with a body out of GRP.

Panache (UK)

Paul Lawrenson designed his first car in 1978. In 1981 he and Peter Robinson founded Panache Kit Cars in Darwen, Lancashire. In 1985 Bob Davies took over the company, renamed it Panache Cars Limited and moved the headquarters to Blackburn in Lancashire. Production ceased in 1987. According to official figures, a total of 131 kits were produced for the reproduction of the Lamborghini Countach.

Panache (1984 – 1987)

The Panache bore a certain resemblance to the Lamborghini Countach, but is not a faithful replica of the original. The basis of the kit is the unmodified chassis of the VW-Beetle. The GRP body was mounted on top. A special feature was the forward opening cockpit above the passenger compartment, similar to the Bond Bug or Nova. By 1985, 71 had been built. After that the kit was mostly mounted on a ladder frame and the car was fitted with a V8 engine.

The Panache has great similarities with the Lamborghini Countach.

Sources:
Harald Linz, Halwart Schrader: Die Internationale Automobil-Enzyklopädie, München 2008, chapter: Panache.

George Nick Georgano (Chefredakteur): The Beaulieu Encyclopedia of the Automobile. Volume 3: P–Z, Chicago 2001, p. 1180.
Steve Hole: A–Z of Kit Cars. The definitive encyclopaedia of the UK's kit-car industry since 1949, Sparkford 2012, p. 191.
Chris Rees, Peter Filby, Classic Kit Cars – A Comprehensive Buyer´s Guide to every Kit Car Produced between 1953 and 1985, p. 82.
Kit Car (magazine), issue 7/1982.

Pantera (BR)

Pantera Design Indústria e Comércio Ltda. from Sao Paulo produced kit vehicles and kits between 1988 and 1992, mainly based on a Volkswagen platform. The first kit was a replica of a 1952 MG TD, which also included a buggy and bodies very similar to the buggy. In 1989, a copy of an AC Cobra

CARS OF THE 1980s

based on the Chevrolet Opala and a replica of a Porsche 911 based on a VW-Beetle were added to the range. After the government opened the Brazilian market to foreign cars, the company was cancelled in 1992.

MG TD (1988 – 1992)

The Pantera MG TD has some similarities with the late version of the MP Lafer. The GRP body is bolted to the shortened floor assembly of a VW-Beetle or VW Brasilia. The 2-seater has a soft top that disappears inside the body when open.

Buggy (1988 – 1992)

The Pantera dune buggy has a very distinctive appearance due to its extremely short wheelbase. The front of the vehicle is characterised by 4 headlights. Behind the driver and passenger there is a roll bar integrated into the bodywork, which is reinforced on the inside with steel tubes. At the rear of the vehicle there are round tail lights. The engine is located directly behind the driver and passenger. The handling characteristics of the Pantera Buggy are very impressive off-road. On the road and at higher speeds, the driver may need a lot of sensitivity in winding situations.

911 (1989 – 1992)

In 1989 the replica of a Porsche 911 was added to the range. The kit is designed to be bolted to the floor pan of a VW Beetle. The engine compartment accommodates the VW boxer engine and air-cooled Porsche engines. Some cars were also equipped with a Corvair engine. Although the sources are rather scarce, it can be assumed that neither the coupé nor the convertible offered for the first time in 1990 were sold in large numbers.

Pickup

The Pantera pickup is probably a licensed version of the Polauto with double cab. At least the idea of the Polauto, which was launched in the early 1980s, seems to have been taken up by Pantera Design.

Sources:
http://www.lexicarbrasil.com.br/pantera-design/
With kind support of João F. Scharinger.

Paragon (AU)

George Pariss and firefighter Peter Swanston first met in 1979. Pariss wanted his Toyota reupholstered and heard from friends that a member of the local fire brigade did this work in his spare time. When they met for the first time, it quickly became apparent that they both had similar dreams. Both had been dreaming of building their own sports car for some time. Five years later, that dream was about to come true.

It started as a hobby for two car enthusiasts, but the response to their first self-designed car turned it into a business idea. With the help of a GRP specialist, the first body was created and mounted on a Volkswagen Type 3 chassis. The Paragon prototype was unveiled to the public at the 1981 Brisbane Motor Show. The two hobbyists wanted to gauge the reaction of the public to see if they were on the right track. The response was surprisingly positive. So the project went ahead with great confidence.

The prototype was then used to make more moulds for a small production run. The prototype was then scrapped. A new GRP body was built and mounted on another used chassis. This second car was sanded, painted and finished in record time. The car was then unveiled in the Grand Windsor Ballroom of the Crest International Hotel.

There is a vacuum tank in the boot next to the original Volkswagen

CARS OF THE 1980s

tank for the headlight lifting mechanism. The bumpers are made from cast aluminium tubes encased in GRP. The front of the car is similar to the Porsche 914, with additional headlights, direction indicators and air intakes for the interior ventilation integrated into the spoiler.

Each Paragon sports car was delivered with a reconditioned floor pan, reconditioned chassis and the customer's choice of engine specification. There was also a choice of sound system, body colour and interior colour. The result was a bespoke two-seater sports coupé.

The Paragon uses the floorpan of a VW Type 3.

Sources:
With friendly support of the members of the facebook groupe „Durchgeboxt"

Petterson Roadster (SW)

The so-called Petterson Roadster was created in 1983. It was based on a 1967 VW-Beetle export model for Sweden, and Mr Petterson was responsible for the conversion. He placed the GRP body on the unshortened floor pan of the VW-Beetle. The result was a two-seater convertible with a roll bar. In 2009, the car was taken to Germany by a Volkswagen AG employee. The restoration was completed in August 2011. In the same year the car received its road registration. Since then, the Petterson Roadster has been driven regularly and can occasionally be seen at classic car events.

The Petterson Roadster is a one-off that was restored in 2011.

Sources:
With friendly support of the members of the facebook groupe „Durchgeboxt"

Porrera (AU)

In the mid-1980s, Creative Cars of Blair Athol, South Australia, offered a kit for reproducing a Porsche 911. It was based not only on the floor pan of a VW-Beetle, but also on large parts of the original Beetle. For the conversion, the roof of the Beetle had to be lowered to match the silhouette of the Porsche. The kit includes new front and rear wings, a boot lid, bonnet with rear wing and bumpers. The original welded nuts in the wheel arches can be used to mount the new wings. Porsche chrome wheels, an exclusive leather interior and Porsche instruments were also sourced to make the car as close to the original as possible. Conversion to disc brakes was only necessary if a more powerful VW or Porsche engine was fitted. According to the brochure, the basic conversion could be completed in 40 hours. It can be assumed that a discerning car builder would spend far more

CARS OF THE 1980s

time to create a beautiful car. With the necessary effort it was possible to build a relatively authentic car.

Sources:
www.carscoops.com
www.autoblog.com/2007/08/14/porrera-beetle-based-faux-911/
Sales brochure of Creative Cars, 1983.

The Porrera brings Porsche feeling to a the driver.

Procar Van (BR)

Procar, based in Rio de Janeiro, was primarily a manufacturer of car accessories. In the 1980s, the company also offered kits for converting a VW-Beetle into a van. Interestingly, the kits were sold by a chain of department stores with branches in the south and southeast of the state of Rio de Janeiro. The mini-van kit was cast in fibreglass, based on a North American model. It was probably modelled on the very successful Vendetta kit from California. The kit consisted of six parts: the inner widened rear fenders, two side-opening rear doors, the rear bumper with rear lights and the load compartment itself.

As an option, hobbyists could get wider fenders and rear windows. After removing further parts of the bodywork from the C-pillar

The Procar Van kit seems to be based on the moulds of the Vendetta that was developed in California.

upwards, the box-shaped body had to be cut to size and joined to the body. This gave the owner of a VW-Beetle a luggage compartment of around 1.8 cubic metres. Thanks to the weight reduction achieved by the GRP parts, the vehicle could be used for a payload of up to 480 kg. With the end of production of the Volkswagen in Brazil, the sale of the kit was also discontinued.

The kit was homologated by the Ministry of Transport. Procar had an FEI approval certificate. Despite this, no significant sales figures were achieved. It is believed that not many more than 10 kits were sold in the early 1980s.

Sources:
Oficina Mecânica (magazine), issue 2, 1982
https://www.lexicarbrasil.com.br/procar/ Mecânica

Proton (BR)

In 1980, Pedro Barbosa Virginio Onofre founded Proton Design LTDA in Fortaleza (CE). The aim of the company was to manufacture vehicles for competition and leisure. The company also produced furniture, playground equipment and GRP lamp holders. During the 1980s, several interpretations of the dune buggy and a sports coupé called the Cucaracha were created. In the early 90s, Pedro Virginio turned his attention to motorsport. This resulted in the first cars designed for competition. The first motorsport creation was the Proton 1600, still powered by an air-cooled 1.6-litre VW boxer engine. After that, only cars with water-cooled engines were produced. Pedro Virginio passed away in January 2012.

Buggy Búzio

Pedro Virginio's first vehicle was a buggy very similar to the Gurgel X10. The car has a hardtop, which can be removed if required. The central instrument of the Beetle was kept on the dashboard. The

The Buggy Búzio has great similarities with the X10 from Gurgel.

floorpan of the VW-Beetle had to be shortened to fit the new body. Only three were built.

Cucaracha

Pedro Virginio's second project in 1980 was a sports coupé called the Cucaracha. The 2-seater coupé was bolted on the chassis of a VW-Beetle and fitted with a 1.6-litre boxer engine. In addition to the speedometer, the dashboard featured a timer, an oil pressure and temperature gauge and a rev counter. The centre console had space for a radio with cassette deck and other instruments that could be retrofitted individually. Behind the driver and passenger was a generously proportioned luggage compartment. The model was so successful at launch that it was featured in a film shortly after the prototype was completed. Despite this, only 10 of the Cucaracha were produced.

The second project is a two-seater coupé called Curacha.

Buggy Tatuí

Pedro Virginios' second buggy was given the name Tatuí. The contours of the vehicle are somewhat more curved, although it still has a relatively sharp-edged appearance. The rectangular headlights sit between the mudguards just above the bumper. Access to the fuel tank was via a lockable flap, under which small items could also be stowed. A removable hardtop was also available for this model.

The second buggy was called Tatui.

Buggy Tatuí 2

A few years after the introduction of the Buggy Tatuí, the car underwent a facelift. The result was a modern looking vehicle with even more pronounced curves in the bodywork. The buggy was called Tatuí 2. The front of the car was now in one piece. The headlights were positioned above the indicators. The roll-over bar was also

After a facelift the Buggy Tatui 2 was launched.

made from two steel tubes that met at the top in an A-shape. Additional headlights on the roll bars added a touch of adventure. However, sales of the second edition of the Buggy Tatuí were not particularly successful either.

Sources:
www.lexicarbrasil.com.br/proton/
Especial Fusca & Cia (magazine),
Guia Histórico Esportivos de Fibra, p. 20ff.

PS 904 (DE)

The real 904 GTS race car was also known as the Porsche Carrera GTS. It is a 2-seater, mid-engined coupe with a plastic body. In addition to the 120 or so built by Porsche with a body by Henkel in Speyer, there is a replica built by Mr Paris and Mr Sanftenberg. After almost 5 years of construction, the home-built car had a GRP body bolted onto a platform frame from a 1972 VW 1300 Beetle that had been damaged in an accident. Disc brakes were fitted to the front axle. Before the body

CARS OF THE 1980s

Replica of the Porsche 804 bolted on the chassis of a VW-Beetle.

could be fitted, the chassis had to be reinforced with the lower strut braces required for Beetle convertible conversions. Sketches, photos and the natural dimensions of the original Porsche served as the basis for the body. A wooden negative mould was made beforehand. The body was then created and reworked several times to get as close to the original as possible. The PS 904's windscreen, seals, windscreen wipers and headlight covers were taken from the Porsche 904 GTS itself. The auxiliary headlights were taken from the Opel GT. The main headlights were taken from a BMW 3 Series and the rear lights from a Ferrari 512 BB.

The PS 904 is a standard 3 seater (2 plus an emergency seat). The front seats correspond to the sports version of the Porsche 911 - model year 1973 - and were upholstered by Recaro. The dashboard features a speedometer, rev counter, oil thermometer, fuel gauge and clock. The PS 904 was powered by a 1.3-litre 44 bhp boxer engine. Koni shocks were fitted instead of the original ones. On 13th April 1983 the PS 904 was presented to the TÜV in Braunschweig and the car was approved without any objections.

Sources:
Hans Joachim Kiersy, Der PS 904 –Porsche-Replik auf dem Käfer-Fahrwerk, Gute Fahrt (magazin), issue 5/89, p. 84.

Pulmonia (MX)

Mazatlán, a few kilometres north of Vallarta, is often referred to as the „Pearl of the Pacific". In this region there are taxis that are specially designed and used for tourist purposes, which look very much like a golf caddy. These taxis are has survived to the present day and refers to the pneumonia, a type of lizard common in the Mazatlán area. A ride in one of the special air-cooled taxis is a tourist attraction that every visitor should try at least once. The first fleet of 16 vehicles any more golf caddies, the man visited the Cushman company in Nebraska and persuaded them to give him a further 8 caddies as part payment. The idea proved popular, but the three-wheeled design proved too dangerous, so after about 100 units the design was changed to four wheels.

Pulmonia taxis were already very popular with tourists in the 1960s, and in the 1980s the body was based on the chassis of a VW-Beetle.

called Pulmonias. The open-top vehicle was built on the chassis of a VW-Beetle for tourist use. When these taxis first appeared in the 1960s, drivers of classic taxis warned tourists not to use them because they could catch pulmonia while driving. The name pulmonia hicles went into service in December 1965. The story goes back to a businessman who bought three golf caddies from the Cushman company to replace the wooden horse-drawn carriages that were popular with tourists at the time. After the bank refused to finance

In the early 1980s, the design was modified to allow the GRP body to be bolted to the floorpan of a VW-Beetle. The design and name were even patented. In 2012, more than 350 Pumlonias were in service. Around 500,000 people were transported in them that year. Shortly after the turn of the millennium, another version with small GRP doors was developed

Sources:
http://latinflyer.com/mexico/travel-video-mazatlan-mexico-the-pulmonia-experience/
www.virtualtourist.com/travel/North_America/Mexico/Estado_de_Sinaloa/Mazatlan-940544/Transportation-Mazatlan-Pulmonia-BR-1.html
www.thesamba.com/vw/forum/viewtopic.php?t=315285&view=previous

for tourism under the name Safari. In 2012, around 230 Safaris were operating in and around Mazatlán. There is even a monthly magazine dedicated to the pulmonias and important events in the greater Mazatlán area. Today, many Mexicans bring their old Beetles to Mazatlán to sell them as spare parts to local garages.

Pulsar (UK)

Pulsar Cars, based at Amplas Chalgrove in Oxfordshire, produced kits between 1984 and 1987 that could be bolted to the undercarriage of a VW-Beetle. In 1985 the rights to produce the Pulsar convertible were also transferred from Amplas to LeMazone in Leigh, Lancashire. In 1987 the company was forced to cease trading for liquidity reasons.

Pulsar 911 (1984 – 1987)

For the Pulsar 911, Mike Parkington used the moulds of a Porsche 911 convertible to develop his kit. The chassis was a 1303 VW-Beetle with a 1.6 litre boxer engine. Most of the engines were fitted with twin carburettors and unleaded cylinder heads. Due to the relatively low total weight of the car, it does not appear to be underpowered. The interior was mostly fitted with Porsche seats. The dashboard and steering wheel were also taken from the prototype. As the bodywork, at least on the outside, is the same as that of the prototype, the Pulsar Cars customer was able to build a car that was very close to the prototype.

Only one right-hand drive Pulsar 911 is known to exist in Germany. The car is powered by a 1700cc Porsche 914 engine with EMPI 40 twin carburettors and 80 bhp. The car was built on the chassis of a 1969 VW-Beetle, but already had disc brakes on the front wheels.

Pulsar Porsche 911 replica.

Sources:
www.volkszone.com/VZi/showthread.php?t=729559
www.covin.co.uk/covinforum/viewtopic.php?t=572
Chris Rees, Peter Filby, Classic Kit Cars – A Comprehensive Buyer´s Guide to every Kit Car Produced between 1953 and 1985, p. 42.

Quiron SP (BR)

The company Quiron -Ind. De Artefatos de Fibra de Vidro Ltda. from Curitiba launched a convertible in 1987 based on the shortened floor assembly of a VW Brasilia. The Quiron SP had a tuned air-cooled 4-cylinder engine with a capacity of 1.6 litres and 64 bhp. The kit consisted of a centre section, boot lid, engine compartment lid, doors and a roll bar made from a metal tube covered in GRP. The Quiron SP was available both as a kit and as a finished car. As well as its design, the Quiron also featured a number of technical refinements. For example, the windscreen wiper was hidden behind the boot lid and the windscreen was removable. The Quiron SP was also sold through dealers such

CARS OF THE 1980s

as Vaticano Car and Maxiauto between 1987 and 1989.

Sources:
www.lexicarbrasil.com.br/quiron/
www.indacarros.com.br/index.
php?option=com_jvehicles&view
=product&cid=&tid=&id=44029:
2013-02-09-22-36-07&Itemid=42

Quiron launched an interestingly designed convertible with a targa roof in 1987.

Ragge (BR)

Júlio Sillas founded Ragge Industria e Comercio Ltda in Rio de Janeiro in 1985. The aim of the company was to develop and sell vehicles using Volkswagen mechanics. The company founder's first creation dates back to 1983. At that time, he developed the Tanger Buggy. Two years later, a Jeep-like vehicle was created, marketed under the name „California" and built on a VW Brasilia platform shortened by 25 cm. In the course of time, the American market was developed in addition to the Brazilian market. The Ragge Long Beach was presented to the public at the XVI International Motor Show in 1990. At the same time, the company was renamed Ragge Industrial Ltda and its headquarters moved to Duque de Caxias, RJ. The new model had a longer wheelbase. This meant that the loading area could be made slightly longer. Ragge's parts suppliers included many manufacturers who were also among Volkswagen's main suppliers. In 1987, the production rights for the Ragge vehicles were acquired by Tanger Industria Ltda, which marketed them under licence. The opening up of the Brazilian market led to a slump in sales. As a result, the company had to cease operations in the mid-1990s.

California
(1986/1987 - 1990)

The Ragge resembles a VW Golf at the front and has a loading area at the rear that can be covered with a hardtop or softtop. The pickup had no rear window, but drove like a saloon with a hardtop. Electric windows and central locking were fitted as standard. The spare wheel is mounted on the rear wall of the cargo area to make room for the load. Access to the engine was via the interior. The first Ragge was delivered with a VW Boxer engine with a displacement of 1584 cc. Later the 1.7 litre engine as used in the SP2 was installed. The rear lights were taken from a Fiat, the windscreen from an Alfa Romeo 2300 and many other parts of the Ragge were borrowed from production cars. The GRP body is neatly finished. The interior is finished with minor imperfections. The Ragge was sold both as a kit

Ragge California pickup with hard top from 1988.

and as a turnkey vehicle. The cars produced by Ragge have reclining seats, velvet upholstery, carpets, a sunroof, fog lights and rubber strips on the bumpers in the luxury version. The standard version is rather spartan. Both versions had too few instruments and poor sound insulation. Nevertheless, the car was a great success. About 200 cars were sold within the first 6 months. Small changes were made in 1987. More space was created for passengers in the rear and the

CARS OF THE 1980s

Technical Details
Ragge California
Engine: VW 1.6 or 1.7 litre
Power: 54 - 64 hp
Length: 3600 mm; Width: 1600 mm; Hight: 1500 mm; Wheelbase: 2.400 mm
Weight: 790 kg (empty)

Long Beach (1990 - 1995)

The Ragge Long Beach can be seen as the successor to the California. Compared to its predecessor, only a few details were changed. Among other things, the rear windows have been redesigned to provide better all-round visibility. Stylised air intakes were added to the left and right edges of the bonnet to improve the look. The Long Beach was also available as a convertible and with a hardtop. The mechanics of this car also came from Volkswagen. The Ragge Long Beach was just as successful as its predecessor. However, after the Brazilian market was opened up, sales dropped and production had to be discontinued in 1995.

The Long Beach from 1990 has generous glazing.

sound insulation was improved. A small spoiler was added to the hardtop and new hinges were fitted. From the 1987 Brasil Transpo show, the car was marketed under the name „Ragge California". From 1988 the Ragge California was also exported to America.

Sources:
Quatro Rodas (magazine), issue 363, October 1990, p.100ff.
Quatro Rodas (magazine), issue 337, March 1988.
https://felipebitu.wordpress.com/tag/ragge-california-long-beach/
www.lexicarbrasil.com.br/ragge/

Rawlson (UK)

Don Rawlings founded Rawlson Racing in 1972 in Dover, Kent. The name Rawlson is derived from the combination of the first syllable of Rawling's surname and the last syllable of co-founder James Henderson's surname. Unfortunately, James Henderson died shortly after the company was formed. Barry Sheppard then joined the team. Over the years Barry Sheppard, Alan Hatswell, Ken Sherman, Mike Lemon, Bruce Swales and Alan Frener have all worked for Rawlson Racing Cars. Don Rawlings spent some time working with GRP before starting to develop a replica of a Ferrari 250LM in 1976. The first car was built with the help of James Henderson. Series production of the kit began in 1982, with kits and turnkey cars also being sold. Some kits were completed and delivered in Faversham, Kent. In 1984 Keith Sharman & Co of Colchester in Essex acquired the rights to the Rawlson 250 LM. After two years the licence was transferred to Classic Replicars of Ashford in Kent. In 1987 the Rawlson 250 LM was added to the range by Western Classics of Bradford-on-Avon in Wiltshire. The 2-seater version of the car was called the 164LM and was developed in conjunction with Jago Automotive with a mid-engined Ford or mid-engined Alfa Romeo Alfasud. Trowbridge in Wiltshire produced the kit from 1987 to 1989. The last manufacturer was Tiger Cars Ltd; Plumstead from London, although it remains unclear whether Tiger Cars ever produced or sold the 250 LM replica as a Rawlson or as a Tiger. However, it is documented that the engineers at Tiger Cars developed the 2-seater version (164LM) and optimised it to accept a 6-cylinder mid-engine from Audi. Depending on the source, production ended in 1990, 1992 or 1998, with a total of around 15 documented examples built over the years.

Rawlson 250 LM (1982 - 1998)

The replica of the Ferrari 250LM was first unveiled at the Birmingham NEC Motor Show, opposite the stand of Maranello, the im-

The Rawlson is a nice replica of the Ferrari 250 LM.

CARS OF THE 1980s

porter of Ferrari cars. The initially confused Ferrari people visited Don Rawling's stand and, after taking a closer look at the car, congratulated him on his creation and wished him good luck. The Ferrari 250 LM, created in 1963, won its first Formula 1 Grand Prix in 1964. In 1965 Jochen Rindt won the Austrian Grand Prix. Only 32 of the Scaglietti-bodied cars were built. Despite considerable success, the car was not homologated at the time. The Rawlson 250 LM looks very much like the original. The car was initially built on the floorpan of a VW-Beetle. From 1987 a ladder frame from Jago Automotive was available. This made it possible to use a Ford engine or an Alfasud engine.

The early VW based version was not only powered by the VW boxer engine. At least one example was equipped with a 2-litre 6-cylinder Porsche boxer engine with 130 bhp. In this case, a Porsche 5-speed gearbox was also fitted. Porsche parts were also used in the car's interior. Later, technology from the Ford Escort and Ford Granada was also used. A total of 13 Rawlson 250 LM were built. It is not known how many were sold over the years. It is interesting to note that the number 12a was used instead of the body number 13 at the customer's request. The existence of exactly one is known. 3 Rawlson 250 LM's are regularly seen at events in England. The 2-part moulds for the Rawlson 250 LM have been preserved.

Sources:
www.madabout-kitcars.com/kitcar/kitcar_details.php?284
www.volkszone.com/VZi/showthread.php?t=435295
Rawlson Racing 250LM, Sports & Kit Car Builder (magazine), issue 3/84.
www.rawlson-racing.co.uk/
George Nick Georgano: The Beaulieu Encyclopedia of the Automobile. Volume 3: P–Z, Chicago 2001, p. 1302.
Steve Hole: A–Z of Kit Cars, Sparkford 2012, p. 207 and 253.
www.collectorsweekly.com/stories/146073-rawlson-250-lm-one-off
http://fiberclassics.org/rawlson-ferrari-250lm-replicar/

Replicar (UK)

Alan Hatswell founded Replicar Limited in Whistable in 1981. The aim of the company was to develop and sell kit cars and neo-classics. Between 1981 and 1995 he produced three neo-classic car kits based on the chassis of a VW-Beetle. The range included a replica of a Bugatti Type 35, a Bugatti Type 43 and a Jaguar SS100. The Replicar Bugatti Type 55 was Replicar's last kit development. Nine Type 55s were built between 1992 and 1995. Unlike previous projects, the Type 55 was the first car to have a custom chassis built. The one-piece GRP body was designed by Alan Hatswell. The Replicar Bugatti Type 55 mainly used components from British Leyland Motors.

Jaguar SS100 (1981 -)

The Jaguar SS100 replica kit was originally developed by Antique & Classic Automotive of Buffalo, NY. Alan Hatswell imported a kit at the very beginning of his business to be the first product on the British market. This laid the foundation for a new standard of quality within the kit car scene in 1981. The proportions of the car are also very well balanced. To achieve this, the Beetle chassis had to be lengthened. This resulted in a wheelbase of 2,700mm, the same as the 1937 Jaguar. With a price of just under £4,000, the kit was also

Replicars Jaguar SS100 replica from 1981.

in the higher segment.

Type 35

In 1981, Alan Hatswell took up the idea, developed in America, of building a replica of a Bugatti Type 35 by bolting the GRP body onto a modified and shortened chassis of a VW-Beetle. The kit was very cheap at the time. However, the manufacturer had to work very hard to achieve a great result. The finished car has a windscreen that folds forward. The side windows could also be folded to the side. For later models, a full-width windscreen was available as an option. A soft top was also developed for the Bugatti Type 35 re-

Technical Details
Type 35
Engine: VW flat four
Power: - hp
Length: 3900 mm; Width: 1600 mm; Hight: 1270 mm; Wheelbase: 2.400 mm
Weight: 800 kg (empty)

plica to provide the driver and passenger with sufficient protection from the weather. The kit quickly became very popular. By 1995, 95 Replicar Type 35s had been produced in both left and right hand drive versions. The rights to the kit were then transferred to Children Motors and shortly afterwards to PBM. Between 1992 and 1995 the kit was manufactured by Lucastore in South London.

Type 43

At the request of an interested party, the Type 35 kit was developed to create a more practical vehicle. The customer wanted space for more than two people. Alan Hatswell modified the rear of a Type 35 and took the opportunity to place the quickly developed one-piece windscreen, which was also used on the Type 35, in front of the driver and passenger. The cockpit was enlarged and moved forward slightly to make room for a second row of seats. A soft top was fitted as standard. The result was a car that appears to have been modelled on the 1927-1931 Bugatti 43 4-seater. Only one example of the Replicar Type 43 was built.

250LM

One of Alan Hatswell's most ambitious projects was the development of a replica of a Ferrari 250LM. This Ferrari had been copied many times before. In terms of workmanship, the Ferrari 250LM replica was particularly

Top: Bugatti Type 35 replica
Middle: Bugatti Type 43 replica.
Above: Ferrari 250 LM replica.

Technical Details
250 LM
Engine: VW flat four
Power: - hp
Length: 4220 mm; Width: 1650 mm; Hight: 1160 mm; Wheelbase: 2.400 mm
Weight: 800 kg (empty)

successful. The car was unveiled at

CARS OF THE 1980s

the 1982 Birmingham NEC Motor Show, close to Maranello, the Ferrari importer. The response to the replica was very positive.

The kit was available in a basic and luxury version. The basic kit included the bodyshell, all lids, doors, windows, assembly parts and instructions. The luxury kit also included all the necessary components for the interior, a roll bar, instruments including sensors, a special exhaust system, fuel tank and front and rear lighting. Sports seats, a sports steering wheel, metallic paint and more powerful engines, including a V8 instead of the VW boxer engine, were available at extra cost.

Sources:
Chris Rees, Peter Filby, Classic Kit Cars – A Comprehensive Buyer´s Guide to every Kit Car Produced between 1953 and 1985, p. 88.
www.sportscars.net.nz/dotcosite/swallow.html
www.replicar.co.uk

Harald Linz, Halwart Schrader: Die Internationale Automobil-Enzyklopädie, München 2008, chapter: Replicar.
George Nick Georgano (Chefredakteur): The Beaulieu Encyclopedia of the Automobile. Volume 3: P–Z, Chicago 2001, p. 1325.
www.popularmechanics.com/cars/a1790/4218480/

Rhino   (UK)

Brothers Don and Terry Mackenzie founded Eland Meres in Birmingham in 1981. They began by designing and manufacturing a vehicle kit. The kit was marketed under the name Rhino. Production ceased in 1983.

The brothers built a GRP body based on a Jeep onto the bare chassis of a VW-Beetle. The body was available in eight colours. Most of the Beetle's technical components were reused. The original wiring harness from the Beetle had to be modified. After a short but intensive production period, about ten kits were produced. In 1983 Alan Breeze bought the production rights, moulds and tools from Eagle Cars. The project was reworked at Eagle Cars. The result was a ladder frame with a Ford Cortina engine. The successor to the Rhino, using Ford Cortina technology, was marketed under the name Eagle RV.

Only ten Rhino Jeeps were built within three years.

Sources:
George Nick Georgano (Chefredakteur): The Beaulieu Encyclopedia of the Automobile. Volume 1: A–F, Chicago 2001, p. 487.

Steve Hole: A–Z of Kit Cars. The definitive encyclopaedia of the UK's kit-car industry since 1949, Sparkford 2012, p. 212.
Kit Car (magazine), issue 9/1982.

Ryder Royale   (UK)

Rob Ryder and Jerry Grolin established Ryder Automotive in Coventry in 1980. Ryder Design & Engineering and Ryder Designs were established around the same time. Two kits were launched within a short space of time. The first kit was taken over by the Pellandini company, which ceased trading in 1978, and was completed and marketed under the name Rembrandt. The second kit is a replica of an MG. At the request of customers, not only kits were sold, but also complete vehicles. The company went into liquidation in 1982. Graham Autos bought the bankruptcy assets at a bargain price and acquired the rights to the two kits. A total of 27 kits were produced by Ryder Automotive.

Rembrandt (1980 – 1982)

The licence to build the Rembrandt was taken over by Pellandini in 1980. The Rembrandt was bolted on the chassis of a VW-Beetle. The arrangement of the

CARS OF THE 1980s

The kit was marketed under Rembrandt, Pelland and Listair.

VW Boxer engine as a mid-engine is remarkable. Production ended in 1982. A total of 15 units were produced before the moulds and rights to the kit were transferred to Graham Autos. The kit was marketed under the old „Pelland" name until 1985. Between 1985 and 1990 the kit was marketed by Listair Cars under the name Listair. Between 1990 and 1993 the kit was marketed as „Dash" by Dash Sportscars of Chesterwood (Hereford).

Listair revised the design in the late 1980s and launched the new car as the Dash.

The Royale is the replica of a Morgan.

Royale (1981 – 1982)

The Ryder Royale is a Morgan replica. It is based on the rear-engined VW-Beetle chassis. The original Morgan radiator grille, windscreen, rear lights and soft top were used. A total of twelve were built. Following the demise of the company, Graham Autos took over the rights to the kit, but in 1984 they passed them on to Sabre Cars of Walland. In 1987 there was another change and Fabrication Design of Newcastle upon Tyne continued production until 1990, retaining the brand name.

> **Sources**:
> Harald H. Linz, Halwart Schrader: Die Internationale Automobil-Enzyklopädie. München 2008, chapter: Ryder.
> George Nick Georgano (Chefredakteur): The Beaulieu Encyclopedia of the Automobile. Volume 3: P–Z, Chicago 2001, p. 1383.
> Steve Hole: A–Z of Kit Cars. The definitive encyclopaedia of the UK's kit-car industry since 1949, Sparkford 2012, p. 209 and p. 221.

Saier (DE)

Alexander Saier founded Automobilbau Saier GmbH in the early 1980s and between 1981 and 1997 the company produced mainly kits for VW-Beetle chassis in Sonnenbühl-Willmand (on the Swabian Alb). Their wide range of products included replicas of the Bugatti, MG, Porsche 356 and Cobra. However, products from trading partners such as Apal were also sold through the dealer network. The AS Catapult (a VW-based Countach) and the AS S1 (a BMW M1 on a Matra-Murena chassis) were particularly popular. Saier also sold the Austrian Tomaszo replicas of the Beetle-Mercedes-SSK to the Ford V8 Streetrod and the pre-war Alfa P35 to the Cobra in Germany. For a long time Apal offered a replica of the Porsche Speedster. The company sold kits and finished cars that could be customised.

MG TD Replica (1988 – 1997)

The MG TD replica was launched in 1988. The body could be mounted either on a bare VW-Beetle chassis with a 1.6 litre boxer engine and 50 bhp, or on a homemade box-section frame. Vehicles built on the Saier frame could also be fitted with Opel engines. In this case the power range went up to the 2.0 litre injection unit of the Manta B with an output of 110 bhp. In 1990, the basic kit cost DM 11,000; with all the available extras, it was estimated to cost around DM 30,000.

MG TD replica lauched in 1988.

CARS OF THE 1980s

Bugatti 35 B (1988 – 1997)

The replica of the Bugatti 35 B was also available on a Beetle base with a 1.6 litre Boxer engine and 50 hp or on a home-made box-section frame. Various Opel engines could be used as an alternative.

Catapult (1990 – 97)

In 1990 a replica of the Lamborghini Countach was created and launched under the name of Catapult. The basic kit consisted of the body, windows, rear wing, doors and tailgate. The kit could be bolted onto the bare chassis of a VW-Beetle. Most Catapult models were powered by the Ford XR3i engine. This engine produced up to 160 bhp, providing plenty of power with a kerb weight of around 900kg. The brake system could be taken from a Porsche 924 or 944. The basic kit was offered for just under DM 13,000. The finished car could cost up to 64,000 DM.

Buggy A1

Among the buggies, the Saier Buggy A1 is certainly one of the most distinctive models. The kit could be screwed onto an unshortened VW floorpan. Particularly worth mentioning is the TÜV approval as a 4-seater vehicle. Several A1s were supplied by Saier with the 75PS engine from the Golf. This power and the relatively low weight of 740kg ensured sufficient driving pleasure. In 1990, the kit for the Saier Buggy A1 cost around DM 8,000.

Apal Speedster

Under licence or with Apal as a trading partner, kits for replicating the Porsche 356 Speedster were also offered.

The Speedster replica was produced under licence with Apal.

Sources:
www.traumautoarchiv.de/html/F1095.html
http://home.arcor.de/bmw-m1/presse/kitcar/bild1.htm
Saier sales brochure from 1991.

The Catapult is the replica of a Countach.

The Buggy A1 is approved as a 4-seater by German TÜV.

Samburá Pickup   (BR)

The Pernambuco company, based in Ceará, launched a pickup in the early 1980s, which was produced in small numbers for several years. The Samburá pickup was built on the undercarriage of a VW Brasilia. The windscreen and doors were also taken from the VW Brasilia. The rectangular headlights are from the VW Gol. The 4-seater vehicle has a loading area with dropsides that can be covered with a tarpaulin. Loading and unloading is possible via the rear wall. This can be folded backwards. The bumpers of the Samburá are laminated to the GRP body and are usually reinforced with additional rubber strips. The Samburá is powered by a VW engine of 1,600 cc, as used in the VW Brasilia. Some cars were also equipped with a 1.8 litre engine from a Gol.

Sources:
http://buggy.forumeiros.com
http://carrocultura.wordpress.com/2010/11/09/orfaos-vw-brasilia-frankenstein/

Samburá Pickup from 1980.

CARS OF THE 1980s

SAM VW (PL)

Bogumił Szuba worked at the Instytut Szybowcowych Zakladów Doświadczalnych in Bielsko-Biala in the 1960s and 1970s as a designer of experimental and high-performance gliders such as the Zephyr 2. In 1958 he bought a 1941 Kübelwagen, which was cheap but in a technically disastrous condition. After work and on weekends, Bogumil Szuba worked on his dream car. This one-off car has been dated to the 1980s, as it was only completed in 1988 by a friend of the creator after a total construction time of 26 years.

The body of the Kübelwagen was largely dismantled and the chassis repaired. Szuba practically rebuilt the suspension. He also completely redesigned the steering and brakes. At the rear, he installed a VW engine with 1,130 cc and an output of 30 bhp. The air filter housing came from a Skoda. Szuba went on to use many parts from the Trabant, VW-Beetle, Skoda Oktavia and Wartburg. At that time it was very difficult to get car parts in Poland. As the leading designer at his institute, Mr Szuba had to make many official trips to neighbouring countries, so he was able to buy the necessary parts. He built the body on a skeleton of steel bars and profiles. The front wings, boot lid and bonnet are made from the same plastic as the gliders. Szuba made the front and rear windows from plexiglass. He paid particular attention to minimising the overall weight of the car. Much of the interior was sewn by his wife, Dante Szuba.

Bogumił Szuba contacted the Volkswagen plant in Wolfsburg. He sent plans for his car and remained in contact with Volkswagen throughout the construction period. This close exchange of information made it possible for the car to be officially certified as a Volkswagen. Nevertheless, it was eventually registered in Poland as a SAM (self-built).

Unfortunately, Bogumil Szuba was unable to complete his creation. After 26 years of work, he died unexpectedly in 1984. Józef Roseger, a family friend, bought the car and put the finishing touches to it. In 1988, he obtained road registration for the Phoenix (Feniks) as a SAM VW. As Szuba had been in contact with the designers in Wolfsburg from the very beginning, the car was recognised as a Volkswagen in an official letter from the Volkswagen factory. The letter was even accompanied by a VW badge.

Other designers from the Instytut Szybowcowych Zakładów Doświadczalnych also built a car. Two other cars were created in a similar way. One is based on the technology of a 1938 DKW and has a SAAB engine and gearbox. The technical basis of the third car is unknown. The VW and the DKW-SAAB have already been extensively restored.

Phoenix / SAM VW was built between 1962 and 1988.

Sources:
http://motoryzacja.interia.pl/samochody-nowe/news-polski-phoenix-vw,nId,1378505
www.drive2.ru/c/288230376152301078/
www.coachbuild.com

CARS OF THE 1980s

Sandbach (UK)

Sandbach Replica Cars, based in Sandbach, Cheshire, started importing kits from the USA in 1983. Shortly afterwards, the company began producing its own kits and kit cars, largely based on American models. Production ceased in 1984 and the company went out of business. It is thought that a total of seven cars were produced between 1983 and 1984. All models offered by Sanbach Replica Cars were originally based on the VW-Beetle chassis. In 1984 Sandbach engineers developed their own chassis using parts from the front-engined Vauxhall Chevette. Various Ford and Vauxhall engines were available until the company was forced to close.

Duke

The Sandbach Duke is a replica of the Jaguar S.S. 100. The body is made from GRP. To build the car, the pedals, gear stick and handbrake had to be relocated. This made it almost impossible for amateur mechanics to complete the kit without outside help.

Saxon

The Sandbach Saxon is based on the Austin-Healey 3000. The kit was available as both a roadster and a coupé.

MG TD Replica

The Sandbach TD is very similar to the MG TD. The 2-seater roadster has „suicide doors" and was built on a bare VW chassis.

The Sandbach TD is very similar to the MG TD.

Sources:
George Nick Georgano (Chefredakteur): The Beaulieu Encyclopedia of the Automobile. Volume 3: P–Z, Chicago 2001, p. 1410.
Steve Hole: A–Z of Kit Cars. The definitive encyclopaedia of the UK's kit-car industry since 1949, Sparkford 2012, p. 223.
Chris Rees, Peter Filby, Classic Kit Cars – A Comprehensive Buyer´s Guide to every Kit Car Produced between 1953 and 1985, p. 90.

Sandwood (UK)

Terry Sands founded Classic Reproductions in 1982, based in Tamworth, Staffordshire. His first project was the Alfa Cassi. This was an alternative product to the traditional Beetle chassis intended for kit cars. A year later, Sands renamed his company Sandwood Automotive Ltd. At the same time he moved to new, larger premises. Together with Thorsren Sodjeberg and Adrian Cocking, he developed a kit car that was shown at the London Motor Show in October 1983. The first production kit car was built on the floorpan of a VW-Beetle, although Sands put a lot of energy into his own chassis project and actually rejected the Volkswagen chassis. The Sandwood California is a replica of a Porsche 356 Speedster which sold very well. The 1983 Scorpione GT was similar to the Avante from Avante Cars. This coupé also had a chassis with an Alfa Romeo engine. The Bugatti Type 49 replica developed between 1983 and 1984 remained a one-off.
Mohrspolt of Tyseley, near Birmingham, took over the rights to the kit cars in 1984 and continued production under the name Sheldonhurst Ltd until 1986. The Alternative Vehicle Centre and Legend Motor Company then took over production for a short time.

Californian / Speedster

The Sandwood Californian was introduced in 1983 and the Sand-

The Speedster replica sold very well in the 1980´s.

wood Speedster the following year. Both kit cars were replicas of the Porsche 356, based either on the rear-engined VW-Beetle chassis or

CARS OF THE 1980s

the in-house chassis optimised for the boxer engine of the Alfa Romeo Alfasud.

Gofer

The Sandwood Gofer (also known as the „Gopher") is a sand track racing car based on the VW-Beetle. The car was available from 1983 to 1984.

Sources:
George Nick Georgano: The Beaulieu Encyclopedia of the Automobile. Volume 3: P–Z, Chicago 2001, p. 1411.
Steve Hole: A–Z of Kit Cars. The definitive encyclopaedia of the UK's kit-car industry since 1949, Sparkford 2012, p.175 and p. 223f.

Saphier (LI)

Jehle was a car manufacturer based in Schaan, Liechtenstein. The company was founded by Xaver Jehle. The company's main activity was the manufacture of truck bodies; Jehle also developed special tanks and runway lighting systems. From the 1970s, Jehle was the exclusive agent for De Tomaso sports cars in the Middle East. A little later, this business gave rise to another branch of the company specialising in bodywork and engine tuning for De Tomaso models. Finally, Jehle produced a small number of its own sports cars until the 1990s. In addition to the Safari, which was based on the technology of the Citroën 2CV, Jehle also produced a sports car based on the VW-Beetle chassis.

The Saphier is very well made and has a hydraulic lifting roof.

Saphier (1982-1991)

In 1982, a wedge-shaped sports car was created, the prototype of which was initially fitted with VW engines of 1,457 cc and 54 bhp. The car went into production with a 75 bhp VW Golf engine and, like the prototype, had a mid-engine layout. A special feature of the design was the lack of conventional doors. Instead, a unit of windscreen, roof and side panels, hinged at the front and opening as a whole, served as the entrance. A foot lever on the outside of the vehicle allows the driver to release the door lock. At the same time, a servo-assisted air compressor is activated, lifting the roof structure upwards. At the same time, the steering column is raised by a total of 18 cm to allow the driver to get in and out as comfortably as possible. Once seated in the Jehle-designed bucket seats, the driver can release the compressed air with a lever. The roof construction lowers and the steering wheel can be pulled down to the desired position. The body is mainly made of plastic. Some struts are made of aluminium. A strong roll-over bar extends over the driver and front passenger, over the side flanks and down to the feet. This makes for an unladen weight of around 750 kg. The relatively large windscreen and generous side glazing turned the car into a mobile sauna in the summer, even with the rear side windows up. To make the interior climate more bearable, an optional sliding roof was available, which could be completely removed. The basic version of the Saphier was

based on the VW-Beetle chassis, while the more powerful versions had their own aluminium double-beam chassis designed by Jehle. The Saphier was designed for various engine configurations.

Sources:
Dieter Günther, Rob de La Rive Box, Max Stoop: Schweizer Automobile. Personenwagen und Sonderkarosserien von 1945 bis heute. Autovision, Hamburg 1992, p. 88–95.
Bill Hartford: Imports & Motorsports In Popular Mechanics (magazine), issue September 1982, p.14.
http://de.wikipedia.org/wiki/Jehle_%28Automobilhersteller%29
Auto Katalog Motorbuch-Verlag 1979 bis 1992.
Lawrence, Mike, A to Z of Sports Cars. Bideford: Bay View Books, 1991, p. 170.

CARS OF THE 1980s

The basic version was powered by a 75 bhp four-cylinder engine from the VW Golf. From 1983, a turbocharged 2,000 cc VW Golf GTI engine with 150 bhp was also available. From 1988, a 5,600 cc V8 engine was available at extra cost. In 1990, a „Super" version of the Saphier with a twin-turbo V12 engine of 6,600 cc was added to the range.

Scheib (DE)

Automobilmanufaktur Scheib, based in Ansbach, Germany, is an automotive company with a long tradition. Ernst Scheib founded the company in 1975 under the name Automobilbau Scheib. Since then, the company has been producing replicas of famous classic cars. The first model released in 1975 was a replica of the Bugatti Type 35 on a VW-Beetle chassis. This was followed by replicas of the MG TD and Mercedes-Benz SS. The kit for the MG cost just under DM 8,000 in 1982. A finished MG cost 29,900 DM. It is likely that the kits offered were mainly licence productions. From today's point of view it is not possible to say more about this. What is certain is that from 1983 onwards, vehicles based on the Opel Kadett and VW Golf were also produced.

The replica of a 356 A Speedster was offered by Scheib until 2003.

Problems with the TÜV or the approval of the conversions could not be solved. The kit cost around 12,000 euros at the time. At least 30,000 Euros had to be budgeted for the finished car with TÜV approval. The most obvious differences to the original are the front indicators, which are orange instead of white, the bonnet cover, the rear-view mirror and the windscreen wipers.

Sources:
Hans Rüdiger Etzold, Der Käfer IV, Eine Dokumentation – Sonderkarosserien, Cabriolet, Karmann-Ghia, Buggy, Auslandsproduktion, 2. edition, Stuttgart 1998, p. 31f.
Harald Linz, Halwart Schrader: Die Internationale Automobil-Enzyklopädie, München 2008.
http://de.wikipedia.org/wiki/Automobilmanufaktur-Scheib
http://christian1503.magix.net
http://thegegeblog.canalblog.com/archives/2010/03/08/17164539.html

Top to bottom: Bugatti P35 replica; MG TD replica; Speedster replica.

Scorpio GT (US)

The company VW / GT Conversion offered a kit very similar to the Bradley GT. It is possible that the moulds were taken from a Bradley GT. The bonnet was then slightly modified so that the car could not be identified as a 100% copy. The kit can be screwed onto the chassis of a VW-Beetle. At the time, the Scorpion GT kit cost $750. A fully assembled car was offered for around $3,000 - the chassis had to be provided by the customer. The GRP bodies were made by a small company in „Old Town" Maine.

When VW / GT Conversion went out of business, the moulds remained with the coachbuilder.

Sources:
www.scorpiongt.com/

CARS OF THE 1980s

Scorpion (CA)

Cormier International, based in Edmonton, Alberta, developed a kit in 1986 based on the Ford GT40. The GRP body can be bolted to the floor pan of a VW-Beetle. Scorpion's brochure was advertised in Kit Car Illustrated. It is not known how many kits were ever sold.

Sources:
www.allcarindex.com
Kit Car Illustrated (magazine), 5/1986.

Advertisement for the Scorion from 1986.

Seidel GT (DE)

During the 1980s, Wolfgang Seidel, who had worked for many years in Volkswagen's design department, created his own design. His car is a sports coupé based on the chassis of a VW-Beetle. For a long time, the car could not be registered because there was no manufacturer's certificate for some of the components that Seidel had designed and built himself. A „self-certification" led to Mr Seidel being included in the register of vehicle manufacturers, and the Seidel GT was able to obtain official road registration. The vehicle consists of a large number of technical solutions, some of them original, which were realised over the course of more than 10 years. Initially, the headlights were controlled electronically via a folding mechanism. On the advice of the TÜV, this mechanism was replaced by a fixed solution. The Seidel GT scores highly in terms of both ergonomics and aerodynamics. Many of the design weaknesses of kit cars, such as the rear, have been elegantly and simply solved. Neither exhaust fumes from the tailpipes nor water swirling around when driving in the rain dirty the rear of the car or the rear window. The coachbuilder's expertise is also evident in the way the removable roof elements have been implemented. The coupé can be transformed into a targa in a few simple steps. Nevertheless, the rain cannot harm the car. The driver and passenger always stay dry.

Wolfgang Seidel designed the Seidel GT is confirmed as the manufacturer of his car.

Sources:
With kind support of Wolfgang Seidel.

S. H. Design (SW)

The Swedish engineer Svenharry Åkesson founded the company S. H. Design in Landskrona in 1987 and began producing cars. Åkesson is known for his numerous creations that have enriched the world of motorsport. Even at a young age, he gained experience in the Formal V. The Spider MK 4 was a commissioned work. Bertils Motor, based in Sweden, supplied the modified VW engines. Based on the first design of the Spider MK 4, a kit for Formula Vee vehicles was created, which sold well.

103

CARS OF THE 1980s

One model series was based on the chassis of the VW-Beetle. However, a lattice frame with a longer wheelbase was also available, in which the engines were mounted in a mid-engine design. Production ended in 1991.

Silver Hawk (1983 – 1986)

Svenharry Åkesson built the Silver Hawk for his eldest son, which could be built on either the unmodified chassis of a VW-Beetle or on a special tubular steel frame. The Silver Hawk had a targa roof and folding headlights. Åkesson presented the car for the first time at the 1983 Uppsala Motor Show. More than 100 orders for the car and the kit were placed within a week. Plastinova was hired at short notice to reproduce the car in kit form. Svenharry Åkesson ordered 225 kits before deciding to sell the tools and moulds to Finland. A total of about 350 Silver Hawks are thought to have been produced.

Top to bottom: Silver Hawk from 1983 with removeable roof element
Below: The Sethera MK I was sold 200 times.

Sethera MK I

As the Silver Hawk sold very well, Svenharry Åkesson came to the attention of the tax authorities. The sale of the rights to the Silver Hawk enabled him to start a new car project. The result was the Sethera Mk.1 in 1987, a car with gullwing doors that could be folded parallel to the car. Åkesson paid particular attention to the windscreen. The extravagantly designed windscreen served as a kind of copy protection for the kit, as the kit-makers were only interested in making a quick profit. They did not want to waste time searching for suitable parts. Around 200 of the Sethera MK I were built. The kit attracted the attention of a French car enthusiast who agreed with Åkesson to modify the kit so that more Ford production parts could be used to build the Sethera. The result was the Sethera MK II, which was exported to many countries. At the same time, the Sethera MK I was also sold as a turnkey car with Audi components.

Sources:
www.elva.com/news/20140208-svenharry.php
www.garaget.org/forum/viewtopic.php?id=280313
www.vwbroukklub.cz/perlicky/vwkity/VWKitCZ.htm
http://de.wikipedia.org/wiki/Sethera
Nick Georgano: The Beaulieu Encyclopedia of the Automobile, Volume 3 P–Z, Chicago 2001.

SN1 (UK)

Steve Collins and Neil Morgan established Steaney Automotive Developments in Chalgrove, Oxfordshire in 1982. The first project was the development of a Eurocco from Embeesea Kit Cars. The result was a kit for a two-seater coupé with a GRP body, called the SN1 (Steve Neil 1). The notchback car has room for 2 + 2 people. The windscreen comes from a Ford Escort, the door windows from a Ford Cortina and the rear window from a Ford Cortina Estate. The headlights are from a Fiat 126 and the door hinges are from a Bedford CF. Only one model remained. The company went out of business in 1984. Between 1984 and 1986, Amplas Ltd. of Chalgrove, Oxfordshire, conti-

CARS OF THE 1980s

nued production under the name SN1. LeMazone of Leigh then took over the rights to manufacture and market the SN 1. In 1986 LeMazone produced eight examples of the LeMazone SN 1.

Sources:
Chris Rees, Peter Filby, Classic Kit Cars – A Comprehensive Buyer´s Guide to every Kit Car Produced between 1953 and 1985, p. 96.

The SN1 was produced by several manufacturers.

SPJ Garra   (BR)

SPJ Indústria e Comércio Ltda. of Rio de Janeiro (RJ) launched a saloon car based on Volkswagen technology in 1988. The 2-door car had room for four passengers. The rear lights were taken from the VW Passat. Options included alloy wheels and radial tyres, electric windows, a car radio with cassette deck and fog lamps. Only a few Garra were built. The company ceased production in 1990.

Sources:
www.lexicarbrasil.com.br/garra/

Only a few Garra were produced by SPJ between 1988 and 1990.

www.lexicarbrasil.com.br/garra/

Sportscoupé   (FR)

A sports coupé was created between 1988 and 1989 and registered in Grenoble in 1990. The car was based on the chassis of a Mexico Beetle. The manufacturer placed a kind of subframe on the chassis, on which the GRP body was mounted. Moulds were made to produce the body, which were destroyed and disposed of after the car was built due to lack of space. A 2-litre boxer engine was fitted to the rear of the car.

The project was financed by the company the car maker worked for. It is not possible to say why only one was built.

The Sportcoupé is a one-off production with removeable roof elements.

Sources:
With kind support of the members of the facebook groupe „Durchgeboxt"

CARS OF THE 1980s

Tanger (BR)

Incofer S.A. Indústria e Comércio, based in Rio de Janeiro, has been in the car body and repair business since 1974. The first complete car was launched in 1983 by Júlio Sillas, who developed the Ragge California two years later. This was a 4-seater dune buggy built on a VW-Beetle platform shortened by 35 cm. In early 1987, the company took over the rights to produce and market further kits. The production rights taken over from Ragge Industria e Comercio Ltda of Rio de Janeiro led to the licensed production of the Ragge California and later the Ragge Long Beach. The kits were slightly revised and offered under the Tanger brand. It is difficult to categorise a car as a Tanger. In Brazil, the Tanger is classified as both an off-road vehicle and a buggy. The only optional extras were a car radio, reclining seats, wide tyres, a hardtop and metallic paint. In 1988, the company moved its headquarters to Duque de Caxias (RJ) and changed its name to Tanger Industrial Ltda. From this point on, different models such as the Tanger Sevetse and Tanger Lucena coexisted. The last product was the Tanger TR, launched in 1993. The recession that began in the early 1990s and the opening up of the market meant that the company had to close in 1994.

Buggy (1983 - 1987)

The rectangular headlights are from the VW Voyage. The windscreen is from a VW Brasilia. The rear lights are borrowed from the VW Gol. The one-piece GRP body has integrated bumpers and fender extensions to give the appearance of a wrap-around body. The slogan „Two for the price of one" was used in advertising, alluding to the car's appearance. The lack of doors made the car look like a buggy. The body is also very similar in appearance to a jeep. Sales of the Tanger Buggy were excellent. After six months, production had reached a good level of 12 units per month. After about two years, sales had reached 20 units per week. At the end of 1984 the car was slightly redesigned. The Tanger Buggy got a front grille, a new bonnet and more space in the back.

Junior (1986 - 1993)

Production of the Tanger Junior started in 1986. This was a children's toy with a GRP body in the style of the Tanger Buggy. This small vehicle has no windscreen, but an air-cooled single-cylinder engine with 3.5 hp. Power is transmitted to the rear wheels via a chain and an automatic gearbox.

California (1987 - 1993)

The Ragge California and its

Top to bottom: Buggy from 1984; Buggy plus Junior Buggy from 1986; California from 1987

cessor, the Ragge Long Beach, already had electric windows and central locking. Only the name was changed. The 1.7 litre Volkswagen engine is the same as in the SP2.

Cabrio (1987- 1993)

The Tanger Cabrio was launched in 1987. The front part of the passenger compartment is closed, while the rear row of seats can be driven open or with an optional

CARS OF THE 1980s

hardtop. The headlights are rectangular. The Tanger Cabrio had a GRP body with integrated bumpers. The technical components are largely derived from the VW-Beetle. The 4-cylinder boxer engine with a displacement of 1584 cc and a central carburettor produced 50 bhp. The Tanger Cabrio had disc brakes at the front and drum brakes at the rear. The interior used seats from the Fiat Tipo. The rear lights were also borrowed from the Fiat Tipo. The dashboard was similar to that of the VW Passat. The boot lid and bonnet of the Tanger Cabrio were slightly larger than those of its predecessor. The Tanger Cabrio had air intakes on the sides of the engine to provide additional cooling air. In November 1987, the kit cost $185,000.00, compared to $378,000.00 for a new car. The running boards, formed from steel tubing and an aluminium plate, also acted as side impact protection. The Tanger Convertible was available with and without doors. Both a hardtop and a softtop were available. The soft top consisted of several parts that could be attached and removed in a few simple steps. The rear part of the soft top slides into a moulding on the roll bar. A comparable number of accessories were already available for this car. Among other things, customers could order protective grilles around the headlights, an electric winch and a spare tyre mounted on the rear of the car. The overall quality of the components increased, making the Tanger Cabrio more attractive to a wider range of buyers.

Sevetse (1988 - 1994)

The new model, with an air-cooled boxer engine at the rear, was presented at the 1988 XV

Motor Show. The name of this Tangiers is derived from the name of its designer, Esteves, who worked for Fiat for a long time. The Sevetse was fitted with a 1.6 litre VW engine as standard. However, the Sevetse was also available with a modified VW Boxer engine of 1.8 litres, as sometimes used in the VW SP2. Recaro seats were often used in the interior, as they were also used in the VW Gol GTI. One of the car's weak points was the electronics, which were not always reliable. Owners of a Sevetse also report water ingress through

the fuel filler cap or the keyhole in the filler cap.

Lucena (1988 – 1994)

The new model with a water-cooled engine was presented at the 1988 XV Motor Show. The Tanger Lucena used the engine from the VW Gol AP, which was mounted at the front. The chassis was developed by Tanger. The body resembled the Emis Art in some respects, and in Europe it had similarities to the Fiat Uno. The Lucena was available with a soft top for the rear or with a hardtop that could be removed if required. The

Top to bottom: Cabrio from 1989; Sevetse from 1989; Lucena from 1990; TR from 1993.

cab is permanently covered, only the load area can be left open, as in a compact pick-up. The boot is located behind the driver and passenger seats. It is not accessible from the outside. There are side zips on the soft top for loading and unloading, but these are optional extras. The headlights and windscreen come from the VW Gol, the rear lights from the Fiat Uno. The 1.8 litre front engine has an electronic ignition system from Bosch (TLDZ). The steering wheel is almost horizontal. The

CARS OF THE 1980s

GRP body is held in shape by steel tubes.

TR (1993 - 1994)

The TR from Tanger is still built in the tradition of the buggy. The one-piece body has relatively low sides for easy entry and exit. The vehicle is very reminiscent of the Hummer, but with much more delicate proportions. The kit could be built on the underbody of the VW Variant. The 4-cylinder boxer engine in the rear is easily accessible via a hatch. The car has a centre bar between the windscreen and the roll bar, so that it can be considered a Targa when fully open.

Sources:
www.planetabuggy.com.br/extintos/tanger/index.htm
www.essevaleumafoto.com/2012/02/ragge-california-1978.html#uds-search-results
Oficina Mecânica (magazine), issue November 1987.
www.lexicarbrasil.com.br/tanger/

Tigress (UK)

The company Autocult from Dunbat, East Lothian in Scotland launched a 2+2 seater sports coupé with diagonally opening doors in 1983. The car was offered as a kit under the name „Tigress". The GRP body could be bolted to a bare VW-Beetle chassis. Stylistically this coupé followed the long tradition of using the Ford GT40 as a model for its own creation. Although the doors of the Tigress were hinged at the front, they had to be tilted up to open, which made it possible to get in and out. The car has manually operated side windows with the Volkswagen mechanism. Unfortunately, the kit was not produced in larger quantities. A few Tigress were probably sold in 1984. The production of the kits seems to have been stopped at the end of 1984, because the commercial success did not materialise and it became more and more difficult to get approval for such vehicles.

Tigress with diagonally opening doors from 1983.

Sources:
Kit Car (magazine), issue 8 from 1984 Nomad Copycat Tigress GP Spyder Acer FF
www.ebay.co.uk/itm/Kit-Car-8-84-Nomad-Copycat-Tigress-GP-Spyder-Acer-FF-/230640881873

Town Car (US)

The idea of a hybrid electric car was born very early on, when it was recognised that the performance of batteries was limited. Several attempts were made to bring a hybrid vehicle to market as a promising technology for the future. In 1980, such a vehicle was developed on the VW-Beetle platform. A 3 kW single-cylinder engine charged the batteries. A 72 volt, 6 kW Baldor DC motor acts directly on the gearbox adapter plate. Six lead-acid batteries are installed in the front of the car and four in the former engine compartment. The batteries are primarily used for energy storage and peak demand operation. The genset was designed for slightly more power than the expected average demand would require. This allowed for a relatively energy efficient and clean car compared to conventional vehicles, and better overall performance and range compared to pure electric vehicles. The Town Car is designed for urban use. It has a top speed of 55 miles per hour with one battery and 60 miles per hour with two batteries in par-

Town Car with hybride drive system from 1981.

CARS OF THE 1980s

allel, and a range of 100 miles. By changing the tuning of the battery, engine and power unit, it was possible to adapt the top speed, range and fuel consumption to different requirements.

The body is made of polyurethane foam composite. First unveiled to the public in 1981, the Town Car was used in the 1990 Hollywood film Total Recall, starring Arnold Schwarzenegger.

Sources:
www.rqriley.com/ev-tech.htm
Mechanix Illustrated (magazine), issue Februar 1981.

Technical Details
Town Car
Engine: DC motor
Power: 4 or 8 hp
Length: 4470 mm; Width: 1830 mm; Hight: 1240 mm; Wheelbase: 2.400 mm
Weight: 1250 kg (empty)

Tupy Mini 175   (BR)

Between 1980 and 1989, the São Paulo company Tupy Veículos Especiais produced several buggies and a small car that remained unique in its kind. The Tupy Mini 175 was built on the shortened undercarriage of a VW Brasilia. The fibreglass body consists of simple geometric shapes. Although the 2-seater car had doors, the side windows were made of transparent plastic, similar to the Jeep, which was sewn into a frame made of soft top fabric. A simple mechanism, similar to that used in Gurgel vehicles, allowed the doors to be locked. The driver and passenger can sit on a bench seat similar to the one in the VW bus. The dashboard has a speedometer, a fuel gauge and several warning lights to indicate the state of the engine (battery, oil pressure). The glove box has a lockable lid. The VW boxer engine is easily accessible through a tailgate. The two pairs of headlights are integrated into the cover at the front of the car. The dipped and main beam lights are split between two headlamps and protected by metal grilles. The front flap opens forward to reveal a small boot, dominated by the fuel tank as in the Beetle. The rear lights come from the VW T2 bus. The front and rear windows are from the VW Brasilia. The bumpers are also laminated. They do not cover the whole width of the car. In the rear is a VW boxer engine with a capacity of 1,300 cc. Due to the lightweight construction of the car, the performance is more than adequate. However, it is doubtful whether the car's tow bar really does a good job. The car seems to be less suitable for heavier transport. The wheel trims look like little black plastic flower pots and have the characteristic holes at the bottom. The 14 inch rims are taken from the VW Brasilia. Owners of this very rare vehicle report that a maximum of 5 were completed and are still in use.

The Tupy Mini 175 is a minimalistic city car.

A yellow car with a tow bar, a red Tupy Mini and an ochre Tupy that was featured in a Beetle magazine (Fusca e Cia, issue 52).

Technical Details
Tupy Mini 175
Engine: VW 1.3 litre
Power: 40 hp
Length: 2630 mm; Width: 1580 mm; Hight: 1460 mm

Sources:
Projeto National, Fucsa & CIA (magazine) issue 52, p. 37ff.
http://autosbizus.blogspot.co.at/p/bizus-das-antigas.html

CARS OF THE 1980s

Vachey (FR)

Paulo Vachey from Saint-Etienne-de Crossey has built his own interpretation of a sports car based on a VW-Beetle. The car has a plastic body and can be seen as a modern version of a Super Seven. The quality of the two-seater convertible is already on a par with the cars of the 1990s. The technique used by the manufacturer to create the body is interesting. The basic shape was created using wire frames. This technique was common in the 1950s, probably reached its peak at the end of the 1960s and was still occasionally used later in prototype construction. The shape of the body is modelled using wires or wire mesh, usually welded together and then coated so that the negative moulds can be removed. The car has survived to this day and is still in a collector's garage.

Application of the wireframe technique; early stage of development; final version as presented at a car show.

Sources:
With support of the members of the facebook groupe „Kit Cars, Replicas, Hot Rods and Clones"

Van Valen Car (NL)

Fer van Valen von Groot-ammers from Friesland built a neo-classic in his private workshop, which he called the Van Valen Car. Between 1985 and 1987, he built the car on the bare chassis of a VW-Beetle. The car's builder drew inspiration for the bodywork from the 1920s and 1930s. The fantasy body was made from 1.5mm thick steel sheet. Styling cues from Ford, Chevrolet and Buick from the period give the car a special flair. The logo above the fake radiator grille reads ‚FVV', the initials of the builder Fer Van Valen.

According to the builder, the car, which remained a one-off, was first shown to the public when it was used as his daughter's bridal car.

Neo-classic car built by Fer Van Valen from 1987.

Sources:
https://conam.info/vraag-a-aanbod/opgeloste-vragen

Villa GT (BR)

Contrary to the opinion of some experts, the Villa GT is a car in its own right. Its closeness to the Lorena GT is due to the fact that a Lorena GT was the starting point. A closer look at the car reveals that the Mirage GT was the inspiration for the Villa GT. Adison Villa added many of his own ideas in 1981, making the car unique. The Villa GT can therefore be seen as the successor to the Mirage GT. The production rights were bought by Paulo Frederico Ippolito Giodano shortly after the first examples were completed. The Villa GT was offered on the Brazilian market as a very inexpensive kit and as a complete car. The kit consisted of body panels, lids and doors, and detailed assembly instructions. The windscreen from the Chevette could be used to complete the vehicle. The bumpers came from a VW TL, the tail lights from a Ford Corcel, the headlights from a VW Brasilia and the dashboard from a VW Gol BX. Any VW boxer engine between 1,300 and 1,600 cc could be used to power the car. A complete Villa GT could be delivered within a maximum of 60 days.

With the abolition of import du-

ties on foreign cars in 1983, sales plummeted to such an extent that production of the Villa GT had to be discontinued. Unconfirmed reports suggest that around 100 examples of the Villa GT were built. One example was also built as a Targa.

The Villa GT with some similarities with the Lorena GT.

Sources:
www.lorenagt.com/
www.classicmagazine.com.br/2009/11/historia-do-lorena-gt.html
Quatro Rodas (magazine), Eschola seu Carro, Issue November 1981.

Vision (US)

Between 1980 and 1985, American Coach Craft Inc. of Lemont, Illinois, offered several kits that could be bolted to the floorpan of a VW-Beetle or Karmann Ghia. Kenneth Marcotte developed a coupé with a GRP body, which was marketed under the name Vision III. Its successor, the Vision IV, never got beyond the prototype stage.

Vision III

The Vision III is a coupé with conventional doors. The windscreen consists of two straight panes, as was the case until the mid-1950s. The side windows are in two parts. The smaller one can be folded up to let fresh air into the cabin. The Beetle's headlamps could be electronically folded outwards. Kenneth Marcotte designed the GRP body. The dashboard, centre console and luggage compartment behind the driver and passenger are also made from GRP. To increase headroom, the floor panel was cut out around the seat slides and at the rear, pressed down and two wedges welded in. This was quite common on the very low profile bodies. There is evidence that one of the remaining cars is fitted with a VW Boxer engine bored down to 1,825 cc. Another Vision III

CARS OF THE 1980s

is powered by a V6 engine from a Buick. The Marcotte Vision was available as a kit and as a finished car until the mid-1980s. It is not known how many Vision III were built. There is an unconfirmed rumour about a further development, which is called Vision IV.

Technical Details
Vision III
Engine: VW engine
Power: - hp
Length: 4620 mm; Width: 1800 mm; Hight: 1170 mm; Wheelbase: 2400 mm

Sources:
Press image of American Coach Craft Inc., 1985.
https://allentown.craigslist.org/cto/5800505925.html
Harold W. Pace, Kit & Specialty Cars, American classics from the past and present, Anaheim 2002, p. 119.

The Vision designed by Marcozze was available as a kit and as a finished car until mid of 1980´s.

Commercial Vehicles (MISC)

There are still many vehicles that use components from Volkswagen or Porsche. Only a few commercial vehicles are shown here, for which hardly any further information is available.

CARS OF THE 1980s

CARS of the 1990s

Cars from the Catalogue

In the 1990s, the government made it largely impossible for people to build their own cars. A wide range of models, from the smallest cars to the compact class, middle class and upper class, all the way to off-road vehicles, sports cars and vans, even confronts the customer with the „agony of choice" when buying a car.

The kit car scene has changed massively. There are now catalogue cars assembled with components from production vehicles. Volkswagen components are now very rarely used because performance was perceived to be more important than price. That is why there are now specialists who offer their services. This means that individuality can still be lived out. Occasionally, vehicles still turn up that have been built to the highest standards by specialists under private management and represent the realisation of automotive dreams. The quality of the turnkey kit cars can often compete with the quality of series production.

Often they are very well known prototypes that are reissued with currently available technology, as neo-classics, so to speak. Examples include the Kübel Lite, the Custom Land Rover and the Bogatti, to name just the most important. Special features such as floatability also often stimulated the imagination and engineering skills of the builders. The Batráquio Anfibio (BR) and the Gator Amphibious (US) should be mentioned in this context.

The Mania Spyder is a remarkably kitcar designed by Ulf Bolumlid in Sweden. Around 50 Mania Spyder kits were sold. Most of the cars were probably finished in Scandinavia.

CARS OF THE 1990s

ACE (US)

In 1996, American Car Craft Enterprises (ACE) of Marietta, Georgia, launched a stretched-looking replica of a Corvette (1968-1982) based on a VW-Beetle. For a short time, ACE also offered a VW-based replica of the Ferrari Dino 246.

The replica of a Corvette from 1968 was offered in 1996.

ACE Corvette

The vehicle is a genuine 4-seater convertible or coupé built on a bare VW-Beetle chassis. The GRP body is very similar to the original, but has been slightly modified to achieve full length.

Sources:
Harold W. Pace „The big guide to kit & specialty cars: Past & Present", p. 169.
http://www.handcrafted-cars.org/Manufacturers.aspx?manufacId=40

Alpha Shark (DE)

Heinz Fuhrmann founded the company CART Design in Kaufering at the end of the 1990s. The first Alpha Shark kit was sold in 1999. The basis for the two-seater roadster is the floor pan of a Mexico Beetle. Over time, however, cars based on earlier Beetles were also created. In these cars, the gearshift linkage had to be modified to prevent the gearshift rod from reaching the dashboard in third gear. The Alpha Shark was the only car sold by CART Design until the company was wound up in 2003. Collectors estimate that just under 30 Alpha Sharks were sold in Europe.

Technical Details
Alpha Shark
Engine: VW engine, 1997 ccm
Power: 100 hp
Length: 3960 mm; Width: 1660 mm; Hight: 1080 mm; Wheelbase: 2400 mm
Weight: 625 kg (empty)

Left: The Alpha Shark was launched in 1999.

Heinz Fuhrmann recommends using a VW-Beetle with a crank axle at the front for the body. The body without doors is made of GRP and is designed in the tradition of buggy kits. The gelcoat surface could be produced in the desired colour. With careful assembly, painting was not necessary. The unique curves of the protruding wings, the large air vents and the wide tyres give the car a very special look. The basic kit was available for around 8,000 Euros. Fuhrmann also supplied turnkey vehicles on request. The dashboard accommodated the most important instruments that could be installed in a Beetle, Type 3, Type 4 or Porsche. If a typical

Beetle engine was not to be installed, the reinforcements for the rear had to be made by the customer. This requires experience. The bucket seats supplied with the kit are also more suitable for smaller people. If the driver is taller than 1.9 metres, you will have to do some tricks to keep him from sticking out too far over the windscreen. The floor pans can be lowered by up to 10 cm. In this case, however, seats with consoles had to be fitted because the full bucket seats supplied did not allow a suitable seating position. The result is a highly individual car that is a pleasure to drive and an eye-catcher.

Sources:
www.alpha-shark.de/
www.1600i.de/1600i-register/257-1.html
Harald Linz, Halwart Schrader: Die Internationale Automobil-Enzyklopädie, München 2008.
https://de.wikipedia.org/wiki/Cart_Design

Beverly Hills 356 (US)

Beverly Hills Motor Cars of San Diego was another company that produced replicas of the Porsche 356 Speedster. Based on the chassis of a VW-Beetle, the kit is a very simplified version of the Porsche 356 Speedster. The body is made of GRP. The technology of the Beetle was largely retained. At customer's request, instruments from the Porsche were fitted.

This replica of a Porsche Speedster was produced in San Diego.

Sources:
https://en.bhmotorcars.com/

By Cristo (BR)

Hamilton Veloso Prado and his son founded By Cristo Indústria e Comércio Ltda. in São Carlos (SP) in 1998. Under the technical direction of FEI Richard Boock, the company produced trikes with Volkswagen engines. The range included a standard model, a sports version and a top model. The trikes were powered by 1.6-litre Volkswagen boxer engines with outputs ranging from 50 to 103 bhp. A tubular frame developed in-house supported the Volkswagen torsion bars. A standard gearbox was used as in the VW Brasilia. Disc brakes were fitted at the rear. The front wheel is unbraked. Clutch and brake are pedal operated. Acceleration is by hand, like on a motorcycle. The By Cristo trikes are 3,800 mm long and weigh about 700 kg. About 1,200 trikes were produced until 2007. The company was then sold. The new owner plans to focus its activities on Latin America and the USA.

By Cristo offered the trikes with 50 to 103 bhp.

Sources:
www.bycristo.com.br

CARS OF THE 1990s

Chesil (UK)

Peter Bailey founded the Chesil Motor Company in Burton Bradstock, Dorset in 1991. He took over a Street Beetle project and started producing kit cars. Angus McCubbin and Jerry Baker ran Chesil from 2004 to 2007. This was followed by Tygan Motor Company of Beaminster from 2007 to 2008, run by Graham Lee. Since 2009 the company has been trading again as Chesil Motor Company under the management of Peter Bailey. A total of around 500 kits have been produced to date.

Chesil is now one of the leading manufacturers of Porsche 356 Speedster replicas. In addition to the kit, the range includes all the components needed to build a Porsche 356. This can save the hobbyist a lot of time when building such a car. Both kits are sold in a variety of configurations, as well as turnkey vehicles on the platform, which the customer pays for. The ambitious car builder can also get help with registration.

The replica of the Porsche Speedster was a great sales success.

Speedster

The first and best-selling model is the Speedster, a replica of the Porsche 356 Speedster. The basis of the kit is the shortened chassis of a VW-Beetle and an additional tubular steel frame. The GRP body is mounted on this frame. The GRP body comes with a grey gelcoat finish. All relevant holes are pre-drilled and ready to accept the chrome parts and instruments. The doors and lids are also pre-installed to ensure a high quality finish. The range also includes the windscreen, side windows and soft top. Since 2010, in cooperation with Inrekor from the USA, a more modern chassis is available, which can be equipped with more powerful engines. The cars are delivered with VW Boxer engines, which can also be ordered with increased power and a displacement of 1.7 to 2.0 litres. The kit is offered in various stages of development up to the turnkey vehicle.

RS 60

The RS 60 was offered between 2005 and 2006 and found two buyers. The Chesil RS 60 is based on the Porsche 718.

550 Spyder

The Chesil 550 Spyder was available between 1996 and 2008. It was an import from Rudolph Perfect Roadster.

> **Sources**:
> UK Kitcar Guide (magazine), issue 2015, Taunton 2015
> Steve Hole: A–Z of Kit Cars. The definitive encyclopaedia of the UK's kit-car industry since 1949, Sparkford 2012, p. 55–56.
> www.chesil.biz/Chesil_Speedster_Evo.htm

Dauphin (US)

In 1994 Redhead Roadsters Inc. released a total of 6 kits. These included the Sterling GT, the Vokaro, the Machette Speedster and the Cute-T Buggy. Redhead Roadsters acted primarily as a distribution channel for the established kits. The Sterling GT was supplied by Solid Sterling. The Machette Speedster is a remake of the Dune Buggy, first released in 1969 under the name Shark. It has similarities to the vehicles used at Indianaplois and stands out from the other buggies developed at the time. The Vokaro was a further development of the Auriga and was taken over by Vopard. In the early 1980s, Vopard produced a longer version of the Vokaro with room for four people. Redhead Roadsters modified the Vokaro 4 and launched the Dauphin 2+2 kit in 1994. This is the only independent creation of Redhead Roadsters Inc.

CARS OF THE 1990s

Dauphin 2+2 (1994 -)

The basic design was provided by the Auriga. Vopard supplied the extension of the design for the body to the unabridged floor assembly of a VW-Beetle. As headlight covers were no longer in demand in the 1990s, and in some cases had already been banned, the Dauphin 2+2 was fitted with round headlights without covers. The change in bumper regulations led to a redesign of the front end. The car was fitted with a bumper painted in the car's colour. To improve the ventilation of the engine compartment, air intakes were fitted to the sides of the car. Although the kit was designed for the mass market, Redhead Roadsters failed to sell in significant numbers.

Sources:
Harold W. Pace, Kit & Specialty Cars, American classics from the past and present, Anaheim 2002, p. 121.
VW-based Kit Car Assembly Manual, Waitsburg 1994.

The Dauphin 2+2 seems to be a modified Auriga; all the other offerings of Redhead Roadsters were kits of other manufacturers.

Delorean Desert (US)

In the summer of 1984, Universal Studios gave the green light to Robert Zemeckis' Back to the Future. The film took years to make. Originally, Doc Brown had converted a fridge into a time machine. Concerns about how the story would work led to a change to a sports car with gullwing doors. The choice fell on the DeLorean, which was converted into a time machine to Steven Spielberg's specifications by the special effects experts at Filmtrix. Three DeLoreans were sourced and converted for the first film. A total of 7 DeLoreans were used in the three episodes.
For the third adventure in 1990's Back to the Future, two DeLoreans were lifted for the film's off-road driving and placed on a specially designed lightweight chassis. The cars, known internally as the „desert" DeLoreans, were designed to look as if Doc Emmet had made a makeshift repair in the 1950s. The car was fitted with whitewall tyres and mooncabs, as seen on the Volkswagen, among others. A new

For the third adventure of „Back to the Future", the Delorean had to be raised and fitted with a powerful VW engine.

119

CARS OF THE 1990s

The Fimset also worked with models. What models could not deliver, the „Desert" equipped with VW power had to do.

Volkswagen gearbox and a tuned air-cooled boxer engine. This resulted in a more favourable weight distribution, which was particularly effective at high speeds. The resulting higher acceleration of the car was further exaggerated in the film by fitting only the front wheels with working brake discs. After the filming, the Delorean with Volkswagen technology was probably stored in a hall for about 15 years. It has now been sold to a collector and is being restored.

front and rear axle were fitted to prepare the car for the challenges of filming. The chassis was rebuilt from scratch, as was common for kit cars in the late 1970s. A Delorean was fitted with a modified

Sources:
www.flat4.org/forum/viewtopic.php?f=3&t=1218&start=100
www.bttf3delorean.com/Where_are_they.html
www.vwheritage.com/blog/2015/10/21/choose-a-vw-time-machine/

Fibreglass Designs   (SA)

Fibreglass Designs, based in Edenvale near Johannesburg, produced several kit vehicles based on the Volkswagen platform between 1990 and 1999. These included a Vandetta-style station wagon (Jirah, Van Wagon), a dune buggy (Kango) and a replica of a jeep (Veep). There are only references to the Jirah, which is also an estate version.

The Kango is a LHD Buggy with a three piece soft top.

The Van Wagon is a license production of the Vendetta.

Kango (1990 - 1999)
The FD Kango is designed in the tradition of the dune buggies and is possibly a more or less official licensed production. The Kango was available with a soft top or with a T-top. In this case, the soft top consists of two elements that extend down over the door area. Another panel with a rear window can be pulled up at the rear. These left-hand drive buggies were built on the shortened platform of a VW-Beetle.

Van Wagon (1990 – 1999)
The kit in the style of Gundaker's Vendetta could also be a licence production. The body behind the B-pillar had to be cut off for the conversion. The GRP rear of the car could be bolted to the remaining parts of the original car. The edge between the metal parts and the GRP parts had to be smoothed with filler and the van was ready.

Veep (1990 – 1999)
The Jeep replica is also produced under licence. Initially, the kits were simply bought in and passed on.

The Jeep replica is called Veep and a license production.

CARS OF THE 1990s

Later the company began to manufacture the GRP parts itself in order to increase profit margins. The rights to the kit were transferred to Kitcar Centre (KCC) when Fibreglass Designs went into liquidation in 1999.

Sources:
www.allcarindex.com/main-index/car-make-details/South-Africa-Fibreglass-Designs/

Hummbug (CA)

The Wombat Car Company, based in Vancouver, is the supplier of a conversion kit made from GRP laminated to a tubular steel frame. The replica of a Humer fits exactly onto the floor assembly of a VW-Beetle and is supplied in such a way that no welding or laminating is required to assemble the vehicle. Only a few parts need to be made to fit. Even beginners can complete the kit. In 3 to 4 months, with 1 to 2 days at weekends, the Hummbug can be ready for its first outing for an investment of around $12,000. Driving a Hummbug is a real pleasure. You only need 2 people to refuel. One person fills the tank and the other answers the

The replica of a Hummer fits on the chassis of a VW-Beetle.

many questions from onlookers. The Wombat has a tubular steel frame that can withstand off-road driving without a trace. The frame around the windscreen is particularly strong. The Wombat Hummbug is also available in an electric

version. In Australia the Wombat Hummbug is sold by XCars.

Sources:
www.wombatcar.com
http://xcars.com.au

Kango Cars (SA)

Kango Cars was renamed Fibreglass Designs in 1990. The company, based in Edenvale near Johannesburg, was already involved in the production of cars and kit cars. Particularly noteworthy are the vehicles that use Volkswagen mechanics. One of the most important models is the Kango. This was a buggy built on the chassis of a VW-Beetle. The range also included a kit for a panel van, a jeep-like vehicle and a replica of a Ford T model. The Silhouette leisure car is built on a specially developed chassis and has a similar engine to the VW Golf. Production ended in 2002. For the years 2000 to 2002, 15 complete vehicles have survived.

The Kango buggy was also marketed with distribution partners such as Fibreglass Designers.

CARS OF THE 1990s

Kango Buggy
The Kango is a buggy built on the shortened chassis of a VW-Beetle. The vehicle is very similar to the Gurgel vehicles that were very popular in Brazil in the 1980s. A soft top can be fitted between the windscreen frame and the roll bar. The doors are also made of plastic and can be fastened with snaps.

MK 2
The Kango MK2 is a classic T-top buggy. The kit is screwed onto the shortened floor assembly of a VW Beetle. The headlights are mounted in the bumper area. The front lid provides access to the fuel tank and can be used for limited luggage storage. The roof is in three parts. The side sections extend down to the entrance. The rear section can be raised to protect luggage.

SS
The Kango SS can be considered a closed version of the Kango Buggy. The vehicle has a fixed roof between the windscreen frame and the roll bar. The rear GRP roof and plexiglass windows can be removed in a few easy steps. The Kango SS was also a bestseller outside South Africa. In England the kit was offered as the Kingfisher Custom Kango. It was also exported to America.

Top to bottom: MK2 is a futher development of the Kango Buggy; the SS kit is a closed version of the Buggy; the Model T is a neoclassic kit in the tradition of the Ford T model.

Model T
One of the many neo-classics in the style of the Ford Model T was also offered under licence as the Model T.

Van Wagon
The kit for the Van Wagon can be traced back to the Vandetta from Grundaker in Metuchen, New Jersey.

Veep
A Jeep-style kit was taken over from another American supplier.

Sources:
George Nick Georgano (Chefredakteur): The Beaulieu Encyclopedia of the Automobile. Volume 1: A–F, Chicago 2001, p. 548.

CARS OF THE 1990s

Mania Spyder (SW)

In 1992 Dalhems, based in Falköping, Sweden, launched the kit for a Spyder. The Mania Spyder was designed by Ulf Bolumlid of Design by Ulf. Behind Dalhems is Henrik Walli, who in the early days built tuned engines for racers such as Gerry Johansson, Sven Arne Persson, Stig Carlsson, Per Hagerman, Karl Ernst Larsson and Bill Taube, helping them to several victories. In the mid-1970s, an outbuilding on a former farm was converted into a workshop. Initially engines were built there, and later GRP parts for the kits. Over time, Dalhems shifted its focus to distributing car parts from England and America.
The Mania Spyder is a kit car that can be screwed onto the bare chassis of a VW-Beetle. The kit consists of the front end, rear end, doors and windscreen. The windscreen frame is an integral part of the front end. A rear spoiler was also available at extra cost. The ambitious car manufacturer had a great deal of freedom in designing the car, so that today hardly any two cars are the same. Anyone willing to invest enough time and money could put a modern looking sports car on the road. According to the manufacturer, the basic version of the Mania Spyder can be built in around 100 hours. It can be assumed that

According to the manufacturer the Mania Spyder can be built within 100 hours.

in-depth knowledge of automotive engineering is required to get the car road-legal. A special tubular frame and hardtop for the Mania kit were launched in 2001. According to the manufacturer, around 50 Mania Spyder kits were sold. Most of the cars were probably finished in Scandinavia.

Sources:
George Nick Georgano (Chefredakteur): The Beaulieu Encyclopedia of the Automobile. Volume 1: A–F, Chicago 2001, p. 548.

Mastretta Sports Cars (MX)

Juan Daniel Mastretta founded Unediseño S.C. with his brother Carlos in 1987. The company was initially set up in rented premises on the south side of the Periferico in Mexico City, in an area of around 120 m2. In 1990, Unediseño became a design consultant for Carrocerfas Toluca SA (CATOSA). This coachbuilder, based in the industrial valley of Toluca in the state of Mexico, was already present on the market with minibuses and coaches. The work on the redesign of the „Urban II" minibus consisted of producing sketches and illustrations of the concept, plans and technical information, as well as supervising the construction of the prototype. The Urban II attracted the attention of minibus transport operators and increased CATOSA's market share in this sector. The management realised

CARS OF THE 1990s

how important Unediseno's involvement would be in increasing demand for the Urban II and how important industrial design would be in their future strategies. They therefore signed a partnership agreement with Unediseño based on a monthly contribution for the renewal of their entire product range.

Development of a Sports Car

Daniel Mastretta, Gumesindo Cuevas and Adrian Tinoco began developing the Unediseño Mastretta sports car in 1991. In the communal courtyard of the residential complex where Daniel's house was located, about 40 metres from the office, the newly acquired chassis of a VW-Beetle, a welding machine and basic hand tools were set up so that Carlos Velez could assemble the body structure of the prototype.

A number of changes were made to the chassis, particularly the overall length, which was reduced by 300mm to achieve the proportions of a two-seater sports car. In addition, a square tube frame was built using bus body technology. Due to the complexity of the project, the financial requirements became a major issue for the small company.

During the development of the body, it became clear that more space was needed to handle the materials and processes. Work on the mechanical elements of the powertrain had to be done in parallel with the modelling of the body. Andres Amaya, a former student of Daniel Mastretta and employee of Unediseño, offered his father's workshop in the centre of Coyoacan. The property had a large garden and the owners were willing to support the project without any intention of making a profit. Carlos Velez moved his welding and grinding equipment there.

1:5 clay model on early stage.

The basis for the development of the prototype was a 1:5 clay model. The 1:1 moulds were made using polyurethane foam and plaster. The fibreglass moulds were taken from the plaster model. The separation of the components and initial troubleshooting in the final assembly were carried out in order to obtain the final fibreglass moulds for the first parts and future series production.

The economic crisis of 1995 also

Prototype of the MXA completed in 1995.

affected the sports car project. Much of the financial resources generated by the projects with CATOSA were invested in the purchase of materials to continue the production of the Mastretta prototype. Some of the workers had to wait a long time for their wages. It was also difficult to pay the suppliers.

The Mastretta sports car, powered by a 1.6-litre VW Boxer engine, was unveiled to the public in the autumn of 1995. That same year, Andres Amaya travelled to Italy to complete a postgraduate course, forcing Unediseño to leave the Coyoacan workshop. The company bought a plot of land near its offices. Despite the small size and precarious facilities of the new premises, it was possible to produce the first three Mastretta cars, the first of which were sold to Alberto Lenz, the owner of Autos Clasicos y Deportivos S.A., who mainly sold Porsche 356 replicas that he had built himself.

During the crisis of 1995 and after the Mastretta project had been published in Kit Car Magazine, Ed Doherty of Bold City Motors in Jacksonville, Florida, visited Mexico with the intention of becoming a Mastretta dealer in the USA. He bought a kit powered by a VW Golf engine and presented it at the Carslisle Pennsylvania Show in May 1996. He subsequently ordered four „kits", which he never paid for, and Unediseno gradually sold them, one of them to Sergio, another of the Mastretta brothers.

A new company name was needed for invoicing the vehicles, so Carlos and Daniel created Tecnoidea SA de CV, responsible for design, and Tecnosport SA de CV, responsible for production. More space was also needed to build the vehicles. An industrial building of around 1,000 m2 was rented on Avenida Alta Tension in the west of Mexico City.

Three of the vehicles built in the new facilities in 1996 were shipped to Germany and purchased by Bonsack Engineering. Bonsack Engineering ordered two cars with VW Golf engines and one with a VW flat four engine, which were built in five months and presented to the German press in the winter of that year. Mr Bonsack sold all three cars but argued that a 5-

speed gearbox and new suspension had to be fitted before negotiations could continue. This was not possible and the relationship was terminated.

Technical Details
MXA
Engine: VW engine, 1598 ccm
Power: 46 hp
Length: 4400 mm; Width: 1750 mm; Hight: 1300 mm; Wheelbase: 2100 mm
Weight: 850 kg (empty)

Tecnoidea's management did not have the resources to cover the cost of these claims. The MXA was offered for $120,000.

MXB (1996 - 1998)
The most noticeable optical differences to the MXA were the headlights. Other than that, the changes were minor. The MXB was probably only delivered with liquid-cooled engines from the VW Jetta or VW Golf with a displacement of 1.8 litres and 90 bhp. The MXB was probably only produced in a limited edition of 2 cars per year. It can be assumed that the total production run was around 15 cars. The MXB was offered for $140,000.

A total of 12 were built, including one kit that went to Barbados in 1997 for Evolution Cars, a manufacturer of beach vehicles who wanted to open up another market with the Mastretta. Because of the country's legislation, the car had to be imported completely disassembled and reassembled in the Caribbean facilities, for which Daniel Mastretta and Gumesindo Cuevas travelled for a week. On the plane, they documented a crate of components for assembly with a volume of around 2m³. The whole project was very complicated and not economically viable for Tecnoidea.

Technical Details
MXB
Engine: VW engine, 1781 ccm
Power: 90 hp
Length: 4000 mm; Width: 1750 mm; Hight: 1300 mm; Wheelbase: 2100 mm
Weight: 900 kg (empty)

Corvette Replica
Robert Arthur (Vetterod) from New Orleans sent an original 1958 Corvette from which the models and fibreglass moulds were taken. A rolling prototype was built in 1996, including the chassis design. The interior dimensions were modified to improve driver ergonomics, and suppliers were found for windscreen frames and door, bonnet and boot hardware. Over a period of two years, 22 kits were built, almost complete, unpainted, without engine, gearbox and suspension. The kit was sold for 12,500 US dollars, which meant no profit for Tecnoidea, but kept the work going during those years of crisis.

Only 12 MXA seem to be built between 1996 and 1997.

MXA (1996 - 1998)
In 1996, two versions of the sports car, the MXA (49 bhp VW flat four engine) and the MXB (90 bhp VW Golf engine), were unveiled at the World Trade Centre during the Mexican Motor Show. Delivery times of three months were promised, but due to lack of organisation and the complexity of production, deliveries were delayed by a further month. There was no coordination in the procurement of components, and the fledgling production line suffered frequent ‚stoppages', requiring overtime to be paid to reduce delivery delays.

Porsche Speedster Replica
Between 1996 and 1999, 23 turnkey vehicles were built for Nambara's Auto Trading in Japan, based on the floor assembly of a VW Beetle. This was a good customer who could not be given enough time as Tecnoidea's attention was divided between this project and the Corvette project.

CARS OF THE 1990s

Sources:
Automóvil Panamericano (magazine), issue 2 1998
Bernd Ostmann: Auto Katalog 1998, Vereinigte Motor-Verlage, Stuttgart 1997, p. 279.

Harald H. Linz, Halwart Schrader: Die Internationale Automobil-Enzyklopädie. United Soft Media Verlag, München 2008, ISBN 978-3-8032-9876-8, chapter Mastretta.
http://www.mastrettacars.com/

Armando Mercado Villalobos, Mastretta, Estudio de Caso, Que para obtener el grado de Maestro en Diseno estrategico e innovavion, Mexico D.F. 2011.

Mc Lela / Blaze (US)

The kit for the McLela was developed and produced by Quality Construction & Engineering in the 1990s. However, distribution was handled by strategic partner Duane Voss of Dynabug Automotive in Tulsa, Oklahoma. At the time, Dynabug was a major VW parts specialist with everything you could possibly need for on-road and off-road use. The kit for an easy to build vehicle with exceptional styling was a perfect fit for Dynabug's offerings. Ray Lombard of Quality Construction & Engineering is the designer of the McLela Blaze, which was conceived as a 2-seater convertible in the style of the MLaren F1.

The kit is bolted to the untrimmed floor pan of a VW Beetle. Alternatively, a tubular steel frame is available for added torsional rigidity. If you are not satisfied with the performance of a VW Boxer engine, you can build your McLela on a custom tubular frame. This is designed to accommodate larger units in a mid-engine configuration. The windscreen of a 1984 to 1986 Honda Civic could be used to build the McLela. A dashboard was available at extra cost to accommodate the instruments of a VW Golf GTI. The McLela was offered in 4 versions. The basic kit was available for 2,740 dollars. The kit mounted on a Beetle chassis with doors fitted cost 3,560 dollars. The kit mounted on the special frame cost 5,300 dollars. The turnkey vehicle was priced at around $12,600. According to the manufacturer, a McLela could be built in 13 days. The intensity of the activities during these two weeks is not described in detail. During the conversion there are two operations that require more experience in vehicle construction. Lowering the floor panel under the seats requires good metalworking skills. Moving the gear lever backwards by about 20 cm is also a job that should be done by a professional. The finishing of the GRP parts shows a high level of quality awareness. The paintwork creates a surface worthy of a show car. The upward-opening doors are remarkable and give the car a special flair. The doors are held in a vertical position by gas pressure dampers. The relatively low seating position was achieved by using Seat sports seats mounted just above the floor pan. The seats were also positioned in a recess in the floor pan. The ambitious carmaker had to cut into the floor pan on the left and right under the seat, press the pan down at the rear and weld triangular recesses into the sides. This created a seating position similar to that of a racing car. The windscreen is from the Honda Civic (1984-1986). The triangular side windows are custom made. The instruments on the dashboard could be used from the VW Golf GTI.

The first kits were offered under the name McLela, based on the original. After the company Jovi

The first kit was called McLela, other kits were labelled as Blaze, 8 to 10 kit were sold in 1996.

When designing the McLela it was important to Ray that the kit could be turned into a finished vehicle as quickly and easily as possible.

in Fort Lauderdale, Florida took over the distribution of the kit, the name of the kit was changed to Blaze. It is estimated that 8 to 10 cars were sold and completed by 1996.

The McLela was offered in 4 different versions: The basic kit, the kit already mounted on a VW floorpan, the kit already mounted on a centre tube frame and the finished car, which was available for 12,650 dollars. There were also a number of engine and transmission options, as well as optional extras such as a hardtop and rear wing. Customers using a Beetle chassis were able to take their first test drives within a few weeks. Dynabug usually supplied 1.8-litre boxer engines and an extended VW gearbox, as with the Beetle in this configuration. With two 44 cc Weber carburettors, an ignition sequence manifold and a sports exhaust, the lightweight car could be driven in a very sporty manner.

After Dynabug Automotive Inc. withdrew from the market, the McLela was marketed under the name Blaze by JOVI in Fort Lauderdale, FL.

Sources:
www.priceofhistoys.com/category/blaze/
www.vwkitcars.com/mclela-blaze-vw-kit-car/
www.allcarindex.com/main-index/car-make-details/United-States-QCE/

Nereia (US)

Nereia Cars, based in Wilmington, North Carolina, built one of the many Nova derivatives as well as boats between 1991 and 1996 or even later. In 1991, Nereia bought the moulds and rights to the Cimbria, which had been out of production for six years. In the same year, cars were offered for sale under the „Nereia" name. The company already had a reputation for supplying high quality GRP boat parts and Corvette spares. It was therefore easy to convince customers that Nereia would live up to their high quality standards. The kit was offered for the Beetle floor assembly or for mounting on a specially designed floor assembly with a special frame and the option of installing a modern and powerful GM drive. The Nereia can be distinguished from the Cimbra SS by its slightly shorter nose. It was available either as a basic kit with all the body panels and a number of critical components such as door hardware and interior trim, or as a luxury kit that included almost all the important components such as leather seats, a wooden dashboard and VDO instruments. Despite these ambitions, many friends of

Nereia Cars bought the molds and rights to produce kits from Cimbria. After a slight facelift the Nereia was launched.

the Nereia were unable to obtain a kit. This explains why no more than 10 kits were produced until 1996. The sales brochures always showed a kind of symbolic picture in the shape of a Cimbria.

Sources:
www.nationalsterling.org
www.sterlingkitcars.com/history_pages/cimbria/history_module_cm.html

Harold W. Pace, KIT CAR, The Car Builder's Authority, 2. edition 2000, p. 87f.
Phillip J Fenton, The Nova/Sterling/Eureka Kit Car, 2007, p. 9ff

CARS OF THE 1990s

Rudolph (DE)

Rudolph Perfect Roadster GmbH, based in Mechernich-Obergartzem, was founded in 1992. The company's history began with the production of plastic wings for classic cars. A short time later, other body parts for the Karmann-Ghia were offered. Soon after, the company concentrated on the development and sale of complete roadster bodies. Basically a two-man operation, the company has over the years produced some interesting classic car replicas. Some of the best known cars in the Ralf Rudolph range are the Rudolph Spyder, the Classic Roadster and the Diardi.

All production steps, from model making to final assembly, are carried out in-house. Each of these cars has been designed and developed over a period of approximately 2 years. It all starts with model making. After initial design studies, 1:1 models are made using special modelling materials. A negative mould is then made for series production. Parallel to the modelling, the vehicle frame is designed. This includes the wheel suspensions, steering systems, brakes, etc. The first finished vehicle is then subjected to a TÜV inspection. Once the necessary certificates have been issued, series production begins. The vehicle frames are hot-dip galvanised and painted, and the bodies are hand laminated from GRP. Most roadsters are powered by Audi, VW or BMW engines.

Notable features

Shortly after its launch in Germany, a kit was brought to England. Peter and Christine Murphy began building their own Evergreen Rudolph sports cars in Cornwall in 1995. The kit, marketed as a „sports car" for short, was available as a convertible and coupé for less than £6,000. Complete cars

were estimated to cost £12,000. The quality of the bodywork was particularly emphasised in the motoring press. At the time, it was not a matter of course that a kit with German TÜV approval, including successfully completed crash and torsion tests, was available. The sports car was fitted with a roll bar integrated into the windscreen frame. The evergreen Rudolph sports car was sold until 1999.

Classic Roadster

The first roadster developed by Rudolph was the Classic Roadster,

The Karmann Ghia replica with GRP body was called Rudolph Classic Roadster. The kit was launched in 1992.

a replica of the Karmann Ghia. The car was unveiled to the public in 1992. This replica was offered as a kit and as a finished car. The one-piece GRP body is mounted on a reinforced VW-Beetle chassis. Due to the initial registration of the chassis, both air-cooled Bo-

CARS OF THE 1990s

xer and G-Kat engines could be fitted.

After some turbulence due to copyright infringements, an agreement was reached with Volkswagen in 2005. With official permission from the group, 15 bodies can be produced each year. The faithful replica of the Karmann Ghia is available with numerous engine variants from Volkswagen, Subaru and Audi. With the longitudinally mounted 1.8-litre turbo engine from Ingolstadt, the car can be registered with 250 bhp.

For a while at least, the Rudolph Classic Roadster could be ordered from the company Agfos near Mannheim. Around 180 of the Rudolph Classic Roadster were sold.

Sources:
www.rudolph-roadster.de
www.roadster-replica.de
www.agfos.de
www.autobild.de/artikel/fahrbericht-roadster-rudolph-spyder-928604.html
Peter Tuthill, Cornwall´s Motor Industry, The story of the many fascinating motor vehicles manufactured in Cornwall from 1981 to date, 2007, p. 59ff.

Savana (BR)

In 1990, a very similar pickup to the Polauto was available for a short time. Compared to the Polauto, the Savana has twin headlights and the option of a cowcatcher to give the vehicle a more distinctive look. The GRP bumper has additional bumpers at the front and rear to the left and right of the number plate. Many of the details suggest that a mould was taken from a Polauto and a separate model was created with just a few modifications. Details of the manufacturer are largely unknown. The name of the town of Sao Joaro da Barra appears in the vehicle documents.

Right: the Savana pickup has some similarities to the Polauto; this car is from 1990.

Sources:
www.essevaleumafoto.com/2012/11/savana-1990.html

Short (BR)

The company Short Motor Sport, Av. Srg. Geraldo Santana 902, São Paulo, began producing road-legal sports cars in 1994. The company used Volkswagen technology. Fábio Taccari had already been working on concepts for customised sports cars during his studies in São Bernardo do Campo, Sao

CARS OF THE 1990s

Paulo. In 1974, he still lacked the money to realise his ideas. Eventually he persuaded a Volkswagen dealer to back him. The economic crisis caused further delays in the development of the 1:1 body moulds. It was not until the 1990s that things began to look up for Brazilian car manufacturers. As in the 1970s, tax rates on car imports were raised, which helped to boost the Brazilian economy. In 1994, a prototype was created and named the Short GT Turbo. The design of the car is reminiscent of the Renault Alpine, Lancia Stratos and Abarth 2000. All in all, the compact wedge-shaped design is predestined for sporty driving. Between 2002 and 2003, Fábio Taccari built a second prototype called the Short EX Turbo. In the course of time, two further models were created, each of which differed from the other in terms of performance enhancements under the bonnet.

Fábio Taccari and his team in São Paulo (SP) produce only two cars a year. But he is trying to increase production with the help of foreign investors. At the moment, he mainly produces car accessories and components for cars and motorcycles. There are also plans to produce an electric car, which can be seen as an evolution of the Short SRT. It will be powered by electric motors coupled to the rear wheels. Part of the energy would come from solar cells that would be integrated into the bodywork.

GT Turbo (1994 - 2002)

The technical basis was the chassis of a VW Brasilia. A 2.2-litre VW flat four engine was fitted. The front suspension is the same as the original Beetle, but with negative camber and caster. Taccari fitted a metal box in front of the front axle to absorb the forces in the event of a head-on collision. The brakes were Volkswagen technology, with disc brakes at the front and drum brakes at the rear. It was not until the late 1990s that the prototype was developed into a production-ready vehicle. Due to the unfavourable weight distribution and the resulting suboptimal handling, the project was abandoned. The experience gained with the Short GT Turbo was used in the development of the Short EX Turbo.

EX Turbo (2003 – 2006)

Fábio Taccari made numerous improvements to the second prototype. The Short EX Turbo was completed in 2003 and by 2006 had covered more than 200,000 kilometres. The Short EX Turbo has an air-cooled 1,800 cc boxer engine at the rear. The gearbox is the same as the SP2. The radiator fan comes from the VW Brasilia. A 0.8 bar KKK turbocharger gives the Short EX a maximum power output of 150 bhp. This results in acceleration from 0 to 100 km/h in 9 seconds and a top speed of just under 200 km/h. Two external oil coolers on the sides of the bonnet

First prototype of the Short GT Turbo from 1994.

ensure efficient lubrication. On the one hand, the speedometer, oil pressure and turbocharger status form a single unit. On the other, the oil temperature gauge, ammeter and fuel gauge are located in the second module. The 2-seater coupé is only 3.5 metres long. The GRP body sits on a chassis with a frame tunnel with a Y-structure at the rear. The front suspension was taken from the VW-Beetle. Perforated disc brakes are fitted at the front and drum brakes at the rear. In the tradition of racing cars, the interior is kept very simple. However, the bucket seats are upholstered in leather. H-belts ensure the safety of the driver and passenger. Small items of luggage can only be stowed behind the seats. The spare tyre, fuel tank and battery are located under the bonnet at the front. The side windows have a two-piece design and are made of polycarbonate. The polycarbonate roof panels above the driver

CARS OF THE 1990s

EX Turbo with 150 bhp and a max. speed of 200 km/h from 1994.

Technical Details
MXB
Engine: VW engine, 1781 ccm
Power: 150 bhp
Length: 4000 mm; Width: 1750 mm; Hight: 1300 mm; Wheelbase: 2100 mm
Weight: 900 kg (empty)

and front passenger are also removable, allowing the car to be driven as a Targa in just a few simple steps. The Short EX Turbo was used as a pace car in the 2006 Turismo GNV World Championship race in Curitiba.

GT AR Turbo (2007 -)

The Short GT AR Turbo was also fitted with the 1.8-litre boxer engine. The turbocharger increases the boost pressure to 1.2 bar. The engine produces more than 180 hp. Acceleration from 0 to 100 km/h is possible in 8 seconds. The Short GT AR Turbo has a top speed of 205 km/h. The front brakes come from the Golf. The rear brakes are perforated discs from the Chevrolet Omega.

GT AP Turbo (2009 -)

The Short GT AP Turbo has the same body as the Short GT AR Turbo. However, a 1.8 litre water cooled VW AP engine has been fitted. The AP turbo builds up a pressure of 2 bar and thus achieves an output of 220 hp. Thanks to the balanced weight distribution (40% front and 60% rear), the Short GT AP Turbo has excellent handling characteristics, even though the AP engine is slightly heavier. The car has a top speed of 237 km/h and accelerates from 0 to 100 km/h in just 6.5 seconds.

AR Turbo with 180 bhp (yellow); SRT from 2013 (black).

CARS OF THE 1990s

SRT (2013 -)
The latest development from Fábio Taccari is the SRT model. The body has been facelifted to make the car more competitive. No significant numbers have yet been produced.

E (2015 -)
Fábio Taccari is developing an electric car based on the Short SRT. Both rear wheels will be driven by electric motors. The project itself is currently (2015) still in the development stage.

Sources:
http://planetarodas.blogspot.co.at
www.carroantigo.com/portugues/conteudo/curio_carros_conceito_nac_6.htm
www.tribunapr.com.br/noticias/automoveis/short-ex-turbo-chega-a-mais-de-200-kmh/
www.lexicarbrasil.com.br/short/
http://shortmotorsport.com

Total Recall (US)

Mike Fennel Enterprises in Saugus, California, produced a series of futuristic-looking Beetle-based vehicles for film productions. For the television series Hardcastle and McCormick, Mike Fennel modified a Manta Montage, which became famous on the show as the Coyote. Creations from his workshop were also used in the feature film Total Recall (1990). Paul Verhoeven's Total Recall is a film based on a short story by Philip K. Dick. The film itself is not a box office hit, but it offers a fairly convincing evocation of a near future on Earth and the colonisation of Mars. Two remarkable vehicles are featured in the film. A relatively independent creation, with gullwing doors and lots of glass, is said to herald a near automotive future. A GRP body has been bolted to the undercarriage of a VW-Beetle, allowing the camera to capture the driver and passenger very well, even in exterior shots.

Beetle based cars featured in the movie „Total Rcall" from 1990.

Total Recall 2
The second vehicle is very similar to a modified Boonie Bug and has

Sources:
www.motortorque.com/blog/2010-02/folly-friday-toyota-total-recall-drivers-outraged-over-fines-rough-justice-8619
http://blog.hemmings.com/index.php/2010/02/03/the-futuristic-cars-of-total-recall/
www.rqriley.com/ev-tech.htm

also been generously fitted with glass surfaces. The Johnny Cap is fully self-propelled. The chauffeur is a mannequin. Passengers simply had to announce their destination and the Johnny Cap would find its way through the dense city traffic. This vision of artificial intelligence was unrivalled for a long time.

Tukano (BR)

Tukano Tecnologia e Design from Fortaleza/CE presented the Convert MCR to the public for the first time at AUTOP'93 - Feira Nacional de Autopecas e Veículos do Ceará, in Fortaleza. The vehicle was built on the platform of a VW-Beetle and, apart from the GRP body, used as many mass-produced components as possible. A further development of the vehicle was launched in 1999 under the name Convert II.

Convert MCR (1993 - 1999)

The Convert MCR is a vehicle that combines many typical features of well-known Brazilian productions. The front of the vehicle has many similarities with the Puma produced in São Paulo. The passenger compartment is very similar to that of a jeep. The rear of the vehicle has a rear wing, round tail lights and a hatch under the integrated bumper to allow access to the engine for maintenance. The GRP doors can also be found in a very similar form on Gurgel vehicles.

The Convert MCR was offered as a kit and as a turnkey version.

Technical Details
Convert MCR
Engine: VW engine, 1584 ccm
Power: 64 bhp
Length: 3570 mm; Width: 1650 mm; Hight: 1660 mm; Wheelbase: 2400 mm
Weight: 650 kg (empty)

A version without doors is supplied with a black and transparent vinyl rain cover. For road approval, disc brakes had to be fitted at the front and drum brakes at the rear. The Convert MCR was offered both as a kit and as a turnkey version until 1999.

Convert II (1999 -)

The Convert II is very similar to its predecessor. The front of the car has been redesigned. The spare wheel under the boot lid has been removed to make room for luggage. Instead of doors, the car has an entrance, as is common with buggies. The Convert II got the headlights from the Opel Corsa. There are only two integrated rear lights - including indicators - at the rear of the car. The back seat can be folded down to create more storage space. The space under the seat could also be used if necessary. The spare wheel is attached to the rear of the vehicle by a metal construction, as was often the case with Jeeps. All in all, the Convert II is a fun car that is suitable for both on-road and off-road

CARS OF THE 1990s

use, and can be comfortably driven by two people.

Front view of the Convert II from 1999 with open access.

Rear view of the Convert II with open loading area and load securing options.

Sources:
www.grupotukano.com.br

Vochoneta   (MX)

In Mexico, the demand for cheap commercial vehicles for transporting goods was met by converting VW-Beetles. These vans were called „Vochoneta". At the beginning of the 1990s, a kind of standard for the conversion of the VW-Beetle into a delivery van developed. The box-shaped body is positioned approximately at the height of the side skirts and protrudes about 40 cm above the Beetle's roof. In most cases, a folding side panel is fitted on the passenger side to allow access to the load from the side. The tailgate also folds upwards.

The Vochoneta was produced in large numbers between 1990 and 1998. Before and after that, private hobbyists did similar conversions. Kits were also available from various kit car suppliers.

Sources:
With kind support of the members of the facebook groupe Vochoneta

CARS OF THE 1990s

Vochos Taxi (MX)

In Mexico, the Beetle has long been part of the street scene. The so-called taxistas dominated Mexico City with their vochos. Eventually, Mexico decreed that all taxis should have a new red and gold livery. A law was passed stating that vehicles registered before 1998 could no longer be used as taxis. At a time when it was becoming increasingly difficult for Beetle taxis, a unique Beetle with an extended passenger door was created. The car belonged to the Volkswagen plant in Puebla for over 11 years from 1996 and was sold to a Mexican Volkswagen fan who used it for several years. The story of the Beetle Taxi ends with its sale to a private collector from Braunschweig, Germany, who brought the car back to Germany and restored it. The Beetle has widened front bumpers and an enlarged passenger door to make it easier for passengers to get into the rear seats. Of course, the rear window and the B-pillar had to be shortened or moved backwards by the same amount as the door was lengthened. The driver's door remained unchanged. Today the Taxi Beetle is in excellent condition with taxi lights on the roof and a „free signal" behind the windscreen.

The Vochos Taxi with extended passenger door was created to react on new regulations regarding passanger transportation.

Sources:
http://commons.wikimedia.org/wiki/Category:Prototyp_mexikanisches_Taxi_at_Sammlung_Historische_Fahrzeuge_Braunschweig
www.volkswagen-classic.de/it/magazin/special/vocho-taxi-in-mexiko/02

ZF98 (PT)

Between 1986 and 1998, João Oliveira was the managing partner of Proto Design in Soito. The company specialised in the production of customised classic car replicas. Its services ranged from the production of moulds and body parts to the complete assembly of vehicles built on a Volkswagen chassis.

ZF98

The ZF98 is one of João Oliveira's more famous designs, created for Expo 98 in Lisbon. Although the vehicle was not presented at Expo 98 as originally planned, it is likely that some units of this sports car were produced. There are some media reports about the ZF98 from that time, but not much else can be learned about the car. Today there are probably still a few ZF98s in Portugal's garages.

CARS OF THE 1990s

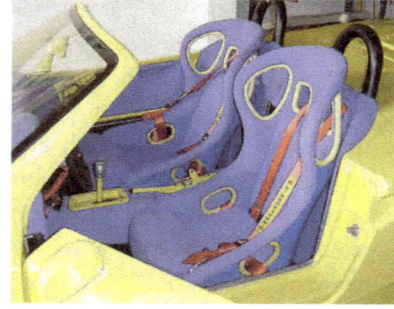

The ZF98 is one of João Oliveira's more famous designs, created for Expo 98 in Lisbon.

Sources:
http://rodasdeviriato.blogspot.co.at/search?q=zf+98
www.allcarindex.com/

www.webcarstory.com/voiture.php?id=4692&PHPSESSID=111ec01d3cf90e391ae7e61ad6c770af&width=1280
www.protodesign.biz

Delivery Vans (MISC)

There are still many vehicles that use components from Volkswagen or Porsche. Only a few delivery vans are shown here, for which hardly any further information is available.

CARS OF THE 1990s

Woodies (MISC)

There are still many vehicles that use components from Volkswagen or Porsche. Only a few woodies are shown here, for which hardly any further information is available.

CARS of the 2000s

Kitcars at the Summit

After 2000, only a few vehicles were built as one-offs or in small series. The quality of these cars is usually outstandingly good. The aim is no longer to build a dream car on the smallest possible budget, but to realise it yourself. The technology is usually customised to the respective project. What is installed is what can be found on the shelves of the series vehicle manufacturers. The design, the idea or the innovation usually take centre stage. The chassis of the VW Beetle is hardly ever used as a basis for new bodies.

The Memminger Roadster 2.7 combines classic shapes with modern technology. With its 210 hp, the vehicle offers a lot of driving fun for two.

CARS OF THE 2000s

Batráquio Anfíbio   (BR)

Near São Paulo, an amphibious vehicle based on a VW-Beetle has been created under the name Batráquio (Tadpole). Erineu Cicarelli was inspired by the restoration of one of the 150 or so surviving Schwimmwagen of the German Wehrmacht. He was able to fund his project thanks to an invention that refills printer cartridges and is sold in 45 countries around the world.

Erineu Cicarelli began the project with scale sketches of the body and technical components. Further design decisions were made on the basis of these sketches. For example, the headlights of the VW Gol were chosen because they worked well with the rear lights of the Chevrolet Corsa.

The Batráquio has a robust chassis made up of Volkswagen components (mainly the shortened floor assembly of a Brazilian VW-Beetle) and a GRP body. It took around 12 years, numerous experiments and improvements before the amphibious vehicle was fully developed. The vehicle's road approval in Brazil can be seen as proof of its suitability for use. The imaginary name „Batráquio" has been registered as a trademark since 2001.

The vehicle has 4-wheel drive and a propeller modelled on the propeller of the Schwimmwagen. Similar to the prototype, the vehicle can use a gently sloping surface to move from water to land and vice versa without the need for complicated conversion measures. Once the vehicle is floating, the propeller can be folded down and locked

The Batráquio was inspired by the historic Schwimmwagen. It can be seen as a modern interpretation of that kind of amphibious vehicles.

in place. This connects to a cardan shaft of sorts, giving a top speed of around 4 knots. The vehicle is powered by a 1.6 litre engine. The windscreen can be folded forward, similar to the prototype.

The Batráquio is a unique model. Although Erineu Cicarelli is now retired, reliable sources report a new vehicle project in his garage.

Sources:
http://portaldoenvelhecimento.org.br/noticias/velhices/empresario-conquista-o-sonho-de-ter-um-carro-anfibio.html
http://revistatrip.uol.com.br/revista/210/salada/isto-nao-e-uma-enchente.html
http://tragaocheque.wordpress.com/2011/10/28/feito-em-casa-batraquio/

Bogatti (US)

In California, a replica of a 1927 Bugatti is still being built on the undercarriage of a VW-Beetle. Finished Bogatti VW kit cars occasionally appear on the Internet. The characteristic front axle of the Beetle shows the origin of this neo-classic. For the conversion, the gear lever and handbrake have to be moved to the rear to achieve the typical Bugatti seating position.

Sources:
http://carslr.com/car/bogatti-vw-kit-car-9075868

This Bugatti replica was built 2015.

Bubbletop Volksrod (US)

Shortly after the turn of the millennium, an ambitious Beetle mechanic near Detroit began a remarkable project that kept him busy for about five years. The basis was the chassis of a 1960 Beetle, but only the frame tunnel was needed for the project. Various Beetle parts, such as the boot lid and front fenders, form the main bodywork components.

The Volksrod had to seat two people. The passenger compartment had to be oval in shape to allow room for the steering wheel and other controls.

There are more space constraints under the hood than the pictures show. remember that the beetle hood slopes down from the centre. that's why i can't get the pivot point more than an inch or two under the hood frame with a passat-style setup, and why the stock outriggers won't work. no matter where the other geometries are with a simple hinge like this, if the pivot point is under the hood fra-

me, it will pull the frame into the hood as it lifts. I thought about burying a central hinge in the top of the dome frame and then using two arm linkages at either end to stabilise and lift the dome, but I thought I was so close with the 4-bar linkages on the A-pillars that it was worth rethinking.

In the end I had to spread the A-pillar pivot points by about 3", raise them another 2-3" and spread the outer rod by about 4". It took a whole afternoon of fiddling with the geometry before we got something that looked promising, and it took a few more iterations on the car to get it to work in 3D and not just on the 2D model. i had forgotten to account for the clearance between the top rod and the bottom of the bladder flange at the top of the arch, and had to move the whole thing down and change the arm lengths again. even an 1/8" makes a noticeable difference in the arch. without the model, it would have taken me

CARS OF THE 2000s

forever to get it right.

In the end, we had to move the pivot points on the A-pillar about 3", raise it another 2-3" and move the outer beam about 4". It took a whole afternoon of fiddling with the geometry before we got something that looked promising, and a few more iterations on the car to get it to work in 3D and not just on the 2D model. i had forgotten to account for the clearance between the top rod and the bottom of the bladder flange at the top of the arch, and had to move the whole thing down and change the arm lengths again. even an 1/8" makes a noticeable difference in the arch. without the model, it would have taken me forever to find the right solution.

The Making of

The design is based on two front mudguards from a VW Beetle.

The creation of the passenger compartment

Many design elements of the VW Beetle can be found on the Bubbletop Volksroad

At the very end, the motor was installed and the bubbletop put on.

Sources:
https://www.thesamba.com/vw/forum/

Bugfire (DE)

Dirk Rosen bought his first VW-Beetle at the age of 18. Over the years he has remained loyal to cars with an air-cooled engine in the rear. Only the type of modifications has changed over the years. Initially, the focus was on tuning, but later kit cars were also built. In 2013, the idea was born for an independent project that would involve more than just buying components, customising them and driving off. With a strong emphasis on a torsionally rigid passenger cell, the 1985 Triumph Spitfire MK IV became the focus of the hobbyist's attention. As is often the case, the first drawings were made on a beer mat while on holiday. Dirk Rosen then produced design drawings based on the original dimensions. The aim was to build the body of the Triumph Spitfire on a Volkswagen chassis. Procuring these two components was relatively straightforward. The complexity of the project only became apparent later. First, the undercarriage was completely overhauled, cleaned of dirt and rust and repainted. Adapting the bodywork required some welding, but in 2016 the revised steel body

CARS OF THE 2000s

was successfully joined to the chassis. The bonnet was a cross between a VW-Beetle and a Spitfire. To ensure that the engine gets enough fresh air, ventilation slots or louvres had to be fitted to the bonnet. The homemade parts are made from 1.5mm and 3mm sheet metal.

As Rosen wanted to use the pedals from the Spitfire, he had to convert to a hydraulic clutch. The Triumph's rack-and-pinion steering gives extremely light steering, even without servo assistance.

Technical Details
Bugfire
Engine: VW engine, 1584 ccm
Power: 50 hp
Length: 3650 mm; Width: 1550 mm; Hight: 1100 mm; Wheelbase: 2400 mm
Weight: 1230 kg (empty)

Power is supplied by a 50 bhp Volkswagen Boxer engine, which

has not been modified to meet the emissions requirements for road use. A Sauer & Sohn exhaust system is used for looks, sound and optimised exhaust flow. Original Triumph Persenning is used when the sun is shining. A Triumph soft or hard top is available for bad weather.

Dirk Rosen made initial contact with the TÜV in 2016. It was particularly difficult to make the front end legally compliant and as safe as possible for passers-by.

The Bugfire is a good example of the VW community's wealth of imagination.

When turning or in the event of an accident, a pedestrian must not be trapped in the front. This requirement alone meant another six months of work for Rosen. Full approval was granted in April 2017, including the H registration plate, as only original Triumph and Volkswagen parts were used. Dirk Rosen opted for a matte red colour to give the car an elegant pati-

CARS OF THE 2000s

na and a classic look. The vehicle, which features a hinged front and removable rear bonnet for easy access to the engine, takes its name from the VW-Beetle and Triumph Spitfire that provided the parts.

Sources:
With kind support of Dirk Rosen, 2017.

Chelo Casas GT   (PR)

José „Chelo" Casas worked for almost 10 years on a sports car that became known as the Chelo Casas GT. The former racing driver and designer from Puerto Rico built the GRP body on the basis of the Avenger. The rear of the car bears some resemblance to the Ferrari 288 GTO. There are also hints of Maserati and Lamborghini. The body was bolted to the undercarriage of a Volkswagen. The car is powered by a Porsche 356 engine. The car can still be seen at car shows in Puerto Rico.

After more than ten years of working the Chelo Casas GT is looking great. It can be spotted at Volkswagen events in Puerto Rico.

Sources:
http://flickrhivemind.net/Tags/autos,guaynabo/Interesting
http://autosclasicosehistoricos.com/index.php/archivo/eventos-especiales/76-6ta-feria-de-autos-clasicos-y-antiguos-del-municipio-de-guaynabo.html

Der Wiger Coupé   (NO)

Norwegian Øystein Asphjell built his own 2-seater coupé based on a 1952 Pretzel Beetle, inspired by the Hebmüller coupé. The front of the car was taken from a 1954 Karmann Beetle convertible and, as with the Karmann convertibles, the turn signals were hand-set into the body behind the doors. The car was completed at Hammerworks in 2009 using the same

The Der Wiger Coupé is based on a VW-Beetle from 1952.

Sources:
www.vwnorge.no/index.php?topic=22340.0
www.volksworld.com

CARS OF THE 2000s

Floating T3 Bus (DE)

In 2019, a T3 bus converted into a Schwimmwagen was displayed at Bremen Classic. The vehicle is a prototype that at least proved that a T3 bus can learn to swim. The vehicle was sealed up to the height of the door handles by welding sheet metal in front of the doors. A bow was added to the front of the bus to provide stability in the water. The drive for the watercraft was installed at the rear of the vehicle at the level of the bumper. A propeller is guided in a tube. The rudder, which can be controlled separately, is at the end of the tube.

A floating T3 bus is an outstanding project that was presented at Bremen Classic in 2019.

Sources:
https://www.classiccult.com/blog/bcm-2019.html

Gator (US)

The company WaterCar launched the Gator Amphibious in 2009. This is a jeep-style vehicle that can be driven both on the road and in the water. The kit consists of a GRP body, additional gearbox, propeller, chassis parts, waterproof headlights and turn signals, steering parts for use in water and various stainless steel parts. A number of interior parts such as seats, mirrors and windscreen can be used from the Jeep CJ8. The

vehicle can be built on a VW-Beetle chassis with a boxer engine and standard gearbox. We recommend the use of a VW Type 4 engine, which provides enough power to reach a top speed of over 45 mph, even in water. With a total weight of 1250kg, the Gator has a top speed of over 125mph on land. With an overall length of 4,950 mm and an overall height of 1,500 mm, the Gator is relatively compact and still offers plenty of room for four people.

Sources:
www.carscoops.com/2010/12/watercar-gator-amphibious-vw-beetle.html
www.autoevolution.com/news/watercar-gator-is-an-amphibious-monstrocity-28097.html
www.fastamphibians.com

The Gator Amphibiuos was launched in 2009.

Kübel Lite   (US)

The Kübel Lite is a cross between a 1940s kübelwagen, built for the German army, and an EMPI Sportster. David Barrett developed the first prototype, which was first shown at a Manx Club event at Calico Ghost near Barstow in early 2010. The vehicle has two rear hinged doors (suicide doors). The Kübel Lite can seat up to 5 people with only children in the back.

The vehicle is built on an extended VW chassis that has been widened by 20cm. The body consists of a stainless steel frame with an aluminium skin inside and out. This relatively lightweight construction results in an unladen weight of around 630 kg. With the passenger compartment fully lined, an additional 100 kg can be added. The windscreen folds forward. So far only one Kübel Lite has been built. David Barrett announced the development of a 2-seater version based on a shortened Beetle floorpan.

The Kübel Lite is a sportster in the style of a Thing.

Sources:
www.ewillys.com/category/volkswagen-kit/
www.thesamba.com/vw/classifieds/detail.php?id=766513
www.kubelite.com/
www.manxchassis.com

CARS OF THE 2000s

Landrover VW (US)

Eric Meyer and Jason Murphy have built some very special cars together. In addition to a lowered and top-chopped Rat Look Kübelwagen with a 2,110 cc boxer engine in the style of 1942, a Land Rover with a Volkswagen heart was created in 2002.

The first ideas and designs were developed 10 years before realisation. The concept was to combine a Porsche Boxter and a 1988 Land Rover. In 2002, Eric Meyer found a damaged body of an 88 Series IIA Land Rover with no engine and no gearbox. To fit a Porsche engine, the wheelbase had to be extended by almost 16cm. The plan to simply move the front axle forward was discarded after the first sketches. The resulting appearance was too oblique. The two hobbyists decided to build a custom chassis to accommodate a boxer engine. To ensure the result had the lowest possible ground clearance, the front ball joint axle had to be modified.

The Land Rover was originally left-hand drive. But that was not spectacular enough for the two tinkerers. So the pedals and dashboard were converted to right-hand drive. A Rancho Pro Street part was chosen for the gearbox. Eric Meyer fitted a 1,600 cc VW boxer engine. With the engine running right up to the rear wall of the body, the exhaust design proved to be very difficult. Jason Murphy designed an exhaust with two equal length pipes and a silencer to give the ‚special' sound.

The wheels come from a 1960s Porsche. Disc brakes front and rear provide the best possible stopping power. As usual with the Beetle, the fuel tank is at the front, where the water cooler fan normally works. Eric and Jason have completely stripped the body of all paint, leaving the aluminium surface to give the car a unique look.

Sources:
www.volksworld.com
www.oldbug.com/rovah.htm

This Landrover with a Volkswagen heart was built in 2002.

Memminger (DE)

Georg Memminger started out as a racing driver and has a number of successes to his name. He competed in the legendary 24 Hours of Le Mans in 1983. In the early days, the company he founded in 1978 was purely a steel construction business. The company was even involved in the construction of the Olympic Stadium in Munich. A 650 metre long catwalk was installed as a viewing platform for visitors. Memminger Feine-Cabrios & Stahlbau GmbH, based in Reichertshofen, only became a Beetle customiser in 1998. The decisive factor was their experience in restoring a Beetle convertible. Original VW convertible doors were not available. Original parts were no longer available and the available reproductions were inferior. Memminger quickly transferred his expertise in steel construction to vehicle construction. Today, his son supports him in this endeavour. Using specially developed steel pressing tools, Memminger now produces numerous parts for the 1302 and 1303 cabriolet and sa-

CARS OF THE 2000s

dant. The two widened fenders, the correspondingly wider running boards and a specially shaped bonnet give the two-seater Roadster 2.7 the desired powerful appearance. The windscreen was shortened at the top, as was often the case with police Beetle convertibles. Behind the driver and front passenger are elegantly integrated roll bars, which end in air domes for safety in the event of a crash. The roadster, which weighs just 800 kg, will be produced in a series of 20.

loon models, including cabriolet doors, side panels, hot air ducts and heating bars and wings for various models. In addition, Beetle convertibles are restored on behalf of customers or for sale and fitted with interesting technical refinements. In this way, each customer receives a tailor-made convertible. In 2018, after more than 20 years of restoring Beetles, the plans for a fully customised car came to fruition. The roadster, to be unveiled in spring 2018, is based on a Beetle platform and powered by a 2.7-litre air-cooled four-cylinder VW Boxer engine with manifold injection. The engine produces 210 hp and a maximum torque of 247 Nm. The top speed is around 200 km/h. Georg Memminger uses a semi-trailing arm suspension at the rear and reinforced wheel carriers at the front. The brakes come from Porsche. The mid-engine layout makes the rear seats redundant.

Technical Details
Memminger Roadster
Engine: VW engine, 2.7 litre
Power: 210 hp
Length: 4040 mm; Width: 1730 mm; Hight: 1250 mm; Wheelbase: 2440 mm
Weight: 800 kg (empty)

Memminger launched their Roadster in 2019. The the engine accelerates the vehicle to a maximum speed of 200 km/h.

Sources:
www.memminger-roadster.de
With kind support of Georg Memminger

Ora Punk Cat (CH)

Volkswagen unveiled a concept for an electric Beetle in 2012. Shortly afterwards, the idea was abandoned in Wolfsburg. Chinese manufacturer Great Wall Motors (GWM) unveiled the ORA Punk Cat at the 2021 Shanghai Auto Show. It is a four-door electric car that looks very similar to the Beetle, with round headlights and a curved bonnet that takes up almost a third of the car. The car has four doors. The bonnet, the curvature of the fenders, the rear, in short, almost all the relevant parts of the car follow the same lines of a VW-Beetle.

Great Wall Motors Company Limited is based in Baoding, Hebei, China, about 150 kilometres south of Beijing. The company was established in 1984. It is China's largest manufacturer of sport utility vehicles and pickup trucks. In 2016, GWM set an all-time sales record of 1,074,471 vehicles worldwide, an increase of 26% compared to

CARS OF THE 2000s

2015. GWM's product range includes the HAVAL, WEY, ORA and GWM Pickup brands. ORA is responsible for the production of electric cars within the Group.

Volkswagen will cease production of the VW Beetle in 2019. The German manufacturer plans to launch an electric van inspired by the classic VW estate in 2024. There are no official plans to bring back an electric version of the Beetle. Perhaps the ORA Punk Cat will make management reconsider, especially if the vehicle is successful in China.

Sources:
https://autoentusiastas.com.br/2021/05/parece-um-vw-fusca-mas-nao-e/

The Ora Punk Cat was unveiled at the 2021 Shanghai Auto Show. It is a four-door electric car looking quite similar to the New Beetle.

Pirassununga (BR)

Officially, Volkswagen produced only three four-door models with air-cooled engines in Brazil: The VW 1600 was created in 1968, the four-door VW 1600 TL with hatchback in 1971 and shortly afterwards the VW Brasilia was launched as a four-door model. In 2009, restorer Milton Ciola from Pirassununga built a four-door version from a ,66 Beetle. His aim was to change as little as possible of the car's design. So he studied the examples from the past. The first big challenge was designing

149

CARS OF THE 2000s

The Pirassununga Beetle with four doors from 2009.

the rear doors without having enough space for a proper B-pillar. A compromise had to be found. This meant shortening the front doors from 94 cm to 79 cm. This made it possible to fit a B-pillar strong enough to support the rear door hinges. The rear hinges, like the front ones, are hinged on the outside. The entrance then had to be extended and reinforced to the rear. Reinforcements were also added to the roof area to ensure the torsional rigidity of the body.

Milton Ciola used as many original Volkswagen parts as possible for the rear doors. Two Beetle doors were purchased and modified accordingly. All doors can be opened to an angle of almost 90 degrees. The side windows are almost the same size, resulting in a harmonious side view. The conversion was completed in just under four months. The rest of the car was then restored. The floor panel was sandblasted to remove rust, the bumpers were replaced and the car, which was originally grey, was painted Granada Red. The previous owner had replaced the 1200cc engine with a 1300cc engine and converted the electrical system to 12 volts. The seat upholstery was replaced and the interior trim for the new doors was modelled on the front doors.

Sources:
www.streetcustoms.com.br/revistas-carros/carros/volkswagen-fusca-4-portas.html
With kind support of Marcello Garcia

Porsche 904 Replica   (NO)

Between 2016 and June 2017, Norwegian Geir Natvig built a vehicle from Porsche parts based on the Porsche 904. The basis for his project was a Porsche 914 chassis, which was cut into two parts for transport to the scrapyard. The parts were welded back together relatively quickly. Natvig welded a tubular frame to the front and rear to connect to the body. The windscreen frame came from a Porsche 911, while Natvig constructed the rest of the body from aluminium sheets, some of which he hammered into shape using wooden moulds. The car is powered by a lightly tuned 2.6-litre Porsche 6-cylinder in-line engine. While the original had a GRP body, the replica has an aluminium body. Normally it is the other way round.

Sources:
www.914world.com/bbs2/index.php?showtopic=298790&hl=epic
With kind support of Geir Natvig Hessisch Oldendorf 2017.

Geir Natvig created a Porsche 904 like car based on the platform of a Porsche 911. While the original is equipped with a GRP body, this car was built with an aluminium body.

RCH   (GR)

Replicar Hellas, based in Katerini, was founded in 2007 by Ilias Gaganelis. The company specialises primarily in the production of Porsche replicas. The cars are hand-built by eleven employees north of Katerini. Most of the components are made specifically for the production of the replicas. Replicar Hellas assembles two cars a month. The average waiting time for a car is three to six months.
The RCH 356 Speedster from Hellas Replicar is a tribute to the original. Type 1 or Type 4 boxer engines are used, depending on the customer's power requirements. The power range is between 60 and 105 bhp.
The RCH 550 is delivered with a power output of between 150 and 250 bhp. The vehicles offer the driving experience of yesteryear with the technological resources of today. The interior is purist but functional and very close to the original.
Gaganelis does not have an official licence from Porsche for his replicas. As a result, the cars do not bear the Porsche badge. Instead, a logo with the initials RCH adorns the bonnet.

RCH 356

The replica of a 1957 Porsche 356 Speedster was launched in 2016 after more than two years of testing. The GRP body sits on a VW Beetle chassis. Instead of the original size axles, stronger versions

CARS OF THE 2000s

are used to allow the installation of powerful engines. Many components such as wiring harnesses, bonnet hinges and parts of the gearbox and engine are manufactured in the company's own workshop. Many other components were supplied by local companies. The first cars are exported to countries such as Germany, Italy and England (from 2021). The vehicles can now also be registered in Greece. The classic version of the RCH 356 is already available for around 49,000 euros. Considering the quality of the product, this is a very interesting offer.

RCH 550

The replica of a Porsche 550 was launched in 2014. The GRP body is bolted to a frame that Gaganelis and his team designed themselves for the 550 Spyder. The car is fitted with front and rear disc brakes. The basic version of the RCH 550 comes with a 1.8 litre boxer engine. Customers can choose from VW's Type 1 or Type 4 engines with capacities ranging from 1.8 to 2.9 litres and outputs of up to 250 bhp. A five-speed gearbox is available as an option instead of the standard four-speed. The basic version of the RCH 550 with a capacity of 1.8 litres and 150 hp is available for around 90,000 euros.

RCH Buggy

At the beginning of 2017, Ilias Gaganelis launched a buggy. The idea of the buggy was not new. The first design was made in 2006, but it took years to develop a buggy that meets today's requirements. The situation in Greece is particularly challenging. The bureaucratic hurdles are often greater than the technical ones. The RCH buggy is designed to carry four people. The

Top to bottom: Porsche Speedster replica from 2022. Porsche 550 replica from 2017. The RCH Buggy was launched in 2017.

GRP body is mounted on the undamaged and completely reworked floor assembly of a VW Beetle. As with the Porsche replicas, various engine options are available.

Sources:
https://www.replicarhellas.com
https://www.facebook.com/Ilias-Gaganelis/
https://thecartell.lu/portfolio-items/cathie-356/
https://www.4troxoi.gr/odigoyme/eidikes-diadromes/rch-buggy-apokalypsi

CARS OF THE 2000s

Rolls Royce VW   (UK)

Nobody knows exactly why things happen, but there are always projects that require a lot of imagination and creative energy to even be considered. When these projects are realised in a beer mood, one of the results is a 1969 Rolls-Royce Corniche with a Volkswagen Boxer engine in the rear. On the outside, the only thing that stands out is the modified front grille. It looks like a monstrous front oil cooler, but has no function. If you wanted to top the project, you would have to leave the original engine in the car and make the rear engine suitable for four-wheel drive.

Rolls Royce Corniche from 1969 with VW flat four engine.

Sources:
With support of the members of the facebook groupe "Unfinished and complete kitcars".

Rosenstiel Roadster   (US)

Dave Rosenstiel built his own Hebmüller replica in Arizona. Eight Hebmüller convertibles were on display at a Volkswagen meeting in America in 1998. At the time, this was a world record. However, Dave Rosenstiel's car caused quite a stir. In 2001, Rosenstiel sold his VW to Randy Carlson, the man behind oldbug.com. He put the finishing touches on the car. He had it painted Agave Green and had the interior rebuilt by West Coast Classic. Most notable, however, is the body, which was hand-crafted from Volkswagen sheet metal based on photographs and drawings of the Hebmüller convertible. Dave Rosenstiel's stated model was the 1948 Hebmüller prototype.

The basis for the car was the floor pan of a 1964 Beetle that had been completely rebuilt. Dave Rosenstiel wanted to get as close to the original as possible. Rosenstiel

took the engine cover from a 1970 Super Beetle and hand-formed the sheet metal into the shape of the original. The design of the rear bonnet meant that a special frame had to be developed to give the rear of the car the necessary stability. The front seat area was taken from a Karmann Ghia and adapted. The upper frame came from a 1960 convertible and the fuel

Dave Rosenstiel created his roadster based on photographs of the Hebmüller prototype.

tank from an Ovali. It took Dave Rosenstiel almost seven years to complete the body.

The roof bars are made of wood and give the car an unmistakable silhouette. The dashboard is also

CARS OF THE 2000s

This Hebmüller replica was based on a VW-Beetle from 1964.

custom-made from steel and modelled on the Pretzel Beetle. The only difference is that the glove compartment is made of papier-mâché. Rosenstiel sourced the seats from Sweden, as well as the bumpers, which were polished. The headlight grilles come from the Porsche Speedster. The steering wheel is a Petri Banjo steering wheel that was modified by Randy Carlson. The horn button is also unique, decorated with the sun and moon. The car is powered by a 36 hp engine with two Solex carburettors. The single tailpipe exhaust is a special design by Rosenstiel and makes for a particularly interesting sound.

Sources:
www.oldbug.com/rosen.htm

Taifun Dream Car   (TH)

The Taifun Dream Cars company in Thailand offers a range of replicas. These are mainly built on a tubular steel frame to allow the installation of powerful engines. The Ferrari P3 and P4 replica is also available for mounting on the floor of a VW-Beetle.

The VW Taifun is a replica of the Ferrari 350. The car is available as

Taifun offers the Ferrari 350 replica based on a VW-Beetle platform. The picture was taken in 2014.

a convertible and a coupé. Other replicas are available on request. The range also includes a Dune Buggy. Only turnkey cars are delivered to Europe. Only engines with 3-way catalytic converters are used for road registration.

Sources:
www.replica-cars-thailand.com/

Wittera (DE)

Wittera, the tuner and tuner of classic cars, sells its conversions and replicas under the label Retro-Ma.de. The Wittera UG range includes a kit for the Porsche 550 Spyder and a Porsche 550 Speedster. The kit for a Lamborghini replica is also suitable for mounting on a Beetle chassis. The GRP body largely matches the dimensions of the original. The customer is free to choose the engine and to specify the interior.

550 Spyder

The Porsche model from the 1950s was already available with either 110 or 135 bhp from a 1.5 litre boxer engine. Wittera offered a standard version and a slightly wider S version that could be bolted onto the unchanged chassis of a VW-Beetle. In the S version, the boxer engine is located between the rear and the rear axle. This results in a design that can be regarded as a mid-engine arrangement. The special arrangement of the engine and gearbox means that more powerful units can be fitted. However, the flat design of the 550 Spyder limits the choice of engine to those that are as flat as the flat twin. In addition to the boxer engines from Volkswagen and Porsche, the Alfa Romeo 33 engine with its 1.7-litre capacity and 132 bhp is also a popular choice. For the more power-hungry, there is also a Subaru turbocharged 254 bhp engine to choose from. To transplant a turbocharged Subaru Boxer into the Spyder, an Audi gearbox is flanged on instead of the original one. Wittera offers the conversion kit, a range of tuning parts and, on request, a turnkey vehicle converted and customised to

Top: the replica of a Porsche 550 is available with eighter 110 or 135 hp.
Below: Lambo replica from 2011.

the customer's specifications. It is estimated that between 40 and 50 Wittera Spyder 550 replicas have been built to date. Around 130 of the original have been produced. Considering the fate of James Dean, who died in a Porsche 550 on 30 September 1955, it is clear that there are now almost as many originals as replicas.

The standard version of the Wittera 550 Spyder can be bolted onto a

CARS OF THE 2000s

steel tubular frame or a shortened floor assembly of a VW-Beetle. The standard version is the same wheelbase as the original.

550 Speedster

The Wittera 550 Speedster has no hood at all. The Speedster's windscreen is also shorter and designed with aerodynamics in mind. All in all, the Speedster is several kilos lighter than the Spyder and therefore more agile to drive.

Lambo Replica

This body can be built on a modified Pontiac Fiero chassis. With a few modifications, the kit can also be built on a Beetle chassis with Porsche axles and a Porsche braking system. As well as Porsche engines, Subaru boxer engines with turbochargers (from 2.0 litres with 200 bhp upwards!) can be used to create a lively racer.
Bodywork and chassis modifications can be supplied by the kit ma-

All you need for this Lambo replica is a Beetle chassis, Porsche axels and a Porsche braking system.

nufacturer for an additional charge. A chassis modification costs approximately 1,500 Euros when a Fiero is delivered. The body with working bonnet and doors costs around 3,500 Euros and includes all the GRP work including fitting the inner fenders and gap adjustment. A very elaborate full paint job costs around 3,000 Euros, all lighting and glazing around 4,500 Euros. Tyres and rims cost around 6,500 Euros. The MOT costs around 650 Euros. With a budget of 25,000 to 30,000 euros, a well-powered Wittera Lambo can be put on its wheels. With 230 hp and an unladen weight of just under 800 kg, it will quickly become a lot of fun.

Sources:
www.retro-ma.de/index.php
www.tuning-stories.de/tuning/porsche-550-spyder-neu-aufgelegt-als-retromodell-von-wittera/
www.wittera.de/cobra/Lamborghini-Countach.html

Stretch Limousines   (MISC)

There are still many vehicles that use components from Volkswagen or Porsche. Only a few stretch limousis are shown here, for which hardly any further information is available.

Hunting Cars   (MISC)

There are still many vehicles that use components from Volkswagen or Porsche. Only a few hunting cars are shown here, for which hardly any further information is available.

Curiosities   (MISC)

There are still many vehicles that use components from Volkswagen or Porsche. Only a few curiosities are shown here, for which hardly any further information is available.

Lively Vintage VW Scene   (MISC)

Beetles, Volkswagens and historic specials have long since achieved cult status. The first meetings took place in Fuldatal near Kassel in the mid-1970s. Since then, the scene has developed enormously. The VW meetings in Germany and Austria are a great opportunity to show off past and present splendour in a beautiful setting, meet friends and have interesting conversations. There is never a shortage of curious visitors. This is only a small part of the scene. Events are held all over the world to showcase the diversity of the VW and Porsche scene.

Germany

VW Vintage Meeting in Hessisch Oldendorf

Only every four years the world's largest VW veterans meeting takes place in Hessisch Oldendorf at the home of the Grundmann family. In 2022, over 1000 participating classic Volkswagens and more than 45,000 visitors made the event a mega-event in the air-cooled scene. While just 80 participants, mainly from Germany, attended the first meeting in 1988, more and more enthusiasts from other continents have been attracted to Hessisch Oldendorf over the years. The longest journey in 2017 came from Malaysia. Seven young VW fans travelled with three old VW buses and a VW Beetle. The journey took three months and one week and covered an impressive 22,500 kilometres. In addition to pretzel Beetles, oval-window Beetles and T1 buses, this meeting often features special models based on Volkswagen. On this special weekend, the Rometsch Museum, also located in Hessisch Oldendorf, is another crowd-puller. The event is hosted by the Grundmann family.

Previous page from top to bottom: The countries of origin of the participants at the VW meeting in Hessisch-Oldendorf; two Dannenhauer & Stauss convertibles; Above: two police convertibles and a convertible from 1952.

Bad Camberg

At the International VW Veterans Meeting in Bad Camberg, the latest date for VW buses is 1955, while VW-Beetles are only displayed up to 1957. For special models based on Volkswagens, the year of manufacture is a little more flexible. Nevertheless, the emphasis is on originality and authenticity. Every four years, around 300 vehicles are on display at the Bad Camberg sports ground. Traditionally, the Petermax Müller Rally is driven from Hessisch-Oldendorf to Bad Camberg before the main day - in memory of a great racing personality. There are guests from all over the world who meet regularly for a cosy get-together. The hosts are the Lottermann family.

Left: The countries of origin of the participants at the VW meeting in Bad Camberg; top right: participants of the event offer spare parts; below: the Hebmüller family in front of their Hebmüller convertible.

1 May Beetle Meeting

Every year in Hanover, Germany, the West Parking Garage of the Hanover Fair is the meeting place for the entire Beetle scene. In 1983 it was just a handful of Beetle fans. In 2023, more than 3,000 Volkswagens came to this traditional event, which is also celebrated by many enthusiasts as the official start of the season. The event also attracts around 15,000 visitors, who come to see the cars and pick up much-needed spare parts and vintage accessories at the parts market.

Top: the festival grounds at lunchtime; **left:** an overview of the parts market; a special kind of racing beetle.

AUSTRIA

1 May - Beetle meeting

More than 600 VW Beetles regularly line the festival grounds at the town hall in Eggenburg, with crowds flocking each year to get up close and personal with these popular vehicles. All Volkswagens powered by the air-cooled VW Boxer engine are very popular there.

Top: the festival grounds; left: „Great 1" the widest buggy in the world (front 345/35x15, rear 570/60x15); right: Baja Bug (green) from Ledl; Custoca Hurrycane (red).

163

Aircooled at the Lake

A relatively new format for fans of historic Volkswagens is the international meeting „Air Cooled on the Lake". Every two years, VW enthusiasts get together at Lake Ebersdorf in the centre of Lower Austria, where the VW Beetle Club Ober-Grafendorf organises a large classic car meeting under the motto „Cooled by the Lake". Around 200 vehicles are regularly on display at the lake. Every Saturday there is a joint excursion. Exotic cars from Brazil are also welcome. There are great prizes to be won, such as a sightseeing flight over the Dirndl Valley or a weekend for two in Carinthia.

Top: the festival grounds at the lake; some impressions; Ledl pickup (brown); Franke Scout Buggy (dark grey).

Puma CoI Europe Meeting

In Europe there is a kind of core team within the Community of Interest for Puma in Europe. Once a year an international meeting is organised, which brings together between 20 and 30 Puma sports cars. The participants come from different European countries. Visitors from Brazil also regularly join in the fun. A Puma GT from Durban (South Africa) is now part of the community.

Top: impressions of several Puma gatherings in Germany and Switzerland; Puma GTS German Edition in red and Puma GTS Swiss Edition in light blue).

National Puma Gatherings in Brazil

In Brazil, regional Puma clubs regularly organise events that the Puma community is happy to travel up to 1000 km to attend. Every year, one of the larger Puma clubs organises a national Puma meeting, to which visitors from Europe are also welcome. In Brazil, the Puma enjoys a status similar to that of the Porsche in Germany. Volkswagen initially supplied Puma Veiculos with rolling chassis, not entirely voluntarily. This has developed into an extremely successful cooperation for both parties.

Some impressions of Puma gatherings in Brasilia, Campinas, Rio de Janeiro and Sorocaba; Jan Balder with a Pumeiro; the author and an early Puma GTB.

Puma Gatherings in South Africa

Production of the Puma GT under licence started in 1973 in Durban, South Africa. To mark the 50th anniversary, a Puma reunion was organised for the first time by the very active local community. The venue was the world's second largest water reservoir in the centre of the country at Gariep. There are now more than 120 Puma GTs on the local Puma register. Considering that some 350 cars were built between 1973 and 2019, it is safe to assume that more than 50% of these elegant sports cars have survived the test of time. Further meetings, with international participation, are expected.

Some impressions of Puma gatherings in Gariep, at the dam of Gariep, Pieter Du Toit and the author in front of Puma GT number 232.

Index

250LM 95
356 Speedster Sebring 72
505 62
550 Speedster 156
550 Spyder 72, 118, 155
550 Spyder S 41
718 RSK 72
911 62, 86
911 Flatnose 49
911 Turbo 49
911 Turbo Replica 39

A

ABR 26, 27
ACE 116
ACE Corvette 116
AC Sportcar 26
AFC Aquila 28
Air Force Bus 26, 28, 30, 31, 32, 33, 34, 35, 36, 37, 38, 40, 42, 44, 45, 46
Akamine 26
Akamine Buggy 27
Akamine Convertible 26
Alfa P3 74
Almenara Buggy 27
Alpha Shark 116
Alto 28
American Fibre Craft Inc. 28
Angelmar 30
Apal Speedster 98
Apollo 79
Aquila 28
ART EMIS 60
Aspen 30
Aspen 550 RSK 30
Aumann 30
Aumann Speedster 31
Aumann Spyder 31
Aumann Van 31
Avante 31
Avante MK 31
Avante MK II 32

B

Badger Jeep 73
Batráquio Anfibio 140
BCW 32
Beck 904 34
Beck Replicas 33
Beck Spyder 33
Beep Netuno 34

Belfusca 35
Belfusca Buggy 35
Beljippe 35
Bernardi 36
Beutler 12, 13, 14, 17
Beverly Hills 356 117
Blasi Cross 36
Blaze 126
British Coach Works Ltd. 32
Briton 71
Bubbletop Volksrod 141
Büffel Koupe 37
Bugatti 35B 74, 98
Bugfire 142
Buggy 86, 106
Buggy A1 98
Buggy Búzio 88
Buggy I 83
Buggy II 83
Buggy Tatuí 89
Buggy Tatuí 2 89
Burly Industries 37
By Cristo 117

C

Cabrio 106
California 92, 106
Californian 100
Can-Am 76
CapCar 37
Catapult 98
CBP 38
CBP 550 Spyder 38
CBP Baja Bug 38
Chalon 40
Chamonix 550 Spyder 41
Chamonix Ind. 40
Cheda 42
Cheda CB 43
Cheda MB Buggy 43
Cheda MC Convertible 43
Chelo Casas GT 144
Chesil 118
Chimo 44
Cintra 959 45
Classic Roadsters 46
Comet 76
Commercial Vehicles 112
Convert II 133
Convert MCR 133
Corbett Countach 5000S 47
Corsair 47

Corvette Replica 125
Countess 48
Covin 48
Crosby 50
Crosby Formel Fun 50
Crosby Manta 50
Crusader 50
CTC Panzer 51
Cucaracha 89
Curiosities 159
CWA Targa 51

D

D'Norbert 54
Dacon 52
Dacon 828 53
Dacon SP3 53
Dauphin 118
Dauphin 2+2 119
Delivery Vans 136
Delorean 119
Der Wiger Coupé 144
Dimo GT 62
Dino GT 71
Dornhai Automóveis Lda. 26
DRB Sabre 55
Duchess MG TD 46
Dukat Coupé 55
Duke 100
Duna Anfibio 65
Duna Buggy 65

E

Eagle 56
Eagle GT1 56
Eagle SS 57, 59
Eagle SS MK II 58, 59
Eagle SS MK III 59
EJ1 39
EMIS 60
EMIS Buggy 60
Enseada 61
Enseada MG TD 61
EX Turbo 130

F

Fibrario 62
Fibreglass Designs 120
Fiera 64
Floating T3 Bus 145
Fortvac Automobiles 36
Fyber 2000 66

168

Fyber 2000W 66
Fyber AP 67
Fyber Boxer 67
Fyber Star 66
Fyber X 67

G

Garra 67
Gator 145
Gofer 101
Griffon LB 68
Gringo 69
GT AP Turbo 131
GT AR Turbo 131
GT Turbo 130

H

Hummbug 121
Hunting Cars 158

I

Invader GT-V 71

J

Jaguar SS100 94
Jipe Fyber 3000 66
Jornada 69
Jornada Convertible 69
Julia 79
Junior 106

K

Kango 120
Kango Buggy 122
Kango Cars 121
Karma 70
Karma 2-PLUS 70
Karmann Porsche 52
Kaylor 71
KCC 72
Kestrel 71
Kitcar Centre 72
Kübel Lite 146

L

L´Autocraft 74
Labate 34
Lalande 73
Lambo Replica 156
Landrover VW 147
Lejin 76
LeMazone 76
Letherbarrow 77

LN-33 77
London Roadster 78
Long Beach 93
Lucena 107

M

Mac Laren 79
Mania Spyder 123
Marauder 80, 81
Mastretta Sports Cars 123
MB Endurance 44
MB Selva 44
Mc Lela 126
Memminger 147
Memminger Roadster 148
MGA 39
MG TD 47, 86
MG TD Replica 97, 100
Mikada 81
Mini Buggy 61
Mitcom Inc 40
MK 2 122
MK I Deserter 80
MK II Chevron 80
MK III Lola 80
Model T 122
Mulholland 82
MXA 125
MXB 125

N

Nereia 127

O

Ora Punk Cat 148
Orion 83
Orion I 83
Orion II 84
Orion III 84
Ostermann GR-C 84

P

Panache 85
Pantera 85
Paragon 86
Peerhouse Cars 28
Petterson Roadster 87
Pickup 86
Pirassununga 149
Porrera 87
Porsche 904 Replica 150
Porsche Speedster Replica 125
Procar Van 88

Proton 88
PS 904 89
Pulmonia 90
Pulsar 77, 91
Pulsar 911 91

Q

Quiron SP 91

R

Ragge 92
Rawlson 93
Rawlson 250 LM 93
RCH 151
RCH 356 151
RCH 550 152
RCH Buggy 152
Rembrandt 96
Replicar 94
Rhino 96
Rolls Royce VW 153
Rosenstiel Roadster 153
Royale 97
RS 60 118
Rudolph 128
Ryder Royale 96

S

S. H. Design 103
Sabre MK I 55
Sabre MK II 55
Saier 97
Salamander 72
Samburá Pickup 98
SAM VW 99
Sandbach 100
Sandwood 100
Saphier 101
Savana 129
Saxon 100
Saxon Austin Healy 3000 46
Scheib 102
Scorpio GT 102
Scorpion 103
Seidel GT 103
Sethera MK I 104
Sevetse 107
Short 129
Silver Hawk 104
SN1 104
Speedster 49, 100, 118
Speedster Replica 38, 42
SPJ Garra 105
Sportscoupé 105

SRT 132
SS 122
Stiletto 29
Stretch Limousines 157
Stripper 48
Super 90 Convertible 42

T

Taifun Dream Car 154
Tander Buggy 75
Tanger 106
Terral 63
Terral 4 63
Tigress 108
Total Recall 132
Total Recall 2 132
Town Car 108

TR 108
Tukano 133
Tupy Buggy 62
Tupy Mini 175 109
Type 35 94
Type 43 95

V

Vachey 110
Van Valen Car 110
Van Wagon 120, 122
Veep 120, 122
Ventura IIIa 75
Ventura LC 75
Ventura RS 74
Ventura RS II 75
Ventura SLE 74

Villa GT 111
Vision 111
Vision III 111
Vochoneta 134
Vochos Taxi 135
VW30 17

W

Wittera 155
Woodies 137

Z

ZF98 135

www.ingramcontent.com/pod-product-compliance
Lightning Source LLC
Chambersburg PA
CBHW080739300426
44114CB00019B/2629